DESMOND KNOWLES

voicing
a thought
on Sunday

HOMILIES AND PRAYER OF THE FAITHFUL
FOR THE THREE-YEAR CYCLE

THE COLUMBA PRESS • TWENTY-THIRD PUBLICATIONS

First edition, 1991,
Second edition, with Index 1992,
This edition, 1996, published simultaneously by
THE COLUMBA PRESS
93, The Rise, Mount Merrion, Blackrock, Co Dublin, Ireland.
ISBN 1 85607 028 X
and
TWENTY-THIRD PUBLICATIONS
185 Willow Street
P O Box 180
Mystic, CT 06355
(203) 536-2611
800-321-0411
ISBN 0-89622-690-5

Origination by The Columba Press
Printed by Colour Books Ltd, Dublin

*For Winifred and Thomas
my first teachers in the faith*

Acknowledgements

Throughout my career dozens of friends and colleagues have advised, assisted and steered me in the proper direction, and I am delighted to acknowledge them here! Thanks to the generosity, enthusiasm and encouragement of such fine people much of the work on this book was transformed into sheer pleasure. Special thanks to Celine McAteer, whose friendship and fidelity, energy and inspiration sustained me throughout and who believed in both me and the book when others remained doubtful.

Contents

YEAR B

YEAR C

Introduction

Preaching is the single most important task a priest performs. The sermon is vital to the deepening of community faith. Effective preaching is very hard work. Put in the simplest of terms, it is the priest speaking in the place of Christ about how a community of Christians should live. Using the language of today, the preacher makes a link between the good news of the gospel and life as experienced by the worshipping congregation. Jesus expressed the most profound truths in the simplicity of plain words using illustrations taken from life. To keep in sight our Saviour and his great eternal truths, the message must come across simply and clearly and deal with the commonplace everyday happenings of life, friends, love, marriage, happy times and troubled times.

These sermons are the fruits of my preaching experience in a busy cathedral parish across a period of ten years. The demands on the time and effort of priests in parochial situations are intense and diverse. The time available for preaching the homily is restricted by many considerations, so I have found it advisable to limit myself to one single theme within the allocated time. I hope that this book may prove useful in assisting busy priests to prepare their own homilies and help pave the way for a better understanding of the word of God among those who open their hearts through listening.

Desmond Knowles
Irish College
Paris
September 1992

Year A

First Sunday of Advent

The new church year is ushered in with the season of Advent. It is primarily a time of spiritual preparation for Christmas – the feast which celebrates the birth of Christ and the beginning of our salvation. This is a time especially blessed by God which summons us to stay awake and to prepare in joyful hope for the coming of our Saviour, Jesus Christ. Advent is an invitation to renew our christian commitment and to start living the life that Christ's first coming, almost 2,000 years ago, made possible in order to prepare for his final coming at the end of time. The reality of life in this world is that everything will eventually end.

If the real meaning of Christmas is to be kept in the forefront of our minds, a conscious decision must be made to enter into the proper spirit of Advent. At the beginning of this season a call to conversion is addressed to all of us because God wants us to grow closer to him and to experience the warmth of his love more deeply. We do this by opening our hearts to receive his Son Jesus Christ into our lives. His presence can be experienced in the people we meet and in the situations that come our way each day. He is around to be seen and welcomed in the poor and needy. However, if God is to do his work in us we must first remove the obstacles which prevent his birth in our soul. Any behaviour which is unworthy of our christian calling demands a rooting out. We give God access to our lives when we set aside the things of the world which bring unhappiness and weary our hearts. Casting off the deeds of darkness affords us the opportunity to live in the light of the gospel.

Unfortunately since human nature will always choose the way of least resistance, many of us pass through Advent without grasping what God wants to do in our lives through Jesus. Our thoughts are all too often centred on the earthly material aspects of Christmas because our senses are bombarded by the glitter and shine of commercial advertisements encouraging us to greed and selfishness. The eternal Son of God seeks an entry into our innermost being so that he may share his life with us. He stands at the door and knocks but will not come in uninvited. This is our opportunity to welcome him and advance on our spiritual journey by walking in the light of the Lord.

Prayer of the Faithful

As we enter the season of Advent we make our prayer to God the Father with all our hearts, so that we can avail ourselves of the opportunity for a new beginning in grace.

1. For the leaders of the church that they may be aware of their unique mission of proclaiming Christ who is the light of the world. Lord, hear us.

2. We pray for ourselves that this holy season may increase our awareness of Christ as we meet him in the poor and suffering people of our neighbourhood. Lord, hear us.

3. That the longing in our hearts for lasting happiness may be fulfilled by following our Saviour on the road which he travelled from the crib to Calvary. Lord, hear us.

4. We pray for the sick of our community that they may be given strength and hope this Advent through God's healing presence. Lord, hear us.

5. That our friends who have died will experience everlasting joy in the company of our Lord and Saviour, Jesus Christ. Lord, hear us.

Almighty God, listen to our prayers. Open our eyes to your presence all around us. May Advent bring us closer to you and each other as we wait in joyful hope for the coming of your Son, our Saviour Jesus Christ our Lord. Amen.

Second Sunday of Advent

For all the world John the Baptist looked the part of a first century hippie with his long hair, rough coat and open sandals. The crowds flocked to hear him preach in stern uncompromising language as he fearlessly denounced evil wherever he found it. His words were clear-cut in their simplicity. He came with a definite mission – to announce to the people that God's kingdom was at their doorstep and if they wanted to enter it their present approach to life needed to be changed.

John challenged people to reform their lives, to repent of their sins and undergo a baptism of purification in the Jordan. When a group of Pharisees and Sadducees approached, he confronted their complacency and warned them not to depend upon the good name of past generations. Being a descendant of Abraham would count for nothing if good deeds were not evident in their lives. As a preacher, teacher and prophet John pointed beyond himself and was a signpost to the coming of Christ into the world.

The call of John to repentance is an urgent invitation for us to prepare a way for the Lord to come into our hearts. And when we come right down to it, that is what Advent is all about. Preparing to celebrate Christmas means renewing our lives by acknowledging our need for Christ who is constantly calling us to higher things. John warns us that the greatest obstacle to the coming of Christ into our souls is sin. We have the freedom to accept or ignore his advice. Our faith reminds us that we have a responsibility to make present the values of Christ wherever we go. This is not possible unless we are making a constant effort to root out the sin that keeps recurring in our lives. To settle for less is to treat Christ as if he were a passing guest and not a forceful presence influencing our actions.

Each Advent is an opportunity for us to come closer to Christ and deepen our relationship with him through prayer and repentance. His power is at work in our lives when we make peace with the family member we have rejected, the relations we don't speak to, the neighbours we have fallen out with, the poor we have no time for and whose plight we don't want to know about. Breaking down these barriers will open the way for Christ to come to us and be born in our hearts at Christmas.

Prayer of the Faithful

Having listened to the message of John the Baptist calling us to renew our lives and bring them into conformity with the gospel, we now pray to our heavenly Father.

1. We pray that the church, like John the Baptist, may always be a light to expose evil and a voice to summon sinners to righteousness. Lord, hear us.

2. We pray for the grace to realise that we cannot really welcome Christ until we first recognise our sins and our need to be saved. Lord, hear us.

3. The starting point in any conversion is to live in patient harmony with our neighbour. Let us pray for a spirit of reconciliation between ourselves and those we have offended. Lord, hear us.

4. We remember the sick, the poor and the marginalised. May they experience love, support and comfort from those around them. Lord, hear us.

5. We pray for the dead. May they enjoy the presence of God in the kingdom he has prepared for them. Lord, hear us.

Lord God, grant that our Advent preparation may make us ready to celebrate worthily the incarnation of your Son. We make our prayer through Christ Our Lord. Amen.

Third Sunday of Advent

One could hardly blame John the Baptist for experiencing doubts about the true identity of Jesus. His outspokenness in front of King Herod had earned him imprisonment in a dungeon and the prospects of death. In his prison cell John had been hearing stories about the peaceful behaviour of Christ which did not fit his own expectations of a stern Messiah ushering in an age of fiery judgment.

Anxious to find out if Christ was the promised one for whom he had prepared the people by his preaching, John sent his messengers to Jesus with the urgent question: 'Are you the one that is to come or are we to await someone else?' The reply given by Jesus indicated that his ministry was one of healing and life-giving. The deaf were hearing; the blind were seeing. People were beginning to experience a new life and the poor were receiving the good news that God was on their side. John would not be slow to draw the conclusion from such an answer that Christ was indeed the long awaited Messiah. He could die with the assurance that his own life had been meaningful and worthwhile.

This gospel poses the problem of our acceptance or rejection of the person of Jesus. The question voiced by John has relevance in every age and is of importance to us, because the basic requirement for entry into the kingdom of God depends on welcoming Jesus and placing no obstacles to his working in our lives. Advent is an opportune time to assess what impact or influence he has on our behaviour by turning over in our minds and hearts the values that are reflected in our actions. Christ had time for failure, for the wounded heart and the bruised soul and we shape his kingdom by bringing his compassion wherever it is needed. His work continues in every age. The many and different guises in which Christ appears never cease to amaze. Very often he comes to us in the flesh and blood of people whose sins are so obvious and who are thirsting for the healing contained in a word of comfort and encouragement. What matters is that we are always ready to greet him. The best kind of preparations for Christmas are deeds of kindness which make Christ's presence felt in a new way in our lives.

Prayer of the Faithful

As we wait in joyful hope for the coming of our Saviour, Jesus Christ, we confidently place our needs before God the Father.

1. We pray that the leaders of the church will always keep faith and be a beacon of joy and hope in a troubled world. Lord, hear us.
2. We pray that the people in rich countries of the world will have the courage and generosity to share their resources with those who are suffering famine and poverty. Lord, hear us.
3. That parents may follow the example of John the Baptist in pointing out Christ and preparing his way in the lives of their children. Lord, hear us.
4. We pray for the sick and the handicapped. May they draw strength and encouragement from those who care for them. Lord, hear us.
5. We remember all our dead friends. May they live forever in the presence of the Lord. Lord, hear us.

Father, in your love, listen to our prayers and make us like John the Baptist; fearless and humble witnesses of your Son's teaching throughout the world. We ask this through Christ Our Lord. Amen.

Fourth Sunday of Advent

Everyone has, at times during life, experienced moments of doubt, confusion and anxiety. In this gospel story we find Joseph in a state of embarrassment because Mary, his betrothed, is with child. Being a man of honour he felt the right thing to do was to break his ties and divorce her informally. At the last moment an angel appeared to him in a dream explaining that the child Mary would give birth to, was the work of the Holy Spirit. He was told not to be afraid to take Mary home as his wife and to adopt her child as his own. There was a divine plan which Mary and he were meant to share and put in motion. With great patience and humility Joseph accepted the vocation for which God had chosen him, even though he felt his unworthiness to act as the foster father of a child who came from God. Joseph played a major role in the events of the first Christmas at Bethlehem. He was a true and loyal servant who, with a husband's love, cherished the virgin mother of God and with fatherly care watched over the child Jesus.

The most striking thing about Joseph is the manner in which he opened himself whole-heartedly to God in quiet faith. No spoken word of his has been recorded but the facts of his life point to a person utterly obedient to the word of God. He was a humble man caring for a young wife and very much at peace in seeing the child Jesus growing in wisdom and maturity. As the drama of life unfolded for the Holy Family, the vision of the angel seemed far away because there were many things which he did not know or understand. His obedience to God's call was not without its difficulties or uncertainties but he welcomed every happening as an opportunity for increasing in holiness.

Joseph was a man who gave everything in the service of Christ. His example gives us courage to face problems in a similar spirit and to keep on believing when all seems hopeless. Along with Mary he is singled out as the one who can best prepare us for Christmas. We are asked to receive Christ as freely and fully into our hearts as he did and to make the major decisions of our lives based on the faith given to us from God.

Prayer of the Faithful

God the Father's love for us is revealed in the coming of Jesus our saviour. In trust we place our petitions before him.

1. We pray for the leaders of the church that they may be a sign of God's merciful presence in the world. Lord, hear us.

2. We pray for the courage and faith of Joseph to follow God's call immediately and unreservedly. Lord, hear us.

3. We remember all married couples and those preparing for marriage that like Mary and Joseph they may build their partnership on the strong foundations of the word of God. Lord, hear us.

4. We pray for the sick that they may experience the compassion of Christ through our caring for them. Lord, hear us.

5. We pray for our departed friends especially ... May they rejoice in the vision of God. Lord, hear us.

Heavenly Father, you walk beside us on our earthly pilgrimage. Like Joseph and Mary we long for the coming of your son into our lives. Hear these prayers of your waiting people. We ask this through Christ our Lord. Amen.

Christmas

Christmas offers us all an opportunity to recapture glimpses of childhood's sacred memories. There is a timelessness about gazing into the crib and coming face to face with the truth that God came down from heaven and dwelt among us as a helpless baby. The gospel story tells us that at Bethlehem on a starry night the Son of God was born. A burst of light startled the shepherds, and angels sang at his birth. It's the simplicity of this happening that captures the imagination. Christmas is more than a story that is told – it's about a birth that brings heaven right down to earth. Love came down at Christmas, broke the sacred barrier between creature and Creator and gave an eternal value to our lives. God has given us the gift of reaching beyond ourselves and discovering the joy of heaven.

There was nothing romantic about the first Christmas. Christ's birth was a hard and bitter experience for Joseph and Mary, two poor people with doors slammed in their faces. They were the picture of poverty with neither room nor lodgings; forced to shelter in a stable outside the entry walls, where animals gave up their manger for the child Jesus. The Christ who was to die on Calvary outside of Jerusalem was born outside of Bethlehem. The message is clear from the very beginning that the love of God is available to all, but especially the poor, the weak, the disadvantaged. The stable is an indication of our need to see grace and goodness in the most deprived of people. As we kneel before the crib, we can pray for the vision during this short life of ours to see things God's way and for the courage to act according to his will. Christmas means something only in so far as we welcome the Lord as he comes to us in the wonder of every human being and as he reveals himself in the value and dignity of every person with whom we live and work. One of the things that makes Christmas very special is being remembered by friends. It's essentially a family feast and an occasion for exchanging gifts and sharing the warmth of our homes in the company of friends. Our hearts and our thoughts are especially with family members who are absent and unable to take part in our festivities. God's presence and love can be experienced in healing misunderstandings, patching up quarrels and letting bygones be bygones. Sometimes removing bitterness can be extremely difficult, but forgiving and forgetting will enable us to enjoy our Christmas happiness to the full.

Christmas is also about kindness, about giving and about the returning of love for love. It's the time of year when our hearts are in the right place and when we realise it is more blessed to give than to receive. We become alive and sensitive to the many needs of the poor who are crying out for our generosity and caring. Spare a thought also for those people who find the going tough and whose lives at this particular time are in the shadow of the crib because of a cross or a recent death. Our joy highlights their sadness. May your Christmas be a holy one because if it is, it will be a happy and joyful one.

Prayer of the Faithful

As the light of Christmas morning dawns upon our earth and the glory of the Lord shines upon us, we pray to our heavenly Father and give thanks for the birth of his Son.

1. We pray that the church throughout the world may be filled with the love of God and show his continuing presence in the world. Lord, hear us.
2. We pray for all people of goodwill who are trying to establish peace in the world, that they may be blessed in their striving for which Jesus the Saviour was born. Lord, hear us.
3. We pray for our families. Keep them in your care and let no harm befall them or sorrow touch them. Lord, hear us.
4. In this season of goodwill let us remember the poor and the needy, the old and the sick. May the joy of Christ sustain them in their struggle. Lord, hear us.
5. Let us remember those who have departed this life and who now rejoice in the greater light of God's kingdom. Lord, hear us.

Heavenly Father, whose light, love and happiness have been shown to us in this Christmas season, give us the grace to walk in your presence. We make our prayer through Christ our Lord. Amen.

Feast of the Holy Family

Within days of the great Christmas festival we are reminded that the child who was God grew up as a member of a human family. Anyone who reads the gospel carefully will see that the Holy Family had their share of troubles and difficulties which caused them great worry. Joseph showed a father's courageous and protective instinct as he did his best to shield the Holy Family from hostility and from the forces of evil. When he learned in a dream of Herod's plot to kill the baby Jesus, he quickly uprooted Mary and the Child and left that night for Egypt where they lived in exile.

The most elementary christian community of our lives is the family into which we are born. The purpose of this feast is to show the importance and sacredness of the family as the basic unit of church life. It provides an opportunity to reflect on the quality of our home and family life, in so far as they imitate the values of the Holy Family of Nazareth. Family life is a full-time job which is not so much about parents and children living under one roof as about their hearts beating together in harmony and love. This will happen if the message of Christ in all its richness is found within its walls. Parents teach their children by word and by example and those who avoid signs of mutual affection and do not show tenderness can scarcely complain if their homes turn out to be empty of love. Such households are not families but a group of people sharing living accommodation. Almost inevitably, conflicts, tensions and misunderstandings emerge when people live in such close confines, so patience and forgiveness are virtues which need to be stressed. Neither can happiness in the home be bought by accumulating creature comforts.

No matter what age young people are, home is the place where they feel free to talk about their troubles and difficulties. Time should be spent with them not only listening to their problems but sharing their visions and dreams for the future. The present age leaves no room for complacency regarding matters of faith. Religion begins at home and parents are the first teachers of their children in the ways of faith. Handing on the faith means handing on a way of life. It's no use parents urging their children to pray if prayer is not part of their own adult lives. One of the great challenges facing couples is to make time and space for prayer in the modern family. This feast is a reminder that Jesus came on earth to make a place for each one of us in God's family.

Prayer of the Faithful

On this feast of the Holy Family we make our prayer to God the Father, hoping that the example given us by the Holy Family of Nazareth may always reign in our homes.

1. We pray for the leaders of the church. May they guide those under their care with the example, strength and constancy of Mary and Joseph. Lord, hear us.

2. That our homes may always be places where we may feel free to share our troubles and anxieties as well as our hopes and joys. Lord, hear us.

3. That we may make our surrender in faith to Jesus Christ the foundation of our family lives. Lord, hear us.

4. For all who are sick. May the God of hope and consolation be with them on their journey and may he bless all those who mediate God's love for them through their care and attention. Lord, hear us.

5. For all who have died and especially for those whom we ourselves have loved. May God the Father welcome them to their true home in heaven, just as they welcomed us to their home on earth. Lord, hear us.

Heavenly Father, you search the hearts of every one and you know all our thoughts. Strengthen the bonds of love in all our families for more honest worship of you and for more willing service of other people. We make our prayer through Christ our Lord. Amen.

Epiphany of the Lord

The story of the Epiphany captures the imagination with its rich mixture of mystery and intrigue. Into the Holy Family's impoverished and temporary shelter come three wise men from the East dressed in majestic robes and bearing gifts of gold, frankincense and myrrh. They had travelled from unknown lands following a star and had experienced the deviousness of King Herod before they were filled with delight in finding the new-born child. After paying homage they left for home by a different route.

The story of the Magi is so colourful we may overlook its significance and fail to see its deeper meaning. The wise men represent all of us. Their journey through desert and mountain following a star reflects our search for purpose and meaning in life, which is not possible unless we are guided by faith which enables us to see beneath the surface of appearances. At the centre of it all is the innocence of the new-born child, surrounded by adoration, wonder and mystery, who is able to stir the emotions, imagination and wills of all those drawn into his presence. The story is always relevant because God sees to it that people who really search will find him. He will shed light into our darkness and make us new.

As the Christmas season draws to a close with faded holly and sagging decorations, the Epiphany reminds us of our journeying into another year following the individual path which we alone are to tread. Life is a pilgrimage, a long journey, but we need not necessarily travel alone, fumbling in darkness in search of our destination. The Epiphany story concerns the wider world and the many varying circumstances of joy and sorrow in which we encounter Christ. It calls for us to look around and search for the Lord who is in our midst, in situations where previously we were unaware of his presence. He comes in people and places we least expect and at times when we are most unprepared for his company. God stands in our midst revealing himself and inviting us to enter his company. Nothing is ever the same again for those who have discovered his light. The responsibility we bear is to let the divine light within us shine through to others. The gospel of love, forgiveness and redemption is not something to keep quiet about, but Good News to announce to the world.

Prayer of the Faithful

By the light of a star, almighty God guided the wise men to the birth place of the Child Jesus. We also seek his guidance as we place our needs before him.

1. We pray for the leaders of the church, that the Lord will guide them in their efforts to bring Christ to all nations. Lord, hear us.
2. As we journey towards God we pray for the grace to be guided by the light of the gospel and so reflect the presence of Christ in our daily lives. Lord, hear us.
3. For all travellers and people who are away from home. May God keep them in his holy care and deliver them from all dangers.
4. For the sick of our community. May they experience the warmth of God's love in their illness. Lord, hear us.
5. For our friends who have died and for whom we have been asked to pray. May the Lord give them peace and eternal happiness. Lord, hear us.

Heavenly Father, we thank you for revealing your son Jesus Christ to us. Grant that we may be always open to his spirit of truth. We make our prayer through Christ our Lord. Amen.

Baptism of the Lord

A solemn moment in the history of salvation is recorded with the incredible scene of Christ joining the queue of sinners who flocked to the banks of the Jordan to be baptised by John. The time had arrived to leave behind his private life at Nazareth and begin his public ministry. John was slightly hesitant at the approach of the sinless one but when Jesus emerged from the waters, the heavens were a blaze of glory as they echoed God the Father's voice, 'This is my Son, the Beloved; my favour rests on him.' Christ's baptism was a statement not only that God's approval was with him in a special way but also of his eagerness to start telling the world openly of its need for redemption. By accepting baptism, Jesus was committing himself to the work of taking away the sins of the world.

Today's feast is a powerful reminder of the vocation to which we are called. It recalls our own baptism in consecrated waters which cleansed our souls from the state of sin and was the beginning of our relationship with God. The seeds of the christian life are sown in baptism which means we belong to God's family, are able to call God, 'Father' and Jesus Christ 'our brother'. Like Christ we have been chosen for a mission in the world of our time. The carrying out of that mission will only be possible if we are prepared to live in accordance with God's will. The truth is, baptism is not over and done with when the priest pours water over our head and the sacred ceremony is completed. The sacrament is the planting of the seed of christian life which grows and bears fruit as we develop our relationship with God.

The start of the new year provides us with an opportunity to review our commitment to Christ and reflect on our calling as a member of God's family. Our special role is to announce Jesus to the world. The ways of doing this are many and varied. We are all called to witness to Christ in our own sphere of living and to make the world a better place by our presence. The lighted candle at the end of the baptism ceremony means we are to show forth Christ by word and deed wherever we go. Do we think of this promise when we are challenged to be honest or to refrain from taking away our neighbour's character? We reflect the glory of God when we refuse to compromise with evil in any of its forms.

In such fashion we make Christ believable in simple ordinary ways.

Prayer of the Faithful

We turn in prayer to the Father who, by our baptism, has made us his children, and present our petitions with confidence.

1. We pray for the leaders of the church that they may receive the guidance of the Holy Spirit so that they may proclaim without fear that Jesus is Lord. Lord, hear us.
2. Let us pray that every member of this parish may recall the meaning and commitment involved in baptism. Lord, hear us.
3. We pray for those who have never known the true faith, that the Holy Spirit may open their minds and hearts. Lord, hear us.
4. We pray for the sick. May they experience the Lord's healing from the spirit of tenderness and patience of those who care for them. Lord, hear us.
5. We pray for our departed brothers and sisters who have gone before us marked with sign of baptism. May they enjoy eternal happiness. Lord, hear us.

Heavenly Father, we thank you for making us your children. May we always honour, trust and adore the name of your Son, now and forever. Amen.

First Sunday of Lent

To begin Lent with the story of the fall of our first parents who disobeyed the word of God by eating the forbidden fruit, should make us aware of our own sinfulness. Before Adam set out on the road of disobedience man and woman knew perfect happiness, and lived in harmony with God. In subtle form the serpent made his presence felt by tempting Adam and Eve to make themselves equal to God. The consequence of their action has cast a long shadow over humanity ever since and created a wall of division between God and ourselves. Their fall cheated humanity of its birthright and burdened it with a sinful heritage. It brought about the kind of world we know so well – a world broken by sin – and it does not take much soul-searching to find evidence of our own sinfulness. There is sin in our lives and will be until the end of our days. We could hardly be true to ourselves if we did not admit this. However, all is not lost because out of the desert comes Jesus to begin his mission of saving people.

Greater than anything lost by Adam's disobedience is the new life won by the obedience of Christ who shared in our weakness so that we might live off his strength. The aimless wanderings of previous ages are given a definite direction in Jesus Christ who is a light shining in the darkness exposing sin for the evil that it is. The story of the temptations of Jesus, where he is enticed to misuse his God-given powers for selfish purposes is well known. When he was tired and hungry it would have been so easy to turn stones into bread and take away hunger. Likewise, throwing himself off the parapet of the temple would have been a spectacular display of his closeness to God. To bow down and worship the tempter would drive a wedge of dis-obedience between the Father and himself. In permitting himself to experience temptation he sets the example we must all follow when we come face to face with the human dilemma of choosing between good and evil. We draw comfort from the fact that the Saviour knew what it felt like to be tempted and as a result can sympathise with us in our weakness.

Lent is a time for new life in Christ. By joining Jesus in the desert of our hearts we focus our attention upon the things which really matter in life. The voice of God is calling us home and we should make a conscious decision to serve the Lord and do what is pleasing to him. This is not so much a season for going off things as an opportunity for returning to the things of God we have neglected. Good habits are hard to keep and easy to lose. Prayer, fasting and almsgiving are the order of the season. At the same time let us avoid those heavy-duty acts of mortification. If we take on sacrifices beyond our limits, we may well end up becoming everyone else's penance.

Prayer of the Faithful

As we begin our Lenten journey we turn with confidence to God the Father who knows our needs, and ask his help in preparing for a worthy celebration of Easter.

1. We pray for our Holy Father and for the leaders of the church that they may be stirred to lead all people to generous service in their local communities. Lord, hear us.
2. For those who are experiencing temptation and are overcome by the difficulties of life. May they be guided by Jesus and given the strength to persevere. Lord, hear us.
3. That this Holy Season of Lent may be a time of renewal and result in our appreciating those things which have real and lasting value. Lord, hear us.
4. We pray for the sick and the dying and those who are faced with life's sorrow, that God may fill any emptiness in their lives with his love. Lord, hear us.
5. We pray for our deceased relatives and friends that they may share freely in the life of God. Lord, hear us.

Heavenly Father, your Son was tempted as we are. Support us in time of temptation, give us strength in our weakness and help us to do your will in all things. We make our prayer through Christ our Lord. Amen.

Second Sunday of Lent

On one occasion, our Lord invited Peter, James and John, three of his close friends, to leave behind everyday concerns and accompany him up a mountain. While at prayer on the summit he seemed to be wholly taken up into another world. When all was peace and quiet they were enveloped in a cloud and given a glimpse of their master's inner power and glory. For a blinding instant the veil separating the visible from the invisible was removed and they had to shield their eyes against the dazzling brightness as the glory of the Lord shone about them. When God the Father's voice thundered from the cloud: 'This is my Son, listen to him,' they were overcome with fear and, filled with awe and reverence, fell to the ground on their faces. The vision passed and they were back to the harsh realities of life. Coming down the mountain Jesus told his inner circle of friends that the road ahead would lead to Calvary and the cross. These three disciples who had witnessed Jesus in glory would shortly see him reduced to a point of deep human weakness during his agony on that dreadful solitary night in the garden of Gethsemane. The transfiguration on the mountain was meant to strengthen their faith and hope and encourage them to persevere through this future ordeal.

The story of the transfiguration is a good example of the strength and assurance we can derive from prayer while facing the difficulties of life. The purpose of Christ's ascent was to seek divine guidance in quiet prayer. If we are to get away from living the half-life, under cover of darkness, and discover what God's plan is for us, we need periods of peace and tranquillity so that God's voice is not crowded out. It always happens that the more we come to know God the better we come to know ourselves. Prayer is about being in the presence of God, listening to him and experiencing his strength in our movement through life. It gives us courage and confidence and helps us to confirm that, as we journey on our pilgrimage from youth to age there is a purpose and an end in view, that God is calling us home. He may not call us to unknown places as Abraham was called but he does summon each of us to trust him as we meet the challenges of daily living.

Prayer helps us to see the world through the eyes of God. While it does not remove or take away our problems it helps us to face them bravely. We are all on the road to Calvary and are constantly tested by disappointments and trials on the way. Christ promises a heavenly future to all willing to share the hardship on that pathway. We can only be true disciples by sharing our faith and assisting others making the journey in our company. God encourages others through us – not in a mysterious way but in the human words and kindly actions we show them. In this way the glory of the Lord shines through our lives and we grow brighter as we are turned into the image of the one we are to   reflect.

Prayer of the Faithful

With confidence in God the Father who has promised us a glorified life in the image of his Son we make our prayer:

1. We pray for our Holy Father and the bishops of the church. May they courageously lead their people as they preach the nearness of God's kingdom. Lord, hear us.
2. We pray for those who are earnestly searching for the truth. May they discover guidance in Jesus who is a light shining in the darkness. Lord, hear us.
3. Help us to listen to the voice of Christ when he challenges us to be patient, kind, charitable and forgiving towards those who hurt and harm us. Lord, hear us.
4. We pray for those who are sick. May they realise how precious their sufferings are in the eyes of God when joined to the sufferings of Christ. Lord, hear us.
5. We pray for the dead. May they enjoy eternal rest and perpetual light. Lord, hear us.

Heavenly Father, enlighten our darkness, show us the path that leads to eternal life. May we never fail to take up the cross which comes to us in so many ways. We make our prayer through Christ our Lord. Amen.

Third Sunday of Lent

A very human picture is painted of the encounter between Jesus and the Samaritan woman at the well. Exhausted from a long walk in the hot sun, he sat wearily down and dismissed Jewish tradition by asking her for a drink of water to quench his thirst. No Jew ever spoke to a Samaritan because a century-old feud kept alive in each generation had embittered relationships. Thirst knows no boundaries so they struck up a conversation, and the woman, taking Jesus literally, was astonished to hear that he could provide her with water that would last forever. She had always wanted to be spared the embarrassment of being snubbed at the well by her neighbours who despised her because of her chequered life-style. As the conversation deepened the woman came to realize that her problem was not the lack of water but an inner thirst that no earthly water could satisfy – a thirst caused by the absence of God in her life. The Samaritan woman had a story to tell because five husbands failed to bring her happiness. Jesus lead her to look at her deeply troubled life and helped her to unburden her soul. Without a note of condemnation he accepted her, and coming to terms with everything she ever did wrong, she was released from her guilt. He gave her hope and offered her nothing less than the living waters of friendship and the Spirit of God which leads to eternal life.

Today's readings focus on water and thirst, but what exactly do water and thirst mean in the gospel context? It's not just water as we know it that Jesus is talking about, but the saving love of God poured out into our hearts enabling us to find life and peace. Thirst stands for the absence of God in our lives – that unsatisfied longing within every human heart. St Augustine talks about 'Our hearts being restless until they find their rest in God.' Since the pleasures of life fail to satisfy the thirsting human spirit, the only remedy is a relationship with Jesus who provides a mysterious type of water producing a well-spring of life within us.

What it took five husbands to teach the Samaritan woman, we learn from the mistakes of over-indulgence in drink, drugs, promiscuity and gambling. Her conversion gives us great hope because in human terms a worthwhile life was beyond her. Yet her past did not hinder her from coming close to Christ. Jesus won her over by gently leading her out of herself and raising her mind and heart to higher things. At Jacob's well a man, by asking for a drink of water, restored a woman's dignity and changed her life. When we were baptised we received this saving water of life for the first time. It was a mere beginning which planted us, seed-like, in the garden of God. As life goes on we need to be constantly in touch with this fountain of living water which Jesus gave us – otherwise we wither and the miracle of growth in godliness does not take place. Today Jesus asks us to have a look at how we are living out our baptism. If we are suffering from thirst his spirit is always at hand to refresh us and lead us in our search for the unending, the unchanging and the eternal.

Prayer of the Faithful

Gathered together as a worshipping community we acknowledge our inner thirst for the things of the spirit and pray with confidence to God the Father who alone can quench that thirst.

1. We pray for our Holy Father and the bishops of the church. May they be effective witnesses to the faith they profess, so that all people may come to recognise Jesus as their Saviour. Lord, hear us.
2. For those who have wandered away from God in the pursuit of earthly happiness. May they realise that all the pleasures of the world cannot satisfy the thirst God has put within the human heart. Lord, hear us.
3. We pray that our lenten penance may make us more open to the spirit of God's redeeming love. Lord, hear us.
4. We remember those in our community who are sick in mind and body. Help us to support them in their weakness. Lord, hear us.
5. Welcome into your eternal home our departed relatives and friends. Lord, hear us.

Heavenly Father, we admit our unfaithfulness and our need for your pardon. Give us all the help we require to live your Son's life to the full. We make our prayer through Christ our Lord. Amen.

Fourth Sunday of Lent

Only a very stony-hearted person would remain unmoved at the sight of a blind man, cane in hand, tapping his way across a busy street. Blindness is one of life's biggest burdens. It's a dead-end deprivation, with a sting of sadness. Life for the blind person is an endless dark night in solitary confinement. Having stated clearly that the man's disability had nothing to do with sin, Jesus mixed a paste, rubbed it on his eyes and resorted his sight. His healing was instantaneous and he returned home to experience the world in a distinctively new way. All his life he had recognised people by their voices. Now, for the first time, he saw what human faces and hands looked like. It must have come as a surprise to him to realise that some of his neighbours did not wish him well of his cure. When the Pharisees brow-beat him and tried to force him into a denial that his sight had been restored, he quickly learned that there was more to sight than seeing the light of day. There is a deeper malady, a spiritual blindness which comes from closing the windows of the soul and putting up the shutters in order to keep out Jesus who is the light of the world.

This gospel is for all time and every day. At a deeper level it reminds us that we were all born blind and were groping in spiritual darkness until at baptism we began our journey of faith in the likeness of Christ. The life we receive at baptism gives us the power to bring Christ to everything we do and to every person we meet. Light is a symbol of life with Christ and darkness is the religious image for sinfulness, shameful deeds and unbelief. Each of us is meant to be a beacon of light showing others how to live and giving direction to their lives by our good example. It is an opportune time to reflect on how we are living out our baptismal commitment and to see if Christ really counts and influences our behaviour. If we are courteous and friendly in our dealings with our neighbours we can be certain that the light of Christ is being reflected through us. Families who are not on speaking terms because of past differences should remember that they have closed out the light of God's love from one another. In its place they have substituted the darkness of hatred and the blindness of jealousy and are unable to see anything good in one another.

Christ is asking us to look at our blind-spots because coming from darkness into light is not an easy journey. It takes time and requires patience because of the many pitfalls on the road. In spite of our best resolutions the light of Christ is inclined to grow dim within us. Jesus knows our weaknesses and is willing to help us provided we come to him for healing. Having been called to walk as children of the light we must keep praying: 'Lord, that I may see.'

Prayer of the Faithful

We turn now in prayer to God the Father and ask him to cure us of our many forms of blindness so that we may lead lives befitting children of the light.

1. We pray for our Holy Father and bishops of the church. May they be so inspired by the light of the gospel as to radiate the happiness which closeness to God brings. Lord, hear us.
2. We pray for ourselves. May our hearts always be open to come to the aid of parishioners who are in need of our help. Lord, hear us.
3. We remember those who have lost their way in life, and are living in the darkness of despair. We pray that they may come to see the light of God in the person of Jesus. Lord, hear us.
4. We pray for all mothers. We thank them for the gift of life, the love they have given us and the faith they have shared with us. Lord, hear us.
5. For those who are sick in mind and heart that they may be healed and comforted. Lord, hear us.
6. We remember our dead. Grant them eternal rest and perpetual light. Lord, hear us.

Heavenly Father, hear our prayers and grant us the grace to live in the light of your truth as we journey on our pilgrimage of faith. We ask this through Christ our Lord. Amen.

Fifth Sunday of Lent

Those who have stood at the grave of parents or beloved ones know all too well the pain and the hurt Martha and Mary felt at the loss of their brother. Even Martha's reproach to Jesus for not being present echoes the anger, bitterness and resentment which many of us feel against God on the occasion of an untimely death. The death of those we love brings into sharp focus what is important. Deep mourning and the pain of separation force us to question the goodness of God, the nature of the hereafter and the meaning of life. They make us realise how frail our grasp of this world is. To people who have no faith, life is just a process from birth to dust and death comes along as the ultimate humiliation to make a mockery of their living, their hopes, plans and dreams. However, we must not allow the darkness of its shadow to cloud all our days because death for the christian is the great moment of life. Our faith is rooted in the central truth of Christ's resurrection.

This gospel speaks to all of us and gives us hope. It tells us that God is stronger than death and he will bring all who are his friends into eternal life. The raising of Lazarus points out that the life we are searching for is not an extension of physical life but eternal life with God. Real death is not physical death but spiritual death which is the destruction of the loving purpose God made us for.

While the iron law of nature dictates that we must all die and go to the grave, the life we share with God is not something which begins after death. It began on the day of our baptism when the seed of God's life was planted in us for the first time. At that moment we were given the power to start seeing as Jesus sees, to love as he loves and to follow him to the right hand of the Father. Once baptised there should be no going back on that relationship. Unfortunately, many of us fail to hear God's daily call to intimacy because we are not fully convinced of being worthwhile objects of his love. Part of our trouble may come from being caught up in the ways of the world and so enticed by its passing pleasures that we refuse to come out of our tombs and be free. We hold on to selfishness, cling to past grudges and stand on our dignity because pride will not permit us to make up past differences. As a result, the life we receive at baptism weakens and we become dead

34

to the voice of Christ calling us to himself and wanting to make his home in us. The story of Lazarus tells us that in dying to sin we are born to eternal life. These last days of Lent are about joining ourselves to the passion and death of Christ by deepening our response to his way of life; prayer penance, acts of charity and personal conversion are the soil in which this life grows. Joining with Christ in his death is a sure guarantee of sharing in his resurrection.

Prayer of the Faithful

We turn now, in prayer, to the Father who through the life, death and resurrection of his Son Jesus, has brought us back to the life of friendship with him and make our requests.

1. We pray for our Holy Father and the bishops of the church. May they proclaim through the witness of their lives the saving power of Christ's resurrection. Lord, hear us.
2. For those who have developed a slavish dependence on drugs, alcohol or gambling. May the warmth of God's love give them courage to rise above their compulsion. Lord, hear us.
3. For those who are recently bereaved and are suffering the loss of loved ones. May the Lord heal their wounds and turn their sorrow into joy. Lord, hear us.
4. We pray for the sick. May they be comforted by recognising the strength of God's love for them. Lord, hear us.
5. We pray for the dead. May they share the company of Jesus who is the resurrection and the life. Lord, hear us.

Heavenly Father, you planted within our hearts the hope of eternal life. Bring us and all those we love to the fullness of that new life of grace. We make our prayer through Christ our Lord. Amen.

Passion Sunday

Holy Week, the most sacred time in the church year, begins today with the triumphant entry of Jesus into Jerusalem. The enthusiastic throng of people gathered in the City for the religious festival of Tabernacles, were in a joyous mood as they spread their cloaks on the road, waved palm branches in the air and openly proclaimed Him as their earthly King. The powerful feeling of those moments resounded in the exuberant chants: 'Hosanna to the Son of David.' Christ has no illusions about this fickle crowd because as the week unfolds, the palm branches will shape themselves into a cross and the hosannas will become the jeers of a treacherous mob calling for his death. 'Let him be crucified, his blood be upon us and upon our children.'

The passion presents the ultimate humbling of Jesus involving far more than the physical cruelty of the crucifixion. There was terror and agony of mind to be endured and this pain was so intense that his sweat became like drops of blood long before the nails were driven into his body on the cross. The loneliness and isolation which he felt when friends deserted the hill of Calvary was nothing to the experience of being abandoned by the Father: 'My God, my God, why have you forsaken me?'

It would be a mistake to comfort ourselves with the thought that it was a group of Jews who killed Christ. The people involved in Christ's death are very like us. The rejection and the crucifixion continue daily. We must never forget that each of us has a hand in Jesus' death when we hurt others through gossip and slander and ride rough-shod over them for our own purpose. Jesus is crucified every time a human being is degraded, treated unjustly and deprived of freedom. This final week of Lent is a great opportunity to celebrate the death and resurrection of the Lord in a way that will change our lives. The simple truth of the christian experience is that sin has marred our lives, has made a mess of our world by leading us to conduct our affairs with hearts hardened against God. The cross is lifted up as a sign of Christ taking the sins of humanity upon himself in order to soften our hearts, by revealing the depth of his perfect love. The fact that God thought we were worth all that pain and suffering should reduce us to silence. We must never forget that Jesus died on the cross so that we might have new life. We should try in our own simple way to imitate him.

Prayer of the Faithful

On this solemn day we place all our needs before our heavenly Father and ask him to deepen our faith, so that we can come to a greater understanding of the passion and death of his Son.

1. We pray that the church throughout the world may be a sign of hope and a source of comfort to all those who are suffering and carrying intolerable burdens. Lord, hear us.
2. We pray that during this week we may be renewed in mind and heart, by dwelling on the passion and death of Christ. Lord, hear us.
3. That we may realise when we help someone else to carry their cross, like Simon of Cyrene, we are ministering to Christ. Lord, hear us.
4. That the sick may draw courage and strength from the cross of Christ. Lord, hear us.
5. We pray for those who have gone before us marked with the sign of faith. May they rest in peace. Lord, hear us.

God our Father, help us to follow in the footsteps of your Son, and keep us mindful of his boundless love. We ask this through Christ our Lord. Amen.

Easter Sunday

The resurrection is the story of the unexpected. On the first day of the week just as the dawn was breaking, Mary Magdalen came to the place where the body of Jesus was laid and discovered that the stone had been rolled back, the linen clothes were lying on the ground, and the body of Jesus was missing. She hurried to tell Peter and John, who were amazed at what had happened. Up until that moment they had failed to understand the teaching of scripture that Christ must rise from the dead. In the months ahead they would recognise more and more the power of his resurrection at work in their daily lives, calling them to live in an entirely new way. In similar fashion, we are filled with hope as we celebrate and proclaim that Jesus Christ is risen, because what happened the first Easter Day has implications for us also. The resurrection is hard to grasp, yet it is the central mystery of our redemption. Christ's victory at Easter breaks all the chains of sin we have ever made for ourselves.

Easter calls us to celebrate the fact that the light of Christ has come into the darkness of our world providing us with hope for a future greater than we dare believe. It challenges us to share a kind of living that goes beyond the expectation of this earth. This is not possible unless we reverse our sinful ways by rising above the things that keep us entombed and imprisoned and become people of the resurrection. Easter has no meaning for us if Christ has emptied his tomb and we are afraid to come forth and put the darkness of sin to flight by exposing ourselves to his light. All our hopes and happiness come from Christ's resurrection. It announces that love is present in the world and is more powerful than the evil any individual may carry out. The good news is that in all the dark and despairing moments of life the possibility of resurrection exists because no defeat is final and no life is written off as hopeless.

We are the builders or destroyers of our own destiny so let us make use of the power of Jesus to ensure that our life grows towards God. It is through our union with Christ in baptism that we share in the glory of his resurrection. This eucharistic celebration provides us with an opportunity of renewing our commitment to Christ personally, by taking a fresh look at the life we vowed to lead. Baptism means letting the word of God dwell in our hearts by doing everything in our lives in the name of Jesus Christ. Lord, we are your people, open up our hearts this Easter Day and increase the gift of your life within us.

Prayer of the Faithful

On this glorious day (night) when Jesus Christ rose from the dead and restored our life of grace we turn to God the Father in prayer asking for all our needs.

1. We pray that the church of God may be renewed in the risen Christ and bring his message of hope and love to all the world. Lord, hear us.
2. We pray for all newly baptised. May they grow in the love and the light of Christ. Lord, hear us.
3. We pray for our parish community. May we experience the joy of the resurrection in the happiness we share with others. Lord, hear us.
4. We remember the sick and the dying. May they be open to the healing life of Christ which has power to comfort them. Lord, hear us.
5. That the recently deceased may have peace and joy forever in the presence of the risen Christ. Lord, hear us.

Father in heaven, hear the prayers we offer with sincere hearts. Increase our belief in the resurrection of your Son so that the joy of Easter may be with us always. We make our prayer through Christ our Lord. Amen.

Second Sunday of Easter

In an age when faith is becoming more difficult and mystery is on the way out, the church puts before us the deeply moving encounter between Christ and Thomas, his doubting disciple. We make a big mistake if we dismiss Thomas as a man of little faith. Who could really blame him for not accepting the disciples' story about the risen Christ without a single shred of evidence? After what happened on Good Friday, it was asking too much of his type of personality. Thomas had seen the Lord, whom he loved deeply, die the death of a criminal, crucified between two thieves and a few hours earlier he had witnessed Peter promise fidelity to Jesus and then deny him three times. He was disheartened, disillusioned and angry which made him hardhearted in his questioning and unwilling to accept the word of others. The episode paints, in dramatic fashion, the journey of many people from a position of total disbelief to one of absolute faith. Having doubts in our search for truth is nothing to be ashamed of and can actually turn out to be a growing point in the life of faith. Thomas was doubtful about the key issues of whether Jesus had risen from the dead and was actually alive. Therein lies the heart of our whole believing. Thomas with his intelligent questioning and his need for satisfactory answers is a good type of person to have in any community, and acts as a defence against the excesses of pious belief. In many ways he echoes moments of our own uncertainty, when we question the religious values handed down to us.

During life, faith is an on-going struggle and there are moments of crisis when our minds are darkened and our vision of God is blurred by clouds of doubt. There is nothing comfortable about believing as it challenges us to change our lives as a result of our encounter with Jesus. The risen Christ is present in our midst as much as he was with the early christians and we are called to live our lives in his name. It is through believing that we enter into a relationship with Christ and enjoy the new life which he offers us.

Faith is our meeting with God and there will come moments in life when all else fails and we have nothing to fall back on except our faith: Lord, help us all. 'I believe, help thou my unbelief.'

Prayer of the Faithful

Gathered together as God's people, with confidence we pray for an increase in faith and seek his help in our struggle with doubt.

1. We pray that the church may always follow the example of Jesus in its striving to make the world a caring place for the poor and the oppressed. Lord, hear us.
2. We pray for this parish community gathered in faith, that our lifestyles will reflect the faith we profess with our lips. Lord, hear us.
3. That in our own lives we may come to enjoy the peace of the risen Lord – a peace which the world cannot give. Lord, hear us.
4. For the sick of our community that they may be comforted in their suffering and pain by the care of those who tend to their needs. Lord, hear us.
5. For our recently deceased. May they receive the fullness of eternal life promised by Jesus to all who believe in his word. Lord, hear us.

God our Father, listen to our appeal for help. May we never be discouraged by our weakness as we live in the hope and trust that you are always with us. We make our prayer through Christ our Lord. Amen.

Third Sunday of Easter

One of the church's earliest memories is the story of the two disciples who fled from Jerusalem after the crucifixion. Jesus was the one person who had meant most to them. With his death their whole world had collapsed and an end was put to their dreams for the future. Struggling to make sense of their disappointment, they felt that there was nothing else for it but to leave the other apostles and to depart from the place where their hopes were severely shattered. On the way out of the city, the two forlorn disciples were joined by a stranger who listened sympathetically to their sorry tale and helped them to see meaning in all that had happened. At every step of their troubled journey Jesus was in their midst but they did not recognise his presence until the breaking of bread at Emmaus. Their faith was restored and they returned to Jerusalem with new-found enthusiasm.

The story of Jesus and the disciples on the road to Emmaus points the finger at us and sheds light on our own situation in times of trial. Their distress is ours in many ways and their sadness sounds familiar to our ears. How many times have we walked the road to Emmaus with downcast face occasioned by quarrels in the home, difficulties at work or the loneliness of being rejected? The troubles and worries of life can so crowd our minds that we lose our sense of direction and are brought to the point of despair. All the time we forget that Jesus is walking with us, at our side ready and anxious to help us if only we would turn to him for guidance, in these moments of quiet desperation. This is an opportunity to reflect on the importance of recognising the Lord's presence in our lives. One way we do this is by growing closer to him through daily prayer and scripture reading.

We encounter the Lord amidst the ordinariness of human life, in the relationships we establish as we work and share together. At Sunday Mass, Jesus invites us to relive the Emmaus experience as we share the eucharist with him. We bring to Mass the joys and sorrows of the week that has gone and Christ speaks to us as he spoke to the two disciples on the road to Emmaus. He will throw light on every moment of joy and show that every bit of suffering has a purpose, giving us a motive for living a deeply religious life.

As we share in the breaking of bread at this Mass, we can pray to have our eyes open so that we can see beyond the sufferings of human living, to the joy that is all around us and ahead of us. Then we are in a position to set out and proclaim the good news to those we will meet in the coming week.

Prayer of the Faithful

Recalling how the disciples on the road to Emmaus recognised Christ in the breaking of bread, we pray to God the Father for a deeper appreciation of the risen Christ as our spiritual food for the journey through life.

1. We pray for our Holy Father and the bishops of the church. May they live lives worthy of their calling. Lord, hear us.
2. That the christian witness of our own lives may bring hope and light to those who are disillusioned and in the darkness of despair. Lord, hear us.
3. We pray for our parish community. May we never take for granted the graces we receive in our eucharistic celebration. Lord, hear us.
4. We pray for our sick. May they be healed and strengthened by the reception of the eucharist and see their suffering as an invitation to share in Christ's glory. Lord, hear us.
5. We pray for our dead. May they enjoy the fullness of life in the company of the risen Christ. Lord, hear us.

Heavenly Father, grant us the deep faith necessary to recognise your Son in all the situations we experience in life. We make our prayer through Christ our Lord. Amen.

Fourth Sunday of Easter

The preaching of Jesus is full of illustrations from the ordinary lives of his neighbours who were farmers and fishermen. In this way he taught of his love for all God's children whom he came to save. But the most appealing image of all and one that stands out from the rest is the figure of Christ as the good shepherd. There is no better loved picture of Jesus in the gospel. In describing himself as the Good Shepherd he is painting a beautiful picture of his loving care for the human family while emphasising how precious we are in the eyes of God. Each one of us has a special place in his heart as he calls us by name and cares for us individually. He is our guardian and guide, constantly calling us home when we are inclined to wander and stray. His everlasting love never gives up on us and keeps knocking at the door of our hearts seeking an entrance until we open. Above all if we cling to him we will not go astray because he will never let us down. There can be no greater grounds for hope than the consoling truth that we are loved by God in such a manner.

This story of the personal love of Jesus Christ for every individual and of his willingness to lay down his life for us, should prompt us to make some response in return for such lavish generosity. If we claim to be part of his family we should be eagerly following him with enthusiasm and generosity. The question for all of us to face is what return are we making as a response for his loving care. Life only becomes meaningful when we live with Christ. Our surest road to safety is to be alert and ready to answer his invitation to come and follow. The compassion of Jesus comes to people through hearts that are full of tenderness and love. We need constant reminding that our calling is to be shepherds after the heart of God, making Christ's presence effective in our neighbourhood. This work is carried out effectively in our families and communities when we respond to the deepest needs of people under our care.

For all our shortcomings we can be the touch of human love for those who have no friends, the tower of strength for those who are helpless and the healer in times of hurt. The caring acts of God are performed in hands that serve. Christ is dependent on you and me to be shepherds of his flock in a caring and loving service of others. There is no other way for the church to be a beacon of hope, a light in the darkness and a sign of salvation for those in need of help.

Prayer of the Faithful

We pray to God our Father with trust and confidence and offer him the deep concern and needs of the church and the world.

1. We pray for our Holy Father and the bishops of the church. May they be true shepherds leading their flocks to good pastures. Lord, hear us.
2. We pray for missionaries that they may be led by God's Spirit as they announce the gospel of peace. Lord, hear us.
3. We pray for those who have wandered away from the paths of righteousness. May they hear the voice of Christ the Good Shepherd calling them home. Lord, hear us.
4. We pray for an increase in vocations to the priesthood and religious life. May the youth of our parish hear the voice of the Good Shepherd calling them to serve God's family in a special way. Lord, hear us.
5. We pray for the sick and those troubled by ill health. May the healing tenderness of the Good Shepherd be present in the loving care they receive from family and friends. Lord, hear us.
6. We pray for the dead. May they share the fullness of life Christ has gained for them in the kingdom of heaven. Lord, hear us.

Father, hear our prayers, bless each one of us in the way you know best. May we follow wherever you lead us. We make our prayer through Christ our Lord. Amen.

Fifth Sunday of Easter

On the eve of his departure from this world, Jesus bids farewell to his disciples who are frightened by the prospect of loneliness and loss of leadership. Calming their anxiety, he tells them not to be troubled by his absence because he has gone off to prepare a home for them in his Father's house. With words of consolation and instruction he offers them a proper remedy for all their troubles. They are to have faith in God and confidence in him. Jesus describes himself as leading the way to God the Father and paints a picture of heaven as a spacious place with room for everybody. The good news is that no matter who we are there is a place waiting for us in the kingdom.

As christians we view life as a pilgrimage to the house of the Father – a journey home. It's a rough passageway through the turmoils of this world, with the inevitable sacrifices, sufferings and grief. Access to the Father is along the narrow road where there is little comfort and a lot of hard work. Jesus travelled it and to negotiate it properly we need his guidance. He is the way, the truth and the life. In every trial of life he is the person who helps us make that leap of faith which points us to our destination. When in the anxiety of the present moment our focus narrows to the problems that hem us in on every side – a sick child, an unpaid bill, an alcoholic partner, unemployment and depression – the list seems endless, his presence and his power give us encouragement and strength. However desperate our situation, faith in Jesus Christ will break the grip that cares and worries exercise upon us. If we really believe in this promise of Christ – not to let our hearts be troubled – a lot of the hustle and bustle will go out of our lives.

The response of Christ to Philip's longing to see the face of God, 'Have I been with you all this time and still you do not know me?' is food for thought. Is it not true that because we are spiritually in a state of dim awareness we often fail to recognise Jesus for whom he really is? It is difficult to hear the gentle whispering of the voice of God in a world of activity and noise unless we develop pockets of silence where we can unclutter our minds and hearts. Only when we find the space and time each day to experience the presence of God in prayer can we look with understanding at the past and with hope and confidence to the future. Then we will begin to know the peace and joy he meant us to have when he said, 'Let not your hearts be troubled'.

Prayer of the Faithful

Gathered together as a people in need, with humble hearts we pray to God the Father, trusting in his great mercy and love.

1. We pray that the church may be a sign of salvation pointing towards Jesus who is the way, the truth and the life. Lord, hear us.
2. We pray for those suffering from pain, anxiety, fear and loneliness, that they may find strength in their trials. Lord, hear us.
3. We commend to you Lord all those who have strayed away from the true pathway that leads to life. Give them the grace to rediscover the joy of walking once more in the footsteps of Christ. Lord, hear us.
4. We remember with compassion the sick of our parish. May their friends and family be a source of help and support in their time of illness. Lord, hear us.
5. We pray for the dead who have gone before us in faith. May they share the fullness of life Christ has won for them. Lord, hear us.

Eternal Father, we thank you for your goodness in calling us to new life in your Son. Grant us your guidance and protection in all undertakings. May we always serve you in our caring for one another. We make this prayer through Christ our Lord. Amen.

Sixth Sunday of Easter

A deeply personal moment is recorded when Jesus speaks in the privacy of the upper room where he is celebrating the Last Supper with his closest friends. His conversation centres around his own personal life and he speaks of the Father, with whom he is in closest union in the most intimate terms. He refers to the apostles, who are his friends, as children with the consoling promise that on his departure he will not leave them orphans but will send them his spirit. This is a remote preparation for Pentecost and the foundation of the church, when the breath of the Spirit will transform them into fearless preachers entrusted with a mission of spreading the gospel. What Jesus is intent upon doing is building up the shattered faith of his disciples for the work facing them after the resurrection.

Jesus did not leave the apostles to struggle with the christian life without the help of his Spirit and he won't leave us either, we have his word for this. The outpouring of the Spirit was not reserved exclusively for those who lived in the time of Jesus. The Holy Spirit is a real person who loves and cares for us and is our strength and encouragement in times of trial, just as much as he was for the apostles.

There is a great mystery of hope contained in today's gospel and we should take courage from it. The church has never been deprived of the truth of God. In the Holy Spirit we have a helper and a comforter who makes Jesus present in each generation to every person in their individual situation. But remember, the Holy Spirit will not arrive unannounced or force an entry into any person's heart.

Jesus can only free and save those who seek to be saved. We will receive the Lord's spirit and grow in our awareness of Jesus only if we request it in prayer and follow the law of God by keeping the commandments.

On at least four occasions during the Last Supper Christ said: 'If you love me keep my commandments.' Jesus invites us to show our loyalty by remaining faithful. Only those who are obedient in carrying out his will are capable of experiencing the fullness of the Spirit. The gospel is not about easy victories. In the struggle to build a better world we are his instruments charged with opening ears, eyes and hearts to what is good, true and beautiful in his kingdom. We do this by living lives of remarkable goodness in unspectacular ways. If we are willing to place our lives in his hands, he will accept and bless them and make such use of them as will be beyond our greatest expectations.

Prayer of the Faithful

With trust and confidence we turn now to God our Father and ask his help in being open to the Spirit as we make our prayer to him.

1. We pray that the leaders of the church may always be receptive to the promptings of the Holy Spirit and seek his guidance in their decisions and actions. Lord, hear us.
2. For families that are divided and suffering because of bitterness. May the Spirit of peace bring reconciliation so that wherever there is hurt there may be healing. Lord, hear us.
3. We pray that our homes may be places of peace and harmony, where parents seek to guide their children in the ways of truth and love. Lord, hear us.
4. For those preparing for examinations; guided by your Spirit may they have full confidence in their ability. Lord, hear us.
5. We pray for the sick. May they be strengthened and encouraged by the love of friends who care for them. Lord, hear us.
6. We pray that our recently deceased may enjoy Christ's gift of peace. Lord, hear us.

Almighty Father, we entrust our lives and our needs to your care. By the gift of your love bind us together as your church so that we may have the courage to live according to our convictions as followers of Christ. We make our prayer through Christ our Lord. Amen.

Ascension of the Lord

Bidding farewell to a loved one is not easy, and is something we never fully grow accustomed to doing. The Ascension marks the end of Christ's earthly mission and his glorious return to the Father. He had achieved the work he was sent to do. While the trumpets were sounding in heaven to greet the arrival of the ascending Lord, the apostles must have been experiencing a deep sadness in their hearts at his departure. However, his final words, 'I am with you always. Go make disciples of all nations,' while full of comfort were urgent in meaning. Not only was Jesus not abandoning them nor depriving them of his presence but he was entrusting them with the mission of making the love of God the Father known, through joyful and selfless lives in the service of others. In Jesus' absence the disciples are not to remain inactive but to move into the future with courage. They have a vital and essential role to play in announcing the salvation Christ has won on Calvary, by transforming death into the dawn of a new life. Jesus will no longer be present in a human body but his place will be taken by the Holy Spirit who will be their guide and strength as they journey through life.

If we ponder within our hearts the meaning of this great feast we may come to grasp something of the confidence which God has in us because the Ascension focuses on what we must do to be with Christ forever. Where he has gone we hope to follow. Like the apostles, we are at the centre of the stage and our call is also to service. We are to continue the work of those who have gone before us and help build up Christ's kingdom. In a world full of homeless and jobless people we turn sorrow into happiness by being his comforting word and his every smile. Our lives may be the only book of the gospel open for people to read. What we are, speaks more loudly than either what we say or what we do. He is counting on us. Our prayer is that he will renew within us the work of the Spirit so that we may know what is true and have the strength to do what is right.

Prayer of the Faithful

On this day of promise we place all our hopes and longings before God the Father and ask his favour.

1. We pray for our Holy Father and bishops of the church that they may grow daily in awareness of their special mission as Christ's witnesses. Lord, hear us.
2. We pray for ourselves as we struggle to live and spread the message of Christ that we may draw strength and take courage from his Ascension. Lord, hear us.
3. We pray for those who have lost hope and are in the darkness of despair that the feast of the Ascension of Christ may renew their vision. Lord, hear us.
4. We remember the sick and handicapped of our community and pray that in their weakness they may discover the power of the risen Christ. Lord, hear us.
5. We pray for the dead. May they be safely at home in the place Christ has prepared for them. Lord, hear us.

God our Father, hear the prayers of your people. Open our eyes and our hearts to the full meaning of the Ascension of your Son. May it bring us to a greater knowledge and closer following of him. We ask through Christ our Lord. Amen.

Seventh Sunday of Easter

After sharing the Last Supper with his disciples Jesus, at the end of his working life, is offering himself unselfishly to the Father. It is the hour when everything is falling apart and the drama leading to his death has been set in motion. Raising his eyes heavenward Jesus sums up the significance of his life by recalling the past. He expresses to the Father his innermost thoughts and deepest desires beginning with the mysterious exclamation, 'Father, the hour has come, glorify your Son so that your Son may glorify you.' On the following day at Calvary, raised on the cross in death, he would be brought to the glory of the resurrection and become the source of eternal life for all who believed in him. As the prayer continues we suddenly get the impression of being party to a very intimate conversation between Jesus and God the Father. He is talking about handing over his mission to the apostles, who would soon be saddled with the burden of spreading the Good News. We listen intently as he prays for the future members of the church in every age because we are included in this prayer. From it we discover that as christians we are united in every generation by a common purpose which is to reflect the honour and glory of God. This is carried out in ordinary everyday occurrences by doing his will, making his name known and by dedicating our work, no matter how insignificant it may seem, to his honour.

Getting to know the will of the Father is never easy and can only be achieved if we become people of prayer. Prayer is an admission of dependence on God's friendship and a realisation that we cannot live life fully without his help. When we pray we talk to God and we express our deepest desires, our hopes and our worries. He is a friend who listens, understands, shows concern and accepts us fully as we are – sins and all. Every time we pray we strengthen our friendship with God who gives us the courage to calmly face the troubles of life. Prayer is the breath of the soul and the life-line of every believing community. Time spent in prayer helps us to realise that we are carrying on the work of Jesus. Remember we can pray anywhere – the time or the place is not important. If Christ needed prayer to carry on his mission how can we continue his saving work without being people of prayer?

Prayer of the Faithful

United with the whole church throughout the world as we wait for a fresh outpouring of the Spirit of Pentecost, we pray in trust and hope to the Father.

1. We pray for our Holy Father ..., the bishops of the church and of all in authority who teach the truth that is Christ, that we may listen to their voice and encourage them by the support of our prayers. Lord, hear us.

2. We pray for the courage and perseverance to continue on our christian pilgrimage and to pass on to our children the hope that has sustained us. Lord, hear us.

3. We pray that we may use TV, Radio and videos in a responsible fashion and not allow them to corrupt the minds of our young people. Lord, hear us.

4. We pray for young people who are preparing for examinations and who are waiting in hope for many things. Guided by your Spirit may they have full confidence in their ability. Lord, hear us.

5. We ask the Lord's blessing on those who are sick. May they be strengthened by the care and concern of those who look after them. Lord, hear us.

6. We pray for our recently deceased. May they be drawn into the presence of Christ and share in everlasting life in heaven. Lord, hear us.

Heavenly Father, you are the source of all good things. Help us to seek only what is pleasing to you so that all may share for ever the happiness of your kingdom. Through Christ our Lord. Amen.

Pentecost Sunday

With this feast we celebrate the birthday of the church because it was on the first Pentecost Sunday that the infant church was launched on course and took on its missionary role. Scripture tells us that while the apostles were at prayer with Mary in the upper room, suddenly there was a roaring wind and the Holy Spirit descended on them in the form of tongues of fire and gave these timid and frightened men the courage to rush into the street and fearlessly preach the word of God to friend and foe alike. The Spirit of the Lord which was poured out and transformed the apostles from a fearful group to courageous men announcing the Good News about the mighty acts of God, was not a one-off happening which only took place at the beginning of the church. Ever since the Holy Spirit has been a permanent presence and a tower of strength in guiding, guarding and directing its course.

The action of the Spirit continues in our time and is first evident in our lives at baptism. It was on that occasion that the seed of eternity was planted within our being bringing us into a loving relationship with God, who invited us to become his adopted sons and daughters. Pentecost and the coming of the Holy Spirit is Jesus announcing that God our Father has breathed his life into our bones giving us an opportunity to share in his eternal life. Heaven has been placed within our reach but entrance into the kingdom does not happen unless we are prepared to change our ways and make room for the Spirit of the living God to dwell within us. The starting point for accepting the gift of the Holy Spirit is to increase our prayer life, which helps put us into a loving relationship with God – the Spirit came upon the apostles while they were at prayer. Without an attitude of prayerfulness it is difficult to discover our special talents and the particular role we are called to play in the mission of the church. Once we discover our own particular gifts there is an obligation on us to use them in building up the Body of Christ.

The story of Pentecost invites us to reflect upon our openness and our response to the outpouring of the Spirit in our own lives.

Prayer of the Faithful

As we gather for this eucharist on the feast of Pentecost which confirmed the apostles in their faith, we pray to the Father for the strength to witness as they did.

1. We pray for our Holy Father and bishops of the church, that they may be ever open to the challenges of the Spirit of God and be an inspiration to all who look to them for leadership. Lord, hear us.

2. We pray to the Holy Spirit for the gift of patience so that we may become more tolerant of the faults of others. Lord, hear us.

3. Conscious that good deeds flow from a pure heart we pray to the Holy Spirit that all our actions may come from a heart filled with grace. Lord, hear us.

4. We pray for the sick and we ask the Holy Spirit to pour out kindness, compassion, peace and love into their lives through the people who are caring for them. Lord, hear us.

5. We pray for all those who have gone before us. May God through the power of the Holy Spirit give them a share in the resurrection of his Son. Lord, hear us.

God our Father, let this day of Pentecost be an outpouring of your Spirit to us all, that we may be a shining light amidst the darkness of the world. We make our prayer through Christ our Lord. Amen.

Trinity Sunday

On the feast of the Most Holy Trinity we come face to face with the inner mystery of God as a family of persons, Father, Son and Holy Spirit, where there is complete harmony, love and total peace. In case anyone is wondering what bearing the mystery of the Trinity has on our lives, it is worth remembering that scripture tells usthat we are children of God the Father who cares for us, that in Jesus Christ we have a brother who died for us and that in the Holy Spirit we possess a friend and comforter who strengthens and protects us when we are in danger. The Trinity is an invitation to discover and deepen the relationship between God and ourselves in the light of what the gospel tells us about his inner life. If we are made in the image and likeness of God then surely we must strive to become like him as much as is humanly possible – because when life is over the fulfilment of our dreams is to be in God's company and to see him as he really is.

However, to come to an awareness of our true dignity as children of God demands a great deal of change and conversion on our part. It requires a basic readiness to let go of everything which binds us to this world. The oneness of God and the unique place he should hold in our lives brings home how easily we can be lured into worshipping false gods. It's frightening the ease with which the trappings of money, power and prestige can take his place. The generosity of the Father in sending his son into the world as a Saviour contrasts greatly with all forms of human selfishness to which we are prone. Christians should not countenance such behaviour.

God is the deepest mystery of our lives and is infinitely more expansive than our tiny minds are capable of imagining. If we had been left struggling on our own to understand God we could never have established that he is a God of tenderness and compassion, slow to anger and rich in kindness and faithfulness. Without the help of Jesus, how would we ever have known that as a community we are linked like a family of people to him? Because God loves us and wants us to return that love, he offers us a share in his own life. That demands that we allow the risen Christ to make his home within our hearts. If our behaviour is to mirror the life of the Trinity, then the grace of our Lord Jesus Christ, the love of God and the fellowship of the Holy Spirit should govern our every word and action.

From the moment we were baptised in the name of the three persons of the Trinity, we pledged to live our lives under their protection and do everything in their name so that, when life is over, we shall go to meet them and live in their company forever. For all this to happen we need to listen to the Spirit inspiring us and drawing us forward in search of the truth.

Prayer of the Faithful

As a community united in faith, hope and charity, we turn to the Father and place before him our needs and cares.

1. We pray for our Holy Father and the bishops of the church, that they may proclaim the one true God by being faithful to the will of the Father, obedient to the teachings of Jesus Christ and sensitive to the promptings of the Holy Spirit. Lord, hear us.
2. That the unifying love of Father, Son and Holy Spirit may draw together in mutual harmony the people of our neighbourhood. Lord, hear us.
3. That by deepening our love for the mystery of the Trinity we may grow in appreciation of the great destiny to which we have been called. Lord, hear us.
4. We pray for the old, the lonely and the sick of our community. May those who care for them be a source of comfort and strength and support. Lord, hear us.
5. We pray for our friends who have died. May they enjoy the fulness of life in God's heavenly kingdom. Lord, hear us.

Almighty God, in you we live and move and have our being. Help us to grow daily in wisdom, truth and love. We make our prayer through Christ our Lord. Amen.

Body and Blood of Christ

Corpus Christi is the feast on which we pay special homage to the real presence of Christ in the eucharist. In a sense we are repeating the beautiful Last Supper gathering in the upper room with the celebration it deserves. This was not possible on Holy Thursday because on that occasion the shadow of the cross loomed large in the background. Jesus Christ, in order to keep alive the memory of his great act of love on the Hill of Calvary, on the night before he died left his body and blood as spiritual food to be received in every generation.

This solemnity is a splendid opportunity to reflect on God's most striking gift to us and a timely reminder to renew our faith and deepen our appreciation of the real presence of Jesus in the eucharist. He is the living bread sent down from heaven as food for our souls to satisfy our deepest spiritual hunger. The eucharist proclaims that Christ died for our sins so that we might have life and salvation. The Son of God could not have given us a greater proof of his love.

As pilgrims on the road of life we suffer from many hungers but the greatest hunger of all is the yearning for a deeper meaning to life. This is something that no earthly bread can satisfy. In our struggle to find purpose, the eucharist is of great help because it is an invitation to follow in the footsteps of Jesus. By setting out on the road he travelled and by doing our utmost to imitate his life of caring and sharing we are gradually brought to see the importance of placing the common good of people before our own self-interest.

If sharing in the eucharist is to mean more than going to Mass and providing nourishment for our own private spiritual lives, we must rise above the divisions and injustices of society which keep us apart and prevent us forming a closer bond within the community. This will mean opening the doors of our hearts and of our homes and accepting people as they are.

In our daily round we are asked to forgive, overlook weaknesses and understand the failure of friends especially when they hurt us. The eucharist means to live as brothers and sisters of Jesus. There is no way we can offer ourselves to God in the eucharist and not try and love our neighbour who has failed us during the week. For God to love through us we must try to be loving also. We are to go out and touch the lives of others, to be the healing presence, the helping hand, the voice of sympathy and words of encouragement when they are needed. In this way we will be shaped and formed by what we celebrate.

Prayer of the Faithful

Celebrating the feast of Christ's own body and blood we stand with confidence in the presence of God the Father and make our petitions to him.

1. We pray that the church throughout the world may grow in appreciation of the eucharist as the Bread of Life by celebrating the sacrifice of the Mass with greater meaning and devotion. Lord, hear us.
2. That, fed on the Body and Blood of the Lord, all the people in this parish may play their part in promoting love, justice and peace, within the community. Lord, hear us.
3. Let us pray to the Lord to bless all children who at this time are making their first Holy Communion. Lord, hear us.
4. Let us pray for those who are ill, that God may help their ailing bodies and heal their wounded spirits. Lord, hear us.
5. That those who have died recently may enjoy eternal life in heaven. Lord, hear us.

Heavenly Father, you give us the body and blood of your Son as food and drink for our pilgrim journey. Grant that through our union with him we may be united with one another as members of his body, through Christ our Lord. Amen.

Second Sunday of the Year

Once more we are reminded of the baptism of our Lord which was the curtain-raiser to his earthly ministry. It began his mission of gathering all people into the one family of God and leading them back to his Father. Jesus went about doing good, touching human lives, healing people, freeing them from the darkness of sin and directing them to lives worthy of their calling. We too have been chosen to continue this saving work which Christ began and to be part of this mission in the world we live in. At the moment of our baptism the seed of God's life was planted within us. That grace-filled day was but the start of our conversion. It takes a lifetime for that seed of God's love to grow, mature and blossom. The only home for a christian to live in is Christ and we should settle for nothing less. If we are to enter into this new and exciting experience as members of God's family we must have a clear idea of what kind of family we are meant to be. To follow the way traced out by Christ,who is our brother, demands a loving personal response on our part. Baptism is a dedication of self to the call of Jesus who went about doing good.

This is a time to reflect on the extent to which Christ has penetrated our thoughts and influenced our behaviour. We are what we do. How many of us can honestly say that we are leading lives which are worthy of our baptismal calling? The power of God shines out where we least expect it and in the most unlikely places. His spirit will be at work and incredibly active in the depth of our person when we open our hearts to those who have lost their dignity through poverty or hard times. We preach not by words only but by the way we live and by the effort we exert to make the world a better place by our presence. The practice of charity and humility spotlights what is wrong with selfishness and arrogance. It exposes evil and sinfulness for what they are. The example we display in our everyday activities paves the way for Christ in others. Today we pray for a greater insight into our role in Christ's mission. God works through ordinary people like ourselves. As the baptism ceremony states, 'We are to walk always as children of the light, keeping the flame of faith burning brightly within our hearts'. Being a disciple of Christ demands outstanding service. It costs no less than everything.

Prayer of the Faithful

God has called us in Jesus Christ to be the light of the world. In need of his mercy and salvation we place our petitions before him.

1. We pray for our Holy Father and the bishops of the church that they may be true to their vocation of leading the church and bringing the warmth of Christ's love to the ends of the earth. Lord, hear us.
2. That all christians may play their part in being a visible expression of the care of Jesus for the unwanted, the unloved and the poor of their community. Lord, hear us.
3. We pray for parents, that they may realise their special mission of discipleship to the community in handing on the faith to their children. Lord, hear us.
4. That all those who are sick and suffering may come to know that God the Father cares for them and that they are precious in his eyes. Lord, hear us.
5. That our friends,who in baptism died with Christ and have now completed their earthly journey,may share in the power and glory of his resurrection. Lord, hear us.

Almighty Father, look on your people with mercy. It is your desire that everyone should be saved. May our lives be a light and encouragement to those who walk in darkness. We make our prayer through Christ our Lord. Amen.

Third Sunday of the Year

Ordinary people like ourselves who are conscious of the conditions of employment must surely be excused for questioning the wisdom of the two sets of brothers, Peter and Andrew, James and John, in leaving their nets to follow Christ. The invitation is direct and simple, 'Come, follow me' with no hint as to where they are going or what is in store for them. Nothing is promised. There is no suggestion of any hesitation or regret on their part at letting go or leaving their boats behind. Only one thing matters – to follow Christ and become fishers of men. This encounter between Jesus and the apostles takes place during the first moments of his ministry and reflects the humble origins of the church. Ordinary people with no special training are called to the extraordinary task of bringing the knowledge and love of God to the whole world. God chooses the weak of the world to confront the strong and the simple to confound the wise.

The mission of preaching, teaching and healing which Jesus began in Galilee is now the responsibility of the church. The call of the apostles is still the model of discipleship and in our generation we have both the privilege and obligation to accept his invitation. As followers of Christ we are called to be servants of God and to struggle in the task of enlarging the church by spreading the Good News of the kingdom. This is not possible unless we have begun living the new life we have received at baptism. There is no such person as an instant christian because coming to faith is a gradual process and a life-long struggle, which is a lesson each generation must learn anew. It involves all the ups and downs of turning aside from a life of sin and self-centred existence to one of obedience to God's call. We begin by getting to know Christ who enables us to cut through the darkness of fear and prejudice which our sins have caused. In order to grow and resolve the tensions within ourselves we need the constant light of Christ which gradually illuminates the way ahead. It is a light that grows brighter as we become more familiar with the gospel.

Right now we stand at a point of opportunity. Christ alone gives us life and hope and we should not be side-tracked in the work of our own conversion by earthly pursuits. We are the hands of God. The power of God is released upon the world by men and women like ourselves in every walk of life who put their spiritual welfare of the community before selfishness in everyday things.

Prayers of the Faithful

Since we cannot remain idle in our efforts to follow through with our faith in the Lord's mission, me pray to the Father for the grace and strength to answer this call.

1.   For the Holy Father, bishops and religious who have been called by Jesus in a special way to bring his message to others. May they carry out their mission generously. Lord hear us.
2.   We pray that our young people may come to a deeper appreciation of the Good News and use their enthusiasm to spread the gospel to others. Lord, hear us.
3.   We pray for all who are called to follow Christ. May we never be tempted to lose heart as we carry on the work of our own conversion. Lord, hear us.
4.   We remember the sick and ask the Lord to give them strength and healing. Lord, hear us.
5.   We pray for our dead. May perpetual light shine upon them forever. Lord, hear us.

Heavenly Father, you have called us to join in the work of establishing the kingdom. Hear us now as we turn to you with our needs. We make our prayer through Christ, our Lord. Amen.

Fourth Sunday of the Year

It may come as a disappointment to ambitious-minded people that God does not look for success gauged and measured in human terms. Nowhere do we hear this message more clearly than in the gospel we have just read, which is the opening passage of Christ's Sermon on the Mount – generally known as the beatitudes. In poetic language they tell us what a true christian should be and spell out the correct relationship of man to God. We might feel uncomfortable as we listen to Christ's perspective on what brings happiness right now in this life and not just in the future. In a startling reversal of earthly standards he puts a high value on mercy, forgiveness and gentleness. He rejects out of hand wealth, rank and freedom to do what we choose, because they give us the impression that we can manage our affairs without taking God into consideration. Every thing the world values as a blessing is absent from what Jesus teaches in the beatitudes and everything the world counts a failure Jesus proposes as a blessing. Human success and power count for nothing in God's eyes. Holiness and wealth do not fit comfortably together.

The beatitudes give us cause for reflection as they turn our normal value system upside down, forcing us to confront whether we are guided by the gospel or by the pattern set by society. Their message contradicts our common sense approach to life yet they are the guidelines of Christ to us on how to spend this life, in order one day to enjoy eternity with him in heaven. At first sight they do not seem to be true, yet it remains a fact of experience that real genuine happiness doesn't come from wealth, power or prestige. There is a fatal flaw in such a manner of behaviour. When we can look back and remember something that has caused us great hurt like a broken relationship or an unfaithful commitment, we may realise that it was often the failure or the disappointment that made us the person that we are. Whatever it looked like when it happened, we realise now that without that set-back we would be a smaller and a less mature person. If we are stronger, more compassionate, tolerant or wiser, it is because we have permitted difficult situations to shape us.

The life of a follower of Christ is not meant to be easy as it calls on us to do things that don't come naturally to us. Remember

Jesus is still speaking to us today and wanting to know: 'Are we kind, considerate and helpful, or are we selfish uncharitable and lazy?' He offers us a joy which shines through sorrow and suffering and which nothing in life or death can take away.

Prayer of the Faithful

Happiness is the most exclusive of all human pursuits. We pray now to God the Father for that peace of soul which entails becoming totally dependent on him.

1.   We pray for the leaders of the church. May they have the courage and strength to proclaim the Good News which is a sign of contradiction to the world. Lord, hear us.
2.   We remember those who are facing persecution because of their witness to the gospel. May they experience the comforting presence of Christ in the midst of their hardship. Lord, hear us.
3.   We pray for our community, that we may take the beatitudes to heart and become blessed and happy in establishing God's kingdom on earth. Lord, hear us.
4.   We pray for the sick and those who mourn the loss of their loved ones. May they be strengthened and healed of their sorrow and pain. Lord, hear us.
5.   We pray for the dead. May they experience the joy and peace of your heavenly kingdom. Lord, hear us.

Eternal Father, we know that you care deeply for our happiness. Strengthen us and keep us close to you who are the source of our peace and joy. We make our prayer through Christ our Lord. Amen.

Fifth Sunday of the Year

When friends compliment us on our goodness and reliability, stating that we are the salt of the earth, they are paying us a great tribute. Just as salt acts as a preservative and adds taste to food,so does christianity lend flavour to life by helping people to live correctly, keeping society wholesome. In the story of the creation of the world God's first act was to dispel darkness and bring order out of chaos by producing light. The gospel reminds us of our noble calling of bringing Jesus into the world. The brightness of our lives as we follow in the footsteps of Christ enlightens the path of God for those around us. Christ's own life was short-lived and his mission was confined to Palestine. The Good News of salvation can only reach others through his followers.

Christ has placed his gospel into our hands and it depends on us whether or not it is proclaimed. His message is seen for what it is when we put it into practice in our lives. Truly good people who take their religion seriously may be quite unaware of the effect they have on others, but their influence does not go unnoticed. There is a warmth and attractiveness about those whose good deeds and actions reflect the image of Jesus, the light of the world. The presence of a genuine Christ-like character enriches the community and enables the best in others to come forth.

We can celebrate the presence of God at home and at work without going out of our way to do anything exceptional. It is evident in ordinary things, like the selfless love of a home-help caring for the every need of a senior citizen or of parents who are loyal to each other and completely dedicated to their children. Likewise, the darkness which is brought about in a community by jealousy, spite and hatred is dispelled and a legacy of shadows lifted when Christ is reflected by neighbours talking and acting in a friendly manner. Such acts of service create an environment where Christ can be known, loved and cherished. These and similar good works are the salt which gives flavour and sparkle to daily life and lets the light of Christ shine forth for all to see.

Prayer of the Faithful

Assembled as a worshipping community, we ask God the Father for the necessary strength and power to bring his light into the world.

1.   We pray that the church may be a beacon of light for all those striving to follow in the footsteps of Christ. Lord,hear us.
2.   That we may realise that we have got to share our bread with the poor and care for the homeless in order to be the salt of the earth. Lord, hear us.
3.   May the light of Christ be reflected in our contact with the people in our community and be a source of comfort to them. Lord, hear us.
4.   We pray for the sick, the depressed and the heartbroken, that they may discover the light of Christ in their suffering. Lord, hear us.
5.   We pray for the dead. May the Lord grant them light, happiness and peace. Lord, hear us.

Heavenly Father, give us the courage to rely on your Son so completely that we may risk everything for the building of your kingdom on earth. We make our prayer through Christ our Lord. Amen.

Sixth Sunday of the Year

One of the main criticisms levelled at church-goers is that their Sunday worship has little influence on their weekday lives. We have only to think of the glaring credibility gap created when members of a congregation, who have not been speaking for years, can gather around the table of the Lord and receive his body, or, on going home from church, refuse to pay outstanding debts, or see nothing wrong with conducting shady business deals. Sincere worship cannot arise from corrupt hearts. Such behaviour by a few can leave an entire congregation open to the accusation that its religious practice is insincere, pure lip-service, and not from the heart.

Jesus is telling us in this gospel that getting by within the letter of the law is not what he has in mind for his followers and spells out clearly what he expects of all those who profess to believe in him. He does not lay down rules and regulations for every situation in life but he asks us to keep a check on our inner attitudes, on our motivation. Thoughts are just as important as deeds. What we say and do must express what is in our hearts because good attitudes produce sincere actions. Anyone can easily perform an outwardly good deed to impress friends, but God is not so readily fooled by such an action. Jesus gives the commandments a deeper meaning, stating that they are to be written into our hearts and into the innermost part of our being. The commandments are a blessing from God and a sign of his care for us. They are for our own welfare and pave the path to inner freedom. If our goal is merely to avoid breaking them then we are not striving for any measure of perfection but simply fulfilling the basic minimum required for salvation.

Christ's teaching about adultery in the heart may seem harsh but when we give the matter some serious thought we see that there is much more needed in creating a good marriage than simply avoiding the evil of adultery. Marriage and happy family life require a whole-hearted and lifelong dedication by both partners. A mutual trust is involved when a couple abandon themselves emotionally, sexually, spiritually and psychologically to each other. Forming a circle of love, in order to stand together and face the world, requires a lot of effort and cannot be achieved through a half-hearted commitment Jesus invites us to relate to God and each other in a new way. Our approach should be based on what pleases God rather than on what we are bound to do. We are not going to be judged on the evil we have avoided but on the good works we have carried out.

Prayer of the Faithful

With confidence we now raise our hearts to God the Father who guides us through the readings of scripture to a deeper understanding of his Law.

1. We pray for our Holy Father and the bishops of the church, that through their teaching and preaching they may challenge us to follow Christ's way of love. Lord, hear us.
2. That we may never put demands on our young people which we are unwilling to carry out in our own lives. Lord, hear us.
3. We pray that all married couples in our community may experience the warmth of God's love in their relationships. Lord, hear us.
4. We remember in a special way the sick and the old. May they be encouraged by the words and comforted by the actions of those who care for them. Lord, hear us.
5. We pray that the faithful departed may enjoy peace and happiness in the kingdom of God. Lord, hear us.

Almighty and everlasting Father, enlighten our lives with your law of love and keep us on the right road which leads to your kingdom. We make this prayer through Christ our Lord. Amen.

Seventh Sunday of the Year

One of the greatest challenges in Christ's teaching is to love those who hate and harm us. This passage of scripture about forgiving wrongdoers and loving our enemies must rank among the most demanding ever preached by Jesus. Forgiving our enemies is not easy. Not to retaliate goes against the human grain and requires great strength and discipline of character.

The gospel reveals the ugly side of human nature and shows us up for what we are – people who are full of petty jealousies, hatreds and spites. A personal remark or a cutting word from a neighbour automatically sparks off a row and revenge is sought immediately. We trade insult for injury and end up out of sorts, nursing hatreds, harbouring grudges and not speaking. Life is full of people with chips on their shoulders because they didn't get the job, were not invited to a wedding or were omitted from a vote of thanks. They carry the scars for years, refusing to let wounds heal until scores are evened out. There is never any shortage of excuses for such behaviour. The world we live in has raised vengeance to the level of virtue and pours scorn on the weakling who doesn't seek retaliation but allows his wife and children to be insulted. Christ rejects this law of revenge and insists on his followers repaying evil with kindness. He warns against giving in to bitterness and being obsessed with feelings of vindictiveness. Hatred never cures any situation. When we grow to hate someone we give that person power and control over us which eats into our heart and destroys our peace of mind. Jesus tells us that such attitudes are not in line with his teachings. People who behave in such a manner have not even begun to appreciate what christianity is about.

Christ's message is one of forgiveness, pardon and generosity urging us to love others irrespective of whether or not we are loved in return. This gospel points to the necessity of having a forgiving heart as a basic essential for loving our enemies. A good take-away thought this morning is-do we pray for those responsible for causing suffering, inflicting hardship and bringing unhappiness into our lives? When we offer pardon and show forgiveness we rise to the level of Christ. The challenge is to decide whether hatred or love is the main motivating factor in our lives. Love of a neighbour is always the distinguishing mark of a christian.

Prayers of the Faithful

We now turn to God the Father for the help needed to follow the example of Jesus who tells us that we are to love our enemies.

1.   For the leaders of the church, that they may give witness to their people in the ways of pardon, love and forgiveness and so reflect God's holiness in the world. Lord, hear us.

2.   That those who are angry and bitter with their neighbours may realise that giving into feelings of resentment and hatred only separates them from God. Lord, hear us.

3.   Let us pray for families who are divided and torn apart because of rows. May they discover their former closeness and warmth. Lord, hear us.

4.   That the sick may attain the peace of mind which grows from appreciating their special role in joining Christ in his suffering. Lord, hear us.

5.   We pray for the dead. May they share in the peace and happiness of God's kingdom. Lord, hear us.

God our Father, you know what is good for us. Rid our hearts of all bitterness and bless our efforts to love all people. We make our prayer through Christ our Lord. Amen.

Eighth Sunday of the Year

Jesus speaks in a very challenging and uncompromising manner when he states that we cannot serve two masters. In a wealth of poetic imagery he points out the danger of seeking security in material possessions rather than putting our trust in God who can be relied upon to provide everything we need. The risk we take when we spend too much time in the pursuit of worldly goods is that God gets precious little space, is easily forgotten and is pushed into the background. The problem facing us is that the world we live in encourages us to set our hearts on acquiring more and more and to seek security in possessions. Our worth is measured in what we own, irrespective of whether we have acquired it honestly or at the expense of pushing people aside and treating them shabbily in the process.

Greed can get to the best of us. It so easily becomes a vicious circle because the more we have the more we want. We fail to remember that a time will come when everything we own and cherish dearly will have to be left behind. On that day human approval will count for nothing. All that will matter then, is how we measure up to God's judgement in the way we have treated others, in the use of his gifts. Because of the constant danger of becoming immersed in the affairs of the world Christ calls for a detachment from material goods with an invitation to a lifestyle based on simplicity and dependence on God. This will mean standing back and turning our thoughts heavenwards so that we can get our priorities right. Sometimes it takes sickness or a hospital bed to make us realise who is the master. In order to relate properly to people we may have to empty ourselves of our selfish desires and personal ambitions.

We could reflect for a few moments on what influence and bearing God has in our lives. The answers can be found in the respect we have for other people and the importance we attach to the image-building symbols of status, power and prestige. To trust in God does not mean sitting back and acting irresponsibly as if food, money and clothes are unimportant. Without food there is no life. Without clothes the body is naked and grows cold. Jesus is not advocating reckless living. As stewards of creation we are to make good use of our human resourcefulness and plan our lives in a responsible manner. However, worry and anxiety, which arise from being over concerned with our own welfare and security are such a wasted effort and betray an outlook which is not based on a deep faith or befitting a disciple. Constant fretting takes all the joy from life and wears out mind and body. Trust in the Father who cares for the whole of creation gives us a freedom of heart, a deep inner peace and a realisation that we are loved. We are made for God and our hearts are restless until they rest in him.

Prayer of the Faithful

Placing aside our worries and anxieties, we bring our innermost needs before God the Father who cares for the whole of creation and in whom we live and move and have our being.

1.   We pray for our Holy Father and the bishops of the church. May they devote themselves tirelessly to the furthering of God's kingdom of truth and love. Lord, hear us.
2.   May we as a community realise that we are carrying out God's will when we show care and concern for the poor. Lord, hear us.
3.   We pray that we may live in complete submission to the will of God and never become over-anxious concerning matters that are not worth worrying about. Lord, hear us.
4.   We pray for the sick. May they experience the love of God through the love and compassion of those who care for life at its weakest moments. Lord, hear us.
5.   We pray for the dead. May they share in Christs' victory over death. Lord, hear us.

Heavenly Father, your love touches our lives at every single moment. Help us to appreciate all the blessings you shower upon us. May we never set our hearts on material things but put our trust in your loving providence. We make our prayer through Christ our Lord. Amen.

Ninth Sunday of the Year

Nothing in the teaching of Jesus is spelt out with greater clarity than that actions speak louder than words. We must practice what we preach because calling ourselves christians without living our beliefs is not going to help us get to heaven. In this gospel Jesus seems to be warning us against over-confidence and self-complacency. We can leave the church feeling good and fail to realise that religion serves no useful purpose if it is confined to the Sabbath, while remaining isolated from our daily lives. The test of Sunday worship is the effect it has on our homes, place of work and the way it influences our relationships with friends and neighbours. Jesus is clearly opposed to us presuming that we have an assured place in God's kingdom, as salvation is not given free but to doers of the word of God and not hearers only. What matters most is our commitment because Christ asks us to become his disciples in a practical and personal way.

This is a call for honest reflection on what the performance of our religious duties means to us. If our profession of faith is something that is merely expressed with our lips, it is a superficial display of belief and of no value. We are in the same league as the man who built his house on sandy ground. On judgement day our bluff will be called and we will be shown up for what we really are. We will be numbered among those who talk and do not act. The reproach, 'I never knew you' will ring in our ears and the consequence will spell disaster and total ruin. God calls for our undivided alleg-iance and asks us to be faithful to all his teaching. He wants us to take his words into our hearts and souls and make them the foundation of our lives. If we base our life firmly on his promise we will become strong enough in the moment of crisis to withstand all assaults and temptations.

A glance at the gospel will show that the worst sins are those of omission, of our failure to show love on a daily basis to one another. There are so many in need whom we can help. We have only to move one tiny step to love and serve someone else and we touch God. The great test is the care and consideration shown to neighbours. On many a day we meet people in need, seldom from want of food but always from the lack of affection, the comforting word of encouragement and the need for forgiveness. When we visit the sick, show concern for the bereaved and help the poor we are engaging in the Lord's work of changing darkness into light. There is no secret about what he wants and there is no better time to begin than now.

Prayer of the Faithful

Holding loyally to the gospel which urges us to build our spiritual house on the will of God, we make our prayer to the Father.

1.   We pray for our Holy Father and the bishops of the church, that they may exercise their responsibility with regard for your glory. Lord, hear us.

2.   We pray for a deepening of our own faith and a deeper consciousness of your presence among the poor, the handicapped and the disadvantaged. Lord, hear us.

3.   We pray for our young people growing up in an unstable and confusing world. Give meaning to their lives and help them to overcome failure. Lord,hear us.

4.   We ask you Lord to send your loving kindness, comforting presence and healing peace upon the sick and all who suffer ill health. Lord, hear us.

5.   We pray for those whom death has taken from us. Grant them eternal rest and perpetual light. Lord, hear us.

Heavenly Father, give us the grace to understand how our lives depend upon the goodness, honesty and courage of fellow human beings, so that we may be mindful of their needs and aware of our responsibilities. We make our prayer through Christ our Lord. Amen.

Tenth Sunday of the Year

The call of Matthew to follow Jesus and leave behind his position as custom post official by the sea of Galilee gives us a deep insight into the ways of God. Matthew was employed by the Romans and earned his living as a tax collector for the government. It was a fast method of making money but to survive in the job one had to be a despicable person, completely corrupt and without a shred of human kindness. People treated tax officials with contempt, regarded them as criminals, avoided their company and refused them entrance to the synagogue. Such a notorious sinner was the least likely person we would have expected Christ to choose as an apostle. It certainly scandalised the Pharisees who, considering themselves the guardians of conventional religion, did not think that they had any thing to learn from Jesus. Their closed minds did not appreciate his compassion and mercy as expressed in his association with sinners.

Nevertheless when Jesus gazed straight into Matthew's eyes he saw beneath a corrupt exterior a potential for goodness and a man who was so unhappy with his old life of shame that he was willing to begin again. Matthew proves what can happen to us once we decide to respond to the call of Christ stirring within our souls. He wastes no time in submitting himself heart and soul to God's word. Joining the ranks of the penniless preacher from Nazareth meant saying farewell to a good life and the start of a long journey through mystery and tragedy towards the resurrection. It was a tough track, dusty and stony, but the pathway was full of surprises as hope shone through moments of hardship and gloom.

In similar fashion God beckons us to open our hearts to his call wherever we are and however it may come to us. Our whole being, body and spirit, should make a courageous response to that invitation. When his voice is disturbing our comfortable, half-hearted, middle-of-the-road christianity we often pretend not to be listening. Sometimes we argue our way out of performing difficult tasks. We forget that discipleship means much more than trailing after Jesus. It means recognising him as someone special, making an act of faith in his presence and throwing our lot in with his way of life. If we are to be the people God wants us to be and do the job he intends us to do, we must live up to the standard of love and truth set out by his spirit in the very ordinary details of our daily behaviour. In whatever way we live and try to share the christian gospel we are living out our vocation. There is nowhere we can walk in life without leaving the imprint of who we are upon the ground we tread.

Prayer of the Faithful

Safe under the protection of God the Father who is the source of every richness and blessing which fill our lives, we confidently make our prayer.

1.   We pray for the Holy Father, and all who are called to leadership in the church. Give them vision to see into the issues of their time and courage to uphold your gospel. Lord, hear us.
2.   We pray for the leaders of our country and those who exercise temporal power in the community that God may grant them wisdom and compassion in all their decisions. Lord, hear us.
3.   We pray for a deepening of our own faith and for a deeper consciousness of the Lord ever present and ever accompanying us. Lord, hear us.
4.   We pray for the aged and the sick. Give them the grace to put their experience of life to good use in your service. Help us to treat them always with respect and affection. Lord, hear us.
5.   Grant Lord, eternal rest and perpetual light to our loved ones. Lord, hear us.

Heavenly Father, direct the minds of those called to make crucial choices in their lives. Give them an understanding heart, sound judgement and a burning desire to do what pleases you. We make our prayer through Christ our Lord. Amen.

Eleventh Sunday of the Year

In this setting we have our Lord sending his newly chosen disciples, whom he selects from a general group, on a trial mission at the very beginning of their ministry. The scope of their activity is limited to looking after their own people – a leaderless multitude who seem to be lost, and deprived of guidance. Christ takes pity on their plight, because they are like sheep without a shepherd, and turns his attention to alleviating their distress. The ministry of these first disciples is gradually unfolded and is one of mercy and forgiveness, accompanied by a vast campaign of physical and spiritual healing. Their role is to be active preachers who proclaim the saving work of God. He gives them authority to expel unclean spirits and cure sickness and disease of every kind. They are the powers that Christ exercises in his own ministry when he goes about teaching and preaching in Galilee.

The strategy of Jesus for realising his ideal of the kingdom of heaven on earth is to employ his followers to proclaim the saving activity of God. It is worth noting that even though time is pressing and the loss of the harvest of souls is imminent, Christ urges his disciples not just to fling themselves headlong into activity but to pray that the Lord of the harvest will help them in their work. Prayer helps us realise that we are called by God and encourages us to live up to our responsibilities as his people. In prayer we come to better appreciate the seriousness of sin, the value of God's mercy and the magnitude of his love for sinners. Only through prayer can we share the life of Christ in the unique way the apostles did.

Removed though we are by 2,000 years from the time of Jesus, we are servants of the church and are responsible for delivering God's message to the world. As christians it is our task to continue the work of Christ. Only with our words can he speak to people and alert them of the nearness of the kingdom. It is with our preaching that he encourages conversion by pointing out the availability of salvation. In the midst of trials, when we look upon human problems with understanding hearts, we bring his encouragement showing that even in the midst of trouble there is one who cares. We preach Christ's message best by reflecting his values in our own lives – actions supplement words and express more fully the genuineness and honesty of what we say. If we are good advertisements for the church, the many non-believers with whom we come in contact may go a step further and discover Christ as a result. It is no small challenge to be Christ's messenger as it demands great effort and hard work.

Prayer of the Faithful

As God's holy people, called in different ways to spread the Good News of the kingdom, we place our needs before our Father who continues to care for us.

1.   We pray for our Holy Father and the bishops of the church, that they may faithfully preach Christ's message to the world and never tire in their efforts. Lord, hear us.
2.   We pray for ourselves. May we always be kind and generous and reach out to others in love for the sake of the kingdom. Lord, hear us.
3.   We pray for farmers and all who work on the land. May they be blessed with favourable weather and gather an abundant harvest. Lord, hear us.
4.   We pray for young people sitting examinations at this time. May their hard work be rewarded with success. Lord, hear us.
5.   We pray for the sick. May they receive comfort and strength from those who care for them. Lord, hear us.
6.   We pray for the dead. May they rest in the peace of Christ's kingdom. Lord, hear us.

Heavenly Father, the harvest of souls is abundant but the labourers are few. In your compassion hear us and help us to take part with joy in the spreading of your message. We ask this through Christ our Lord. Amen.

Twelfth Sunday of the Year

In these days of indifference to the gospel message, it is good to recall the instruction Jesus gave to his apostles as he prepared them for their mission of preaching. Opposition to the gospel is inevitable so he points out the danger they will face. People whose evil stands to be exposed will not tolerate their preaching and will behave in an aggressive manner towards them. Their mission in a world that does not readily accept the good news will meet with resistance. This gospel is a reminder that we cannot expect the community around us to receive the teaching of Christ with open arms. Jesus makes no secret of the fact that bearers of the word of God will suffer ridicule and rejection, yet he urges us to bear witness to him openly and to be fearless in making a stand for truth and justice however unpopular this may make us.

Fear is an emotion with which we are all familiar as it often cripples our lives and hinders us from being the people we want to be. We can think of so many situations in life where our response to Christ is feeble and half-hearted. Because of the fear of being laughed at, being out of fashion or regarded as weaklings we often fail to stand up for what we know to be just and right in our hearts. Maybe in the company we keep there is a danger of losing friends, by going to church, refusing to take part in idle gossip that drags someone's name through the mud, or saying no to drink or drugs. For evil to triumph, all that is required is for good people to remain silent. The pressure in the face of temptation to abandon our christian principles because of the smirks and sneers of others arises daily and challenges our loyalty to the teaching of Jesus Christ.

The mission of Jesus was to proclaim his Father's love and he never failed in carrying out that task. No one can be a follower of Christ without making an act of confidence in his work by announcing the message of the kingdom. If the word of God is to free us to act according to our deeper convictions then we must pray for the grace to overcome our fears. There are many situations in life when it is supportive to remember those words of the Lord, 'Fear not.' Whatever happens, God is always in control. It is his world. His power and his Spirit are at work in our midst and we can be sure of his steadfast love. When we have completed our earthly journey of professing the Good News, he will claim us as his own before the Father.

Prayer of the Faithful

Gathered together as a community to celebrate the mystery of our salvation, we turn now in prayer to God our eternal Father, conscious of his love for each of us.

1. For our Holy Father, our bishop and all who have been called to guide God's people. May they direct humankind to a knowledge and belief in Christ. Lord, hear us.

2. We ask for the grace to face difficult situations with courage knowing that you are always at our side to give us strength. Lord, hear us.

3. For the poor, the oppressed and those whose lives are crippled by fear. May we respond to their voices with compassion as they cry out for help. Lord, hear us.

4. For students sitting examinations at this time. May they give of their best and receive the reward of their hard work. Lord, hear us.

5. For the sick and the disabled that they may experience the healing and comfort that only Christ can bring. Lord, hear us.

6. For all our faithful departed. May they reap the reward of their labours in God's eternal kingdom. Lord, hear us.

Heavenly Father, you are the source of all life. We offer you our prayers. Dispel the darkness of evil from our hearts and fill us with the brightness of your blessing. Amen.

Thirteenth Sunday of the Year

In an age when people are growing further apart there is a greater need for friendliness than ever before, and the traditional value of hospitality is once more being rediscovered. Far from being an optional extra, hospitality is regarded as a sacred duty and the equivalent of welcoming the Lord himself. The delightful story of the couple who made the prophet Elisha welcome under their roof and as a result were rewarded with the gift of a son, is an indication of how precious hospitality is in the eyes of God. The gospel reminds us that all small ways of giving and caring which we avail of, even a trivial act of kindness, like the giving of a cup of cold water to a stranger on our doorstep, will win God's favour, and result in a great blessing. The world we live in is crying out for small acts of kindness, which cost little but are sadly missing, like a smile, a word of appreciation or a phone-call. In extending a welcome to other people we are following in the footsteps of the Master who has room for everybody in his heart.

Inviting Jesus into our lives and putting him first in our preference is a demanding task as it involves a re-shaping of our attitudes. It may mean coming to grips with years of inbuilt selfishness which goes against the grain. Christ comes to our doors in many disguises and is not always recognisable. If we have not cracked open the hard shell of indifference to others, we run the risk of letting slip so many opportunities for soul-making. When a stranger comes looking for help, our natural instinct tells us not to get involved or put ourselves to any trouble. Unless we have made a conscious decision to reach out to those in want, we will resent the disturbance such intrusions make on our privacy and run the risk of neglecting a genuine needy person.

Following Christ involves putting his way of life into practice and in a christian community this means everyone should feel welcome and there should be no strangers or outcasts. Hospitality means showing a generosity of disposition and a willingness to interrupt our personal lives in order to perform some unrecorded act of kindness because it is not what is given that counts but the heart with which it is given. The least we can do for Christ, who has accepted us in our sinfulness, is to receive one another with open arms. In this way we respond to his compelling call for discipleship and allow his word to take hold of us.

Prayer of the Faithful

Mindful of God's steadfast love for humanity, we come with open arms and lovingly place our petitions before him.

1.   We pray that the church may become a community of love where all are welcome and no person feels rejected. Lord, hear us.
2.   We pray for everyone in our parish community. Inspire them to search for the good in one another and to show the generosity of an open heart towards all who are lonely and in need of company. Lord, hear us.
3.   For all those who are on holidays at this time. May God grant them an enjoyable break and a safe return to their homes. Lord, hear us.
4.   For the sick at home and in hospital. May they have the courage to accept whatever cross the Lord may send their way. Lord, hear us.
5.   For all who have died. May the Lord welcome them into his kingdom of love and peace. Lord, hear us.

Heavenly Father, we thank you for listening to our prayer. You know our needs better than our words can express. Grant what is for our good and your glory. We ask this through Christ our Lord. Amen.

Fourteenth Sunday of the Year

From time to time, as the problems and worries of the moment overpower us, we all find life difficult and discouraging. As the signs of stress and tension become visible on our faces, we sit up and listen to those reassuring and comforting words of Jesus: 'Come to me all you who labour and are overburdened and I will give you rest.' Jesus presents himself as the friend and consoler of the weary and oppressed. In the middle of trying situations he seems to invite us to come to him with our worries saying all will be well. This giving of our hearts to Christ implies complete trust and childlike dependence, qualities which are missing in our adult world. When we were young we spent our childhood days in a simple carefree setting, relying completely on the love of those who cared for us. Growing up meant casting aside this childlike trust and exchanging it for reliance on material possessions. We have lost our paradise of childhood innocence and as a result find it difficult to cast our cares upon the Lord with the confidence that he will sustain us.

Christ leaves us in no doubt that humility is vital in our search for God. It is not a prized quality in our society where success is measured on arrogance, ambition and ruthlessness and, where the house we live in, the car we drive and the company we keep are indicators of our esteem. The humble person does not have to complicate matters by projecting such a false self-image or deceiving himself with the trappings of grandeur. He realises that without God he is nothing. Because we are lacking in humility, we are robbed of that inner peace which comes from putting our hand in the hand of God. Humility enables us to let go of self and make space for God in whom we find our strength. When we come to Mass on Sunday morning laden down with the problems and troubles of the past week, Christ meets us at our own level. As we unload our difficulties and sufferings before him, he makes them into an acceptable offering to his heavenly Father.

This gospel speaks to us of the tender personal and human qualities of Christ's love for us. God is full of mercy and compassion and a great comfort in times of sorrow and distress. There is a great capacity for goodness in each one of us, provided we accept the invitation to build up our lives with Christ as our model.

Prayers of the Faithful

Gathered together as a worshipping community we bring all our needs before our heavenly Father, confident of his loving care.

1. We pray for our Holy Father and the bishops of the church. May they guide us in the ways of peace and reconciliation. Lord, hear us.

2. We pray for those who are tempted to despair under the crushing weight of their problems. May they seek refuge by placing their anxieties and worries in the hands of Jesus. Lord, hear us.

3. We pray that our own words and actions may convey a deep trust in the generous love of Jesus. Lord, hear us.

4. We pray for all those who are weighed down by sickness. May they find comfort and healing in the care and concern of those who nurse them. Lord, hear us.

5. We pray that all those who died recently may enjoy everlasting happiness in the kingdom of God. Lord, hear us.

Heavenly Father, your Son promised to give us rest when overburdened. Grant that we may always respond to his guidance and strengthen us to be instruments of his peace. We make our prayer through Christ our Lord. Amen.

Fifteenth Sunday of the Year

Jesus paints a very familiar picture from everyday agricultural life in Palestine and draws a lesson from it. It's the story of a farmer who goes out to sow seed in the rich soil of his field but unfortunately some seed accidently falls on rocky ground and among thorny briars and fails to take root. Seed needs soil and showers for growth. It needs protection from birds, wind and frost until it takes root and shoots forth to produce plants, flowers and fruit. The harvest will depend on the quality of the soil and the care and attention the seeds receive.

Jesus compares the word of God, which is intended to produce fruit in our lives, to seed sowed in the earth by the farmer. At baptism the delicate and demanding seed of the word of God is first planted in our hearts. If it doesn't get our whole-hearted attention by finding a home in our lives, it withers and dies. Often when the Lord comes knocking on our door we fail to make him welcome because we are so preoccupied with the meaningless pursuits of the moment. To be a cultivator of goodness, we have to dig deep within ourselves. God does not want part-time or half-hearted followers. His word never blossoms alongside greed, snobbishness and the love of the easy life.

Growth in the life of Christ is not always a smooth, gradual and straightforward process. The different types of soil can well be the varied response we make to his word, depending on the twists and turns our fortunes may take. When we meet with setbacks and disappointments, obstacles may stack up against our good intentions and weaken our firm resolve. Moments like this call for deep faith. No matter what the situation, we have to struggle to believe. The word of God has an immense and mysterious power to change us. The hard thorny patch that our lives may be currently experiencing, could be Christ's way of calling us to a deeper union with him. Experience tells us we have to work for anything that is worth having. Reaping the rich harvest of God's goodness depends on our openness to receive his word. So often, when God is sowing the seed of his love around us we are cold, off-hand and too proud to allow ourselves to be won over. However, there is good soil in every human heart and given time and effort and a considerable degree of pain, the Spirit of the living God will put down deep roots in our lives, assuring us of salvation.

Prayer of the Faithful

We now place our prayers and petitions before God the Father with the great confidence that they will be heard.

1. We pray for our Holy Father and the bishops of the church. May they be guided by God's spirit in their efforts to produce a harvest of justice, love and peace. Lord, hear us.

2. We pray that as a parish community we may grow in tolerance, understanding and forgiveness. Lord, hear us.

3. We pray that unchecked ambition and selfishness may never smother the word of God in our lives. Lord, hear us.

4. We remember our sick. May they experience the healing power of Christ giving them hope. Lord, hear us.

5. May those who died recently enjoy light, happiness and peace in heaven and may those burdened with grief have courage to overcome their loss. Lord, hear us.

Heavenly Father, help us to recognise the seed of your word at work in our lives. May we never get distracted by the cares of this world but be active in your service and so produce an abundant harvest. We ask this through Christ our Lord. Amen.

Sixteenth Sunday of the Year

We can see from the gospel passage that the people Christ was preaching to were country folk, close to the earth, aware of the rise and fall of the seasons and with a keen eye for harvest time. Christ compares the church, the people of God, to a field where wheat and weeds grow side by side until the harvest. Only then are the good separated from the wicked. In the world around us, good and bad people mix like wheat and weeds growing in the same field. This prompts the question asked by many upright and impatient believers: Why does God who is good allow evil to flourish? They want to see vice rooted out immediately. Such an attitude too readily forgets that every human heart contains a mixture of good and evil. We are a sinful people and should be conscious of our failings. Life is more complicated than drawing clear cut lines between saints and sinners. The church is not an exclusive community of the virtuous. It is here because we are sinners looking for salvation. The patience and tolerance extended by God to our personal sinful situation is to be shown to those whose faults are known to us.

This gospel story gives us an insight into the life of God whose power is best displayed in leniency and endless patience. He is at all times concerned with the conversion of people but never with their destruction. With him no one is ever written off or considered beyond redemption. His mercy is more urgent than his judgement and his nature is best revealed in his tolerance towards the wayward in our midst. God cares for everybody, but especially for those whose lives are choked by sin. The Pharisees were highly critical of Jesus choosing to break bread and share the company of people who highlighted weakness. By wanting to right the wrongs of society we can easily forget that it is God's world. He is in control and it is not our business to judge others before he does. It should suffice to know that in the end good will triumph.

The emphasis in this gospel is on exercising patience and showing tolerance until God makes his great gathering on judgement day. In the meantime, as members of the church, we all share the task of revealing the patience of God by forgiving the faults of others. Many of us will find this challenging, as we may be harsh or judgemental by nature. It's all so easy to categorise people and pin the label 'sinner' on them, forgetting how appearances are so often deceptive. This does not mean cultivating an attitude of indifference towards evil. While we must abhor sin we must never stop loving the sinner. Judging others before God does is a very foolish and risky business. We are weak in many things and have enough to contend with in the swampy patches of our own lives where wild weeds are growing. God has lost ground there and we have no one else to blame but ourselves for sowing these weeds. The good news is that it is never too late for a sinner to turn back to God and be accepted. Weeds can never become wheat, but by the power of God a sinner can become a saint. Let us all be thankful that on the last day we shall be judged by God and not by one another.

Prayers of the Faithful

As a frail and weak people we bring our petitions before our heavenly Father who in his mercy and love wants us to be saved and come to a knowledge of the truth.

1.   We pray for our Holy Father and the bishops of the church. May they always work for the good of all the people under their care being especially aware of the poor and less privileged. Lord, hear us.

2.   We pray that as a parish community we may recognise the goodness in each other, show charity to all we meet and refrain from judging or condemning the wayward. Lord, hear us.

3.   We remember especially all who have lost their way and are feeling the pain of loneliness, anxiety and rejection. May their hope in the mercy and love of God be restored. Lord, hear us.

4.   We remember the sick, the housebound and those who are suffering. May they be encouraged and their lives blessed in the knowledge of God's love for them. Lord, hear us.

5.   We commend to the mercy of the Lord all who have died. May their sins be forgiven and may they rest in the peace of heaven forever. Lord, hear us.

Heavenly Father, may the power of your love always sustain us. Help us not to get distracted by the cares of this world and not to be overcome by the evil in our lives. We make our prayer through Christ our Lord. Amen.

Seventeenth Sunday of the Year

Each person has a different set of values in life. Some people crave for fame and popularity. Nothing pleases them more than to be recognised in the street and to have their photographs in the newspaper. For others the pursuit is status and respectability within the community. They are not happy unless they've got a luxury home, money in the bank and drive an expensive car. Their big push is for material goods. But the readings in today's liturgy issue a direct challenge to all types of worldly life-styles and tell us to get our priorities right. Many married couples find out the hard way that it is more important for a family to be happy than to live in plush surroundings. Time spent with children is of more value than money spent on toys. We may live in the age of the instant, but rearing a family and teaching them how to get along with one another are things that cannot be rushed. Experience teaches us that there are no short cuts in these important matters because anything that is worthwhile cannot be achieved without a lot of effort.

The treasure the gospel is referring to is our faith which tells us we are heirs to the kingdom of God. It is so import-ant and valuable that everybody must give it absolute priority. This should be our only interest and chief concern in life. At the end of the day nothing else matters because worldly values are destined to pale into insignificance. Our search should not be for superficial happiness but to develop a good relationship with God.

One of the encouraging aspects of this gospel story is that such a treasure can be found in ordinary places. God is constantly speaking to us in the simplicity of our lives. What we've got to do is to open our eyes to his presence and search for him in the bits and pieces of everyday happenings. This will only come about with prayer and by taking a good look at ourselves and trying to discover what God is saying to us at any given moment. We can stumble across the treasure, in suffering bravely borne and properly accepted or when a serious illness leaves us invalided and our entire future is put in jeopardy. Such times of crisis with everything falling apart may be a call to new growth and an adventure in holiness.

It's a day to reflect on the depth and the value we put on our faith in Christ. How many can honestly say that nothing else matters but this precious gift handed down to us by our parents and by a previous generation at so great cost? Does it mean anything to us that Jesus died on the cross for our sins so that we could share in his glory? If we really want happiness there is no point in turning to the passing things of life hoping that they will fill our emptiness and loneliness. We must invest time and energy in detaching ourselves from such superficiality. Our great destiny is to share in God's glory so our sole preoccupation should be to stake everything on Christ and the values he stands for and portrays.

Prayers of the Faithful

Knowing that our heavenly Father in his wisdom provides for all our needs, with confidence we approach him in prayer.

1. We pray for our Holy Father and the bishops of the church, that they may be guided and inspired by the wisdom of the gospel. Lord, hear us.
2. We pray that we may use the material gifts necessary for our well being in a proper way and not become victims of greed, selfishness and the pursuit of wealth. Lord, hear us.
3. For ourselves, and all those who are searching for the truth, that we may come daily to a deeper appreciation of our faith in Jesus Christ as the pearl of great price. Lord, hear us.
4. We remember all in our community who are sick and housebound. May the Lord fill the hearts of those caring for them with love and compassion. Lord, hear us.
5. For all our friends who have departed this life and for all the faithful departed. May they rest in peace. Lord, hear us.

Heavenly Father, source of all that is good in life, help us to use your gifts wisely and to rejoice in the treasures of your love. We make our prayer through Christ our Lord. Amen.

Eighteenth Sunday of the Year

On hearing of the death of John the Baptist, Jesus was deeply up-set and in need of finding a quiet place where he could share his grief with the apostles. However, when he stepped ashore there were thousands waiting to reach out and touch him and they were not disappointed. He began teaching and nourishing them in mind and heart and finally towards evening, when they had been without food for a long time, he satisfied their hunger by working the miracle of the loaves and fishes. It was clearly a miraculous event, a marvellous happening and a pointer to the fact that God, who creates the world, provides us with food and takes care of our every need. The crowd returned to their homes satisfied and spiritually refreshed from the time spent in the com-pany of Jesus.

Here we have a picture of the church as it acts in every age. Jesus did not feed the stranded crowd at the edge of the sea of Galilee all on his own. He accomplished it with the help of his dis-ciples who were reluctant to accept responsibility for the hungry people. Their first reaction was to send the crowd away to fend for themselves, and let somebody else deal with the problem. Challenged by Jesus to use their own resources, they remembered having five loaves and two fishes which they brought to him. The little they had when placed in the hands of Jesus turned out to be more than enough for all. The five loaves and two fishes are sym-bols of the power for goodness which we all possess. In our own eyes it may seem of little account but it is what the Lord has given us and expects us to use in his service. The gift may be our ability to be a good neighbour, a caring listener to a sorrowing widow or a willing member of a parish organisation. In whatever way we minister to the needs of others, we show forth the compassion of Christ and extend his friendship. Jesus sets before everyone the task of communicating his love through the qualities they possess.

When we gather around the altar to celebrate the eucharist by our presence we make an offering of self and show that with the rest of the church we accept the challenge of Jesus to do what we can for the good of others. He receives our gifts in the same manner as he accepted the five loaves and two fishes from the disciples and offering them to the Father, gives them eternal value. On their own our efforts may seem small and insignificant but when placed in God's hands and fitted into his plans, they become part of the great saving mission of the church and give a deeper meaning to our lives. The Lord not only invites us here to be nourished at his table but sends us forth to give as we have received, to forgive as we have been forgiven, and to love as we have been loved.

Prayer of the Faithful

Gathered like the crowd in the gospel and hungry for the word of God, we turn now with confidence to our heavenly Father who never fails his people in their need.

1.   We pray for the church throughout the world, that it may witness in word and deed to God's love and concern for the hungry and needy. Lord, hear us.

2.   We pray that as a community we may be men and women of prayer and that we may be prepared to give of our time and talents to help those searching for the meaning of life. Lord, hear us.

3.   We pray for world leaders and all who hold positions of great power. May they help distribute the world's resources in such a way that no country may be in danger of famine. Lord, hear us.

4.   For the sick and the suffering. May they experience in their lives the sustaining love of God. Lord, hear us.

5.   We remember those who have died. May they enjoy forever the eternal banquet of heaven. Lord, hear us.

Heavenly Father, be mindful of us who are in need of your mercy. Fill our hearts with your love and never allow us to be separated from you. We make our prayer through Christ our Lord. Amen.

Nineteenth Sunday of the Year

This gospel episode takes place while the disciples are returning by boat, having left Jesus on his own to spend some time in prayer. Suddenly a storm blows up and their boat is in danger of foundering. Experienced sailors though they are, they find themselves battling hopelessly for their lives against the raging elements. Panic grips them at the sight of Jesus walking ghost-like towards them across the waters. In their distress they appeal to Jesus who beckons Peter to come and walk on the waters also. He starts out with the greatest confidence but quickly loses his nerve as he becomes conscious of the force of the wind and the power of the waves. His faith and his courage fail him and he starts to sink. Jesus promptly answers his cry of distress, comes to his aid but rebukes him for his lack of faith. The storm dies down – the crisis is resolved. Christ's presence produces a great calm on the waters and a deep peace in the disciples' hearts.

When confronted with stress and pressure of various kinds we are very much like Peter and can identify with his temptation to despair. A sudden turn of events in life and we are faced with storms which threaten the peace and security of our families and homes. At such moments our faith fails and we need to hear those encouraging words of Christ, 'Don't be afraid.' Life is a perilous journey and we need the help of Christ to guide us to our true destination. Peter's mistake was that he turned to Jesus in real prayer only in a moment of crisis when he was paralysed by fear and in danger of drowning. There is a lesson for all of us who tend to forget about God when all is going well and who only become serious about prayer when problems and tragedies arise. The saying, 'All we can do now is to pray,' betrays an attitude which regards prayer as a last resort when all else fails. Christ is prepared to help us at all times and not just in our hour of desperation. If we turn to him in all the circumstances of our lives he will show us how different his presence makes everything.

The gospel highlights the importance of faith and prayer in the following of Christ. When Peter accepted the Lord's invitation to come to him across the waters he was taking a risk – it was a leap in the dark, a journey into the unknown. Likewise, we have been invited by Christ to leave our relative security and follow him with conviction and courage through the storms and trials of life. We need not become casualties on the sea of life because the Lord is always waiting for us with outstretched arms.

Prayer of the Faithful

With renewed confidence in the love of God whose help is always close at hand, we humbly place our requests before him.

1.   We pray for our Holy Father and the bishops of the church. May the power of the Lord's presence continue to guide them in the storms and crisis that face the church. Lord, hear us.

2.   We pray for an increase in the gift of faith so that we may have the courage to trust in your presence amidst the problems of daily life. Lord, hear us.

3.   We pray for those who are drifting aimlessly on the stormy seas of life. May they find in the church a haven of peace. Lord, hear us.

4.   Help us to bring Christ's compassion to the sick by being channels of his loving care. Lord, hear us.

5.   We pray for the faithful departed. May they have heavenly rest in your presence. Lord, hear us.

God our Father, increase our faith so that we may enter more fully into the life of your church, and so accomplish your holy will. We ask this through Christ our Lord. Amen.

Twentieth Sunday of the Year

At the heart of this gospel is a lively exchange between Jesus and a Canaanite woman of great faith, who suffers so much from the illness of her daughter who is possessed by a devil. Totally convinced that Jesus can be of assistance in her hopeless situation she comes forward, kneels at his feet and asks for her daughter to be cured, crying out: 'Take pity on me, Son of David.'

Unable to cope with her cry of desperation, the disciples are embarrassed and want Jesus to send her away as quickly as possible. At first Jesus seems reluctant to have anything to do with her and keeps her at arm's length, but the woman persists, refusing to take no for an answer. In her humility, she claims no rights but pleads further reminding the Lord that even dogs can feed on the scraps that fall from the master's table. Her prayer of faith wins through and in the end she gets what she so desperately needs.

This is one of the rare occasions when we find Jesus in conversation with a woman who is not only a Gentile and a pagan but belongs to a nation noted for its traditional hostility to the Jewish people. Nevertheless, Jesus does not regard this as an obstacle. He puts her faith to the test and grants her request because she has shown more trust in him than his own people. It must have gone hard with Christ that he was not accepted among his own to whom he devoted his life's mission. This encounter between Christ and the Canaanite woman indicates that God has no favourites and nobody is excluded from his company. His message was not the exclusive property of the Jewish people but the Good News to be shared among all peoples and nationalities. His whole mission is to break down barriers and to remove walls of division and prejudice between Jew and Gentile.

This gospel confronts us with our own tendency to cause conflict by promoting exclusiveness. Many of us are biased against people simply because their political and religious outlook differs from our own. We fail to remember that no seats are reserved in heaven for any particular following. What is necessary if we are to get there, is to have faith in God and reliance on his mercy. God does not discriminate but welcomes all who believe in him, who ask for his mercy and seek to do his will. In a church-going community everyone should be made welcome no matter how they may be dressed, how un-attractive they may be or how low in esteem society may hold them. The good news is that everyone can call upon God in their need and receive his mercy because, unlike us, he has time for everybody.

Prayer of the Faithful

United in love we turn with confidence to God the Father knowing that a request made with faith will never be refused.

1. We pray for the church throughout the world, that it may be a channel of God's mercy, peace and love. Lord, hear us.
2 We pray that as a community of believers we may not be divided by petty barriers of hatred and prejudice. Lord, hear us.
3 We remember especially mothers who are anxious and deeply worried about their children's health. May they never fail to turn to Jesus for support and comfort. Lord, hear us.
4 For the sick of our community, may they be consoled and loved by those who care for them. Lord, hear us.
5 We pray for those who have departed this life. May they rejoice forever in their heavenly home.

Almighty God, our refuge and our strength, your wish is to unite all people. May we always be sensitive to the needs of others and never exclude anyone from our company. We ask this through Christ our Lord. Amen.

Twenty-first Sunday of the Year

Peter must surely rate as one of the more interesting characters in the gospel. In many ways it's amazing that Christ selected him as the leader of the church because his record would not even have impressed his own contemporaries. By human reckoning he was a disastrous choice and should never have been appointed. You could hardly describe him as a stable person because at times he was brave while on other occasions he displayed complete cowardice.

During Christ's arrest in the Garden of Gethsemane he was hot-headed and with his sword cut off the soldier's ear. Some time later in Pilate's courtyard,when taunted by a servant girl, he was so weak that he denied ever knowing Christ. Yet on the road to Caesarea Philippi Jesus appointed him as leader of the christian community. His call to lead was a most important step in the development of the church. Christ had confidence in him, released a great power within his being and entrusted him with a mission which was crucial for the continuation of his work. The choice of Peter as head of the church is an example of the power of God at work – using the weak things of this world to confound the strong. Before his encounter with Christ, Peter's life had little meaning.

On life's pilgrimage, it's a source of great comfort that God has invited us to be members of his church built upon the rock of Peter. People of every age listen attentively to the leaders of the church because of the promise Jesus made to Peter. There's a very human aspect to Peter's life story to which we can easily relate. His weakness and moments of betrayal are common-place in our own lives. However, his deep-seated trust in the person of Christ more than compensates for any failure as will a similar trust on our part.

The question put by Jesus to Peter: 'Who do you say that I am?' resulted in an inspiring declaration of faith. As followers of Christ this question confronts us daily and calls us to judge ourselves as to how we are living our lives, working at our marriage and rearing our children. What is the point in saying the word of the Lord is our light and our strength if we do not live accordingly? Being christian commits us to live in a particular manner and involves having moral standards which differ from so many in society. One thing is certain – a neutral stance to Christ's vision of life is not possible, because to follow him is to live decisively and to take an active responsibility for our behaviour.

Prayer of the Faithful

As we ponder on the foundations of the church, we pray with open hearts to God the Father for our own needs and the needs of the world.

1.   We pray for our Holy Father. May he be inspired by the Holy Spirit as he continues the work of St Peter in guiding the church through difficult times. Lord, hear us.

2.   We pray for bishops, priests and all who maintain positions of authority in the community. May they grow in the love of God and willingly accept the responsibility entrusted to them. Lord, hear us.

3.   We pray for all believers especially in times of trial. May they never lose sight of Christ as the cornerstone and foundation of their lives. Lord, hear us.

4.   For the sick and the aged. May they be supported and loved by their families and friends. Lord, hear us.

5.   We pray for all those who have parted from this life. May they find rest in the kingdom of God. Lord, hear us.

Heavenly Father, enable us to place our lives in your hands. Purify our hearts and keep us always faithful to your command. We ask this through Christ our Lord. Amen.

Twenty-second Sunday of the Year

Peter found it difficult to accept that the mission of Jesus would end with the cross and crucifixion. He did not see why pain and suffering were necessary for discipleship, and was anxious that the Lord avoid this course of action. He was outraged at the idea that such happenings should take place. Like most of us, he failed to grasp the role of suffering in God's plan. He thought that being part of the kingdom was a matter of power and success. Words were powerless to rid him of the idea of a Messiah of earthly splendour and glory. Peter had yet to learn that the standards of Christ were not those of prosperity and privilege. The outcome was a reprimand from Jesus who cautioned him against adopting the stand-ards of the world, 'The way you think is not God's way but man's.' The gospel ends with a challenge from Jesus to welcome hardship and to embrace pain and personal suffering, for to hold on to this life is to lose eternal life and everlasting values.

In the grand scheme of things we are set a whole series of tests. The road is never a straight one and suffering is a reality of human life. In the world greed, cruelty and sickness are the order of the day. Our earthly pilgrimage is so beset with trials and tribulations that it is aptly named a 'valley of tears'. We have all experienced our share of hardship in the form of sickness, loss of job or death in the family. Down the ages the problem of pain has been the debating ground of so much human thought and the torment of so many noble souls. When things go wrong and affliction comes our way we cry out and protest in bitter rebellion. It's a natural tendency to turn one's back on trouble but running away from pain can never bring joy, for to hide from it is to pretend that it does not exist.

Being a christian is a demanding honour because God's way of doing things is contrary to human expectations. In the gospel, Christ tells us plainly that discipleship involves denying ourselves, taking up the cross in trust and confidence and following his footsteps across the hill of Calvary. It's a hard teaching but the measure of greatness in the kingdom of heaven is the stand-ard of the cross.

This is an occasion to reflect on our own commitment to Christ because it's easy to lose sight of our final goal in life. Our hearts are tempted to seek comfort in material things and to avoid hardship. Many church-goers think only of themselves and reluctantly give God forty minutes on Sunday morning, yet if asked to identify themselves would profess to be christian.

Prayer of the Faithful

Called as prophets to bear witness to our faith we turn with confidence to God our Father and ask in prayer for what we need.

1. We pray for the church. May the Holy Spirit continue to renew her in the search for fresh ways of bringing Christ to our world. Lord, hear us.
2. We pray for those who are suffering and heavily burdened. May they never forget that the Lord is with them in their struggle. Lord, hear us.
3. For all young people and their teachers who are beginning a new school year. May Christ be their model and inspiration. Lord, hear us.
4. For the old, the lonely and the sick of our community. May they embrace their cross willingly and offer up their sufferings for the sake of Jesus. Lord, hear us.
5. We pray that the Lord will bring the faithful departed safely into his kingdom. Lord, hear us.

Heavenly Father, look with mercy upon our feeble efforts. Give us the strength and courage necessary to model our lives according to the commands of your Son. We make our prayer through Christ our Lord. Amen.

Twenty-third Sunday of the Year

The readings carry a very clear message concerning our responsibility towards the salvation of others within the community. No man is an island and in Christ we are all brothers and sisters and members of the one family. Life is short and we all have to take seriously the duty of doing good while we can by helping those who are weak or in need of our assistance. This does not mean we are to be prying busybodies, interfering in people's lives. The love of our neighbour has to be prudent and tactful and let us not forget that the best portion of a good life is those little nameless, un-remembered acts of kindness.

There is no living together without pain and the gospel brings us the delicate question of counselling those adults in the community who are misbehaving, doing wrong and going astray. It goes without saying that correction is seldom welcome and those who need it most always like it least. This is a matter in which great caution must be exercised because the wrong word or undue interference can cause far more damage than the original fault. Correction is never easy and can be embarrassing as it may carry with it the risk of losing a long established friendship. Normally, silence is golden but there are occasions when failure to speak out is to condone an evil practice. Like it or not, situations arise where failure to get involved is not an act of love but an unkindness. At those specific moments, what we have to say should be expressed in a spirit of charity and not for the sake of finding fault or telling a few home truths.

Love is the one thing that cannot hurt our neighbour. If we have the ability to convey a genuine concern, a little honest talking can often clear the air and change the situation for the better. It is worth remembering that none of us is perfect, so when we point out the faults of others, we should be prepared to hear about our own. As we can all give offence unwittingly, we should make it our business if we have a difference with anyone, to settle the matter and be reconciled. Harsh words and an aggressive attitude have no place in a christian community. Christ himself emphasised the importance of being reconciled with our brothers and sisters when he said: 'If you are offering a gift at the altar and on the way find that your neighbour has something against you first go and be reconciled with your neighbour and then come and offer your gift.' (Mt 5:23-24). How many of us really take these words to heart?

Prayer of the Faithful

Mindful of his many blessings, we turn to God the Father in prayer and ask for a strengthening of care and concern within our community.

1.   We pray for the bishops of the church. May they be fearless in speaking the truth and give witness in their lives to the words they proclaim. Lord, hear us.
2.   We pray that our parish community may be drawn closer together in promoting a truly christian atmosphere. Lord, hear us.
3.   For all of us gathered here in eucharistic worship. May we have the courage to speak the truth with love and accept criticism honestly. Lord, hear us.
4.   We pray for the sick, the aged and the housebound. May they see God's comfort and consolation in the compassion of those who care for them. Lord, hear us.
5.   We pray for the dead. May the Lord welcome them into everlasting life. Lord, hear us.

Heavenly Father, grant us the grace to lead truly christian lives. Increase the love of our neighbour in our hearts. Keep us sensitive to one another's needs as we live our lives together. We ask this through Christ our Lord. Amen.

Twenty-fourth Sunday of the Year

There is no mistaking the theme of this liturgy which is all about forgiveness and mercy – basic attitudes that every christian must put into practice. Apart from the command to love one another there is no obligation which Christ taught more forcefully than that of showing forgiveness. In the actual circumstances of every-day life, forgiveness is more often talked about than put into practice because it is difficult and demanding and it takes a great deal out of us. Within families small incidents get blown out of proportion, become major flash-points and rifts develop. Among neighbours, children playing, animals straying and rights-of-way, can cause unholy war. In any community differences brought about by thoughtless words, selfish actions and jealousy inevitably provoke clashes. As a nation we prefer to nurse old sores rather than reach out the hand of reconciliation.

No wonder the first reading tells us to reflect on death which is the great leveller, and puts all human affairs into the proper perspective. As one walks the long granite corridors of a cemetery, forgiveness takes on a new dimension. Neighbours who were with us not so many yesterdays ago and who for a life-time remained unrepent-antly hostile over a boundary hedge are now buried a short distance from one another. There is no need for a fence between them now. In the light of eternity and the shortness of our span of life, harbouring old grudges is pointless. The great christian cry of forgiveness which comes from the heart was first echoed on the hill of Calvary. What Jesus proclaimed in words from the cross, he had lived out in deeds. The purpose of his life and death was to win forgiveness for all people.

What comes through with blinding clarity is that our ability to forgive is the measure of the depth of our christianity. The forgiveness that we offer others is the the indispensable condition which makes it possible for us to receive God's forgiveness and to meaningfully pray: 'Forgive us our trespasses as we forgive those who trespass against us.' It is in pardoning that we are pardoned. Our failure to offer pardon means that we have forgotten God's goodness or have not fully appreciated the unconditional forgiveness we have received from him.

In the actual circumstances of daily living we are seldom put to the test of forgiveness, in matters which are heart-breaking or emotionally crippling, like the betrayal of a friend. Real pain is felt in the slight hurts and petty envies which tempt us to be vindictive and strike back in a harsh and unyielding manner. What is required is limitless forgiving and an ability to gloss over faults and to keep on loving even in the face of insults. If we are to be true channel of the Lord's grace then Christ must be the standard by which we measure and shape our conduct.

Prayer of the Faithful

Aware of the loving forgiveness of our God, we place our needs before him with heartfelt trust.

1. We pray for our Holy Father, and the bishops of the church that they may reflect the kindness and mercy of Christ. Lord, hear us.
2. We pray that those who have been embittered by injuries and wrong-doings may remove resentment from their hearts and be open to the peace of Christ. Lord, hear us.
3. For those among us who find it difficult to forgive. May the realisation of God's generous mercy to humankind touch their hearts and enable them to extend the hand of friendship. Lord, hear us.
4. Give comfort and healing to the sick. May the care and concern of their families strengthen them. Lord, hear us.
5. We pray for the faithful departed. May they rest in peace. Lord, hear us.

Heavenly Father, look with compassion on our failings, deliver us from hardness of heart and grant that we may be always ready to forgive injuries and heal divisions.

Twenty-fifth Sunday of the Year

Our picture of God is influenced to some extent by our ordinary way of looking at things and that is why, as we listen to this gospel, we are tempted to react and share the grumble of the workers who have laboured since early morning. In human terms it seems a bit unfair that after slaving all day in the hot sun they got the same pay for their efforts as those who were taken on at the eleventh hour. If we get too uptight about the injustice of the situation, we miss the point of the story. The parable is not dealing with equal rights for all, or an honest day's work for an honest day's pay. Its main thrust is to show the generosity of God in throwing open the doors of the kingdom of heaven to Gentiles and sinners on equal footing with the Jews. For their part the Jews resented what was happening and envied the good fortune of these late arrivals. After all, they were God's chosen people and expected preferential treatment.

Unfortunately this selfish and begrudging attitude towards the salvation of sinners is not confined to the Jews. It is sometimes found among people who would regard themselves as devout christians, yet make comments about eleventh hour and deathbed conversions which are anything but charitable. They cannot accept that after struggling all their lives in the service of God, giving time to prayer, Mass and the sacraments they end up no better off than those who don't bother with religion out turn to God at the last moment. Apart from the fact that nobody can judge how any person stands before God, such an attitude betrays a complete lack of understanding of the christian mission on earth, which is to bring salvation to all people. Entry into heaven sooner or later, regardless of the date or time, makes no difference because it is given to all who do the will of God the Father. All who enter ought to be grateful for their own good fortune and should not express displeasure when God's favour is shown to others.

This gospel fills us with an inspiring image of a generous, gracious and forgiving God whose love for us has no bounds and whose mercy extends both to those who have laboured all their lives in his service and to those who have broken faith but turn to him in their dying hour. Before the Almighty we all stand like beggars and can never boast that we have earned our salvation. Everything we have is a free gift of his love and mercy. We cannot explain his generosity, but one thing is certain – God's ways are not our ways.

Prayer of the Faithful

Encouraged by the Good News that 'The Lord is close to all who call upon him,' we place our needs before our heavenly Father, with that hope in our hearts.

1.   We pray for our Holy Father and all those entrusted with the responsibility of preaching God's word. Give them the strength to proclaim the truth joyfully. Lord, hear us.
2.   We pray that as a community we may open our minds and hearts to the needs of others and so lead joyous and generous lives. Lord, hear us.
3.   We pray for those who are out of work. May they not lose the hope of being able to provide for themselves and their families. Lord, hear us.
4.   For the sick and the suffering. May they be comforted by the compassion and understanding of their family and friends. Lord, hear us.
5.   We pray for those who have died recently. Touch them with your love and bring them peace. Lord, hear us.

Heavenly Father, help us to be always thankful for the many gifts you have showered upon us. Bring us closer to one another in understanding and love. We make our prayer through Christ our Lord. Amen.

Twenty-sixth Sunday of the Year

No matter who we are, we possess the freedom to say 'yes' or 'no' to God and the ability to repent and change the direction of our lives. One way or another we are responsible for our conduct and accountable for our behaviour. One day we will stand before the judgement seat of God answerable for our goodness and our failings. The Good News is that with the help of God's grace we can change the direction of our lives for the better. The varying attitudes of the two sons give us cause to think carefully because whether we like it or not, there is a mixture of both personalities in our make-up. Very few of us can say that when the Lord called us we were ready and eager to answer, 'Here I am Lord, I have come to do your will.' The gospel is telling us that actions speak louder than words. If regular Sunday church-going is not accompanied by upright christian living, what we profess to believe has no value and amounts to no more than lip service or idle promises which are worthless. We are uttering words but are not changing our hearts.

The liturgy points out that there must be a connection between what we say and what we do. Jesus criticised the religious leaders of his day because they shirked their responsibility and only thought that they wanted to do God's will. Their promises were empty because they did not keep them and as a result their journey to God was going nowhere. In a ringing denunciation Christ stated that their observance of the law was an outward show and that there was more honesty and a greater readiness to accept the call for repentance among outcasts. 'I tell you solemnly, tax-collectors and prostitutes are making their way into the kingdom of heaven before you.'

This is a story for all ages. The trail of broken promises that each of us leaves behind points to the inconsistency between what we promise and what we do. In the early christian community the scandal of professed church members who did not fulfil their promises was deeply felt. The lesson the gospel offers us is that we may be saying 'yes' to God on Sunday and turning our back on what we profess during the rest of the week. Many of us who say 'yes' to the Body of Christ don't realise that we are saying 'no' to the community of Christ when at the church door, an age-old difference between families prevents us from speaking to a neighbour. Newly married couples have no problems saying 'yes' on their wedding day but find it increasingly difficult to keep their promise through the ups and downs of life. The test of our allegiance to Christ is in keeping the promises that we have made and accepting his will whatever it may be.

Prayer of the Faithful

Trusting in God the Father's unfailing generosity, we now place before him our many needs.

1.   We pray for our Holy Father and the bishops of the church, that they will have the courage and strength to respond generously in guiding the faithful under their care. Lord, hear us.
2.   That as a community we may base our lives on the mercy and compassion of Christ and not on outward appearances. Lord, hear us.
3.   That in our own lives we may be honest and sincere and respond to the will of God with unquestioning obedience. Lord, hear us.
4.   Comfort the sick and the broken-hearted. May they experience the love and compassion of Christ in those who take care of their needs. Lord, hear us.
5.   For those who have died. May they experience everlasting joy in your kingdom. Lord, hear us.

Heavenly Father increase your grace within us. Help us to carry out the promises we make in words with a sincere heart. We ask this through Christ our Lord. Amen.

Twenty-seventh Sunday of the Year

When parents are in deep distress after being let down or rejected by their children they may well voice the lament of Isaiah in the first reading: 'What more could I have done for my children that I did not do?' There is no pain more intense or distressing than that of being rejected. Like a sword of sorrow it pierces our heart and leaves us deeply wounded. Rejection is something we all encounter on our journey through life and Jesus was no exception. The terrible truth is that the Son of God came to earth, showed his love in every possible way and was rejected. In this very hard hitting gospel we are exposed to the blunt truth that God has done everything possible for us as a people by sending his Son to live among us. In return we have turned our back and offered him nothing but black ingratitude and cold indifference.

It does not take a great deal of imagination to see ourselves in this parable. Each of us is a tenant, cultivating a small portion of God's vineyard and when harvest time arrives we are expected to produce the fruits of right living, by displaying a brotherhood of caring, sharing and showing forth the charity of the gospel in our daily lives. By doing this we put into practice during the week what we profess to believe at our Sunday morning celebration of the Mass.

This parable challenges us to keep working in God's service and not to become complacent. We can examine our conscience to see if we are producing the gifts of God's love. The Lord is bitterly disappointed when we lazily sit back and fail to appreciate the beauty of our lives, the joy of our families and his loving care. There will be a day of reckoning for all of us. A time will come when we will be answerable for the way in which we have carried out the task God has given us to do. What then if at the end of life we have nothing to offer the Lord but the sour grapes of a pagan lifestyle? We will have smothered a beautiful being with indifference, ingratitude, selfishness and neglect and have become useless to God. Christ is concerned that we respond to his appeal to bear fruit and become an immense and beautiful harvest.

Prayer of the Faithful

Reflecting upon the warning in the gospel about the need to bear fruit, we place our requests before God the Father.

1.   We pray for our Holy Father. May he receive light, strength and support in guiding the church in these difficult times. Lord, hear us.

2.   For an increase of the spirit of prayer in our families so that our minds may be filled with the peace of God which brings eternal joy and lasting happiness. Lord, hear us.

3.   That in our own lives we may bear the fruits of love, forgiveness, justice and peace. Lord, hear us.

4.   We pray for the sick and suffering of our parish. May they never lose heart in the midst of their trials but be strengthened by the word of God. Lord, hear us.

5.   We pray for the dead. Grant them eternal rest in your kingdom. Lord, hear us.

Heavenly Father, we thank you for your steadfast love. Help us to serve you generously and to live lives worthy of our calling. We make our prayer through Christ our Lord. Amen.

Twenty-eighth Sunday of the Year

Our hearts go out in sympathy to the poor man in this gospel story who has been hauled off the street into a wedding reception where he is a complete stranger, and immediately finds himself in serious trouble because he is not suitably dressed for the occasion. How could he be expected to have the necessary clothes at such short notice? We miss the point if we think that the parable is about wearing the right outfit at a wedding. The message goes much deeper because the banquet referred to is eternal life in the kingdom of heaven. Jesus is saying that, while God the Father has opened wide the doors of heaven and invited everybody into his kingdom, entrance is by no means automatic and should not be taken for granted. It is not as easy as that, for we've got to work our passage, be spiritually prepared, and prove ourselves worthy of the invitation. Furthermore there is no room for complacency because membership of the church does not guarantee salvation.

Our invitation to God's kingdom was issued for the first time as we wore our christening robe. The priest pronounced that we were clothed in Christ. Yet baptism was only the beginning of that call to spend our lives like Christ. We are invited every day to follow God more closely and our response is the work of a life-time. The wedding garment is a symbol of a life in the footsteps of Christ. The question we must ask ourselves is: how are we living that life? The Jews made the fatal mistake of banking too much on their special role as God's chosen people and failed to take the offer seriously. This can be our story if we think that because we are baptised and are regular church-goers that we have done enough. As we go about our daily struggle of trying to make ends meet it's so easy to leave God out of the picture.

This gospel should cause us to pause and think about the wonderful future that is within our reach. It is telling us that God is longing for our homecoming in the next world. Meanwhile the one thing necessary is to make sure that we will arrive safely by responding to his love. We are never nearer that love than when we come forward at Mass to receive the Body of Christ in Holy Communion and when in our daily lives we avail of the opport-unities of sharing in Christ's life. By beginning our day with a prayer or asking his blessing before we eat our food, offering encouragement and support to our neighbours in the small circle of our living, we are extending this brief spell of eucharistic celebration into every detail of our day. In this way we are not facing life alone. We are walking with one another and with Christ.

Prayers of the Faithful

In faith we now make our petitions to the Father whose concern is that all people accept his invitation to the banquet of eternal life in heaven.

1.   We pray that the church throughout the world may be seen as a sign of hope and encouragement by all who journey on their pilgrim way. Lord, hear us.
2.   God's invitation is not to be treated lightly. May we realise that membership of the church is not a guarantee of salvation unless we change our lives and put on Christ. Lord, hear us.
3.   May we respond to the love of God by continually wearing the wedding garment of repentance and good works given to us at baptism. Lord, hear us.
4.   For those who are sick or disabled. Help us to bring your compassion to them through our acts of kindness, Lord, hear us.
5.   Bless and reward with eternal life those who have departed this world. Lord, hear us.

Heavenly Father, touch our lives more deeply so that we may avail of the opportunities that daily come our way to receive grace and share in your life. Grant this through Christ our Lord. Amen.

Twenty-ninth Sunday of the Year

When the Pharisees dragged the name of Caesar into their dispute with Jesus, it was a clever attempt to trick him into making an incriminating statement. He was in a no-win situation because to state that tax should be paid would have made him appear a traitor to his country, while a denial would have left him behind bars as an enemy of Rome. Aware of their malice, he sidesteps the issue and draws attention to Caesar's image on the tax coin saying: 'Give to Caesar what belongs to Caesar and give to God what belongs to God.' He challenges them to take their responsibility to God as seriously as their obligations to the state. While God and Caesar each have a claim over us, neither allegiance should cancel out the other. Jesus does not specify what constitutes the dividing line between our duty to God and our obligation to society.

The gospel reminds us that we are members of God's kingdom and citizens of the country in which we live, with obligations to both. As christians we are not only members of the church but also members of society. Tensions can exist between our loyalty to God and our duty to our country especially when political questions touch upon faith and morality. Religion and politics do mix and overlap, so crucial issues of conscience occasionally emerge. In these instances we must put God and his laws first even if it brings us into conflict with the state. We are obliged to bring the gospel of Jesus into every aspect of our life. Normally conflicts of interest are rare and our loyalty to the laws of our country need not contradict our obedience to God. A good christian, by keeping his thoughts on heaven while having his feet firmly planted on earth, can love God and country and be faithful to both.

Christian life in the world should result in giving a certain tone to society. We are chosen to be the saving hands of Christ and are called to spread the good news in different ways, on many levels. Every person must show a proper interest in the well-being of society. Living in an imperfect world highlights the need for christian men and women in public life who are not afraid to express their allegiance to God in social and religious affairs. Their fresh vision points out spiritual values which others would fail to take into account. The most important goal for all of us is to work out our salvation. It takes a lifelong effort to give to

God what is his due. This is something we must keep uppermost in our minds. By remaining steadfast in our faith, at home and in public life, we show that our reward is not to be sought in this world. If we have been neglectful in these matters we can start now by coming before God at this Mass in faith and offer ourselves completely to him in union with Jesus Christ on the altar.

Prayer of the Faithful

In our weakness and need, we turn in prayer to God the Father who as the source of all worldly power and authority must be served and obeyed.

1. We pray for Our Holy Father and the bishops of the church. Bless and inspire them in their efforts to explore new ways of spreading God's kingdom. Lord, hear us.
2. For civil leaders who hold public office. May they openly and courageously recognise their dependence on God and never pass laws which are contrary to justice and peace. Lord, hear us.
3. We pray for our community, that we may recognise our obligations as citizens of the state and be honest in all our dealings. Lord, hear us.
4. Comfort and support those who are sick. May we be channels of Christ's love and compassion to them by our caring. Lord, hear us.
5. We commend to the Father's love all the faithful departed. May they rest in peace. Lord, hear us.

Heavenly Father, everything we have and are is yours. Renew us in your love so that we may serve you generously and humbly. We make our prayers through Christ our Lord. Amen.

Thirtieth Sunday of the Year

The gospel highlights the two commandments which Jesus describes as the greatest: Love of God and love of neighbour. No matter how often we hear these words we are struck by the demands they place upon us. Jesus brings together the love of God and love of our neighbour as something inseparable like two sides of the one coin. Love of God, whom we cannot see, is false if it is not complemented by the love of the people whom we rub shoulders with every day on the street where we live. Our neighbour is not thrown in as an afterthought because it is through people around about us that God makes contact with us on a daily basis. Scripture keeps constantly hammering home the message that 'anyone who says he loves God and hates his brother is a liar.' (1 Jn 4:20-21) We cannot call ourselves christian and continue crucifying our neighbour.

Loving our neighbour as ourselves is a necessary element in giving our hearts and minds to God and that is where the challenge lies. It is wonderful in theory but difficult to put into practice. To love one's neighbour can be challenging especially when the people next door are inquisitive and their children downright bad-mannered, not to mention the work-mate who is trying on our nerves. To show love in such circumstances is dreadfully difficult and demands great effort and yet, more often than not, we meet God in such an encounter. Make no mistake, our religion becomes an escape and our holiness an illusion if we pray daily, go to church on Sundays, yet cut ourselves off from the people who are worshipping under the same roof as ourselves. God cares about how we treat others. Everyone is made in his image and likeness.

This morning we are being asked to have a good look at those shadowy nooks and crannies of our lives which are sealed off from God. To profess that we love God while remaining indifferent to the plight of others is a contradiction. We all want love to be a thornless rose, smooth and velvet to the touch but if we are following Christ we will find that it involves sacrifice and the shadow of the cross. Love is, waiting upon the aged, nursing the sick, patching up quarrels and taking the time to listen to the broken-hearted. Very few expect to discover love in weakness, powerlessness and suffering and yet that is the heart of Christ's message to the world. From his birth in a stable as one who was homeless, to his death on the cross as a common criminal, Jesus always identified with the spiritually, physically and materially poor of this world. This gospel is not an ideal to be admired but a way of life to be lived if we are to walk humbly with our God. There is an old saying that the night is over and the day has begun when we recognise other people as our brothers and sisters.

Prayer of the Faithful

Recalling the love of God for his people ,we now place before him our concerns of the present moment.

1. For our Holy Father and the bishops of the church. May their preaching and example be instrumental in bringing the faithful to a deeper knowledge and love of God. Lord, hear us.
2. May we never forget to show compassion to those in our community who are underprivileged and feel unwanted and unloved. Lord, hear us.
3. In our own lives help us to be models of forgiveness, mercy and kindness. Give us the grace to love tenderly, to act justly and to walk humbly with our God. Lord, hear us.
4. By the gentle touch of your Spirit help us develop a deeper compassion for the sick and elderly. Lord, hear us.
5. Grant eternal life in your heavenly kingdom to our recently deceased ... May they rest in peace. Lord, hear us.

Heavenly Father, look with pity and mercy on all who are in need. May your Spirit guide us in the ways of joy and peace. We make our prayer through Christ our Lord. Amen.

Mission Sunday

Mission Sunday is a time when we remember, in a special way, those who have taken to heart Christ's call to make disciples of all nations. They have left their native land, their family and friends and have gone to foreign parts labouring to plant the faith among the great masses who know nothing about Christ. It is not easy to be an exile, a stranger constantly adapting to the ways, culture and language of another country. Living conditions are often primitive – a shanty hut without running water or electricity. It is easy to despair when the hot climate becomes unbearable and leaves the preacher's weary body with little resistance to disease. Without our support, generosity and prayers it would not be possible for missionaries to carry on the good works which they are doing. What encourages them most is the sure knowledge that their home church is fully interested in their apostolic endeavour to preach and teach the word of God and be bearers of the Good News. In many mission countries the local church is still very poor and unable to survive without help from outside. People in these countries differ from us in colour and culture, but they are our brothers and sisters in Christ who depend on our aid.

A Sunday like this is also intended to remind us that to be a missionary you do not have to travel away from home. There is no place on earth where the church is not missionary because every parish, home and work-place is a mission field. There are neglected corners in our own community where the Good News needs spreading. In this mission field so close to home we are all chosen, by virtue of baptism, to be active. It is a duty and obligation entrusted to every generation of believers by Christ the Lord. Our task is to make everyone aware of the need for salvation by the witness of a good life, because those who are searching for truth are more impressed by what we are than by what we profess to be. Since we bear silent witness by our lives, it is important to get our own house in order as this may be the only book of the gospel open for people to read. 'Let me preach to you without preaching, not by my words but by my example.' (Cardinal Newman)

The message we preach depends to a certain extent on our manner of life and on our ability to reach out to others through the spirit of love. God is constantly working in and through us announcing a message of hope and spiritual salvation. The challenge facing us is made all the more difficult because of the current decline in religious practice, coupled with an indifference to the message of the church. Many who profess to be christian make no serious attempt to let gospel values influence their everyday activities. Our faith, which bears the mark of our fore-fathers and is a reminder of things more lasting than life, is for sharing and for handing on to the next generation. It is not a treasure to be hoarded up in miserly fashion. We ask God to make our faith strong enough so that we may be eager to share it with others.

Prayers of the Faithful

Confident that God the Father wants all people to be saved and come to a knowledge of the truth, we make our prayer in the hope that grace will be given and sinners reconciled.

1.   We pray that our Holy Father and the bishops of the church may be filled with the Holy Spirit and show forth to the world the beauty of the christian way of life. Lord, hear us.
2.   We pray for our foreign missionaries especially those from our own parish and diocese. May their courage never fail and may their preaching be received with gladness. Lord, hear us.
3.   We pray that as a community we may support the foreign missions by our prayers, our concern and our generosity. Lord, hear us.
4.   Console and encourage those who are sick and house-bound. Help them to realise the effectiveness of their prayers in opening hearts to the love of God. Lord, hear us.
5.   We commit to the loving care of our Father, the souls of all missionaries who have died during the last year. Lord, hear us.

Heavenly Father, enlighten our minds and strengthen our wills so that we may never fail to appreciate the faith given to us at such a great price. We make our prayer through Christ our Lord. Amen.

Thirty-first Sunday of the Year

Jesus was very severe in denouncing the religious leaders of his time who were far from being examples of integrity. What made him harsh in his criticism of the Scribes and Pharisees was that they failed to practice what they preached. He pointed them out as pious frauds, people who were good at pretending and who loved to be the centre of attention. Their long prayers were merely a good outward show because they neglected the much more important matters of faith, justice and mercy. Instead they were empty and hollow, neither good nor holy. Their way of life pointed to a display of vanity and self-importance and was not directed to the glory of God. As a result, their preaching lead people astray. Christ saw through their pretence and accused them of blatant hypocrisy.

It would be wrong for us to poke fun at the unflattering picture of the Pharisees painted in the gospel. What Jesus says is important for us too. There is plenty of food for thought for everyone because to some extent we are all tainted with hypocrisy. Very few of us can truthfully say that our deeds always match our words. We may not be as hypocritical as the Pharisees but we can very easily put on a show to hide our short-comings and appear virtuous. Most of us are good at presenting one face for the public and displaying a different one for our own family and friends. Christ hated hypocrisy in all forms. Sincerity and openness of character appealed to him. He was in no way fooled by appearances as he could see into the depths of the persons heart. Jesus wants his followers to avoid the obvious mistakes of the Pharisees which emptied God's word of its power and content.

This gospel is a challenge to all christians about the quality of their worship and the witness of their faith. If we are to live up to what we profess as followers of Christ we must mean what we say and do what we mean. All of us are in constant danger of not living up to our ideals. Those of us who are in the public eye are being asked if we perform good works for the glory of God or to seek our own advancement. We have lost our way when the search for human approval becomes uppermost in our lives. As parents, any correction of children falls on deaf ears when our own behaviour is irresponsible and our language foul. As actions speak louder than words we must match our external behaviour with an inner genuineness. In all circumstances of life we lead by example and that is what will bring others to Christ.

Prayer of the Faithful

Coming together as God's people, we confidently place our needs before the Father assured that he will grant our requests.

1. We pray for our Holy Father and the bishops of the church that they may be totally dedicated to their high calling of preaching the gospel. Lord, hear us.
2. May parents and teachers instruct those under their care by the good example of their lives. Lord, hear us.
3. May we always seek to do what is right and may God's word be a living power influencing our actions. Lord, hear us.
4. Look with compassion on the old, lonely and sick and ease their suffering. Lord, hear us.
5. We pray for the dead. Grant them eternal rest and new life in the kingdom of God. Lord, hear us.

Heavenly Father, deepen our faith so that we may grow in your love and always serve you with generosity and a sincere heart. We ask this through Christ our Lord. Amen.

Thirty-second Sunday of the Year

Parables are never as simple as they appear on the surface. They always carry a deeper meaning which is applicable to daily living. On first hearing this parable of the bridesmaids who were excluded from the wedding feast and forced to remain locked out in the dark, we could easily be forgiven for regarding their sensible companions, as a selfish lot in refusing to share their oil with them. To our way of thinking the punishment of having the door of the wedding banquet slammed in their face is too severe. At worst they deserved a reprimand for their last minute rush. However the gospel story is not about forgetting to bring along extra oil for a lamp, but about how we view the invitation extended to us all to take our place in the kingdom of God. We have only ourselves to blame if we fail to arrive or are unprepared when the time comes. Being ready beforehand is what matters most and a last minute hurry to get ourselves into spiritual shape is not to be recommended. If we are to have an eternity of joy we shall have to prepare for it whole-heartedly. Admittance to the banquet of eternal life cannot simply be taken for granted. Christ teaches this parable as a warning because the day of the Lord will come with startling suddenness like a thief in the night.

In a strangely appropriate way, the church has associated the end of the liturgical year with the month of November. The leaves have fallen, nature is dying and there is no more growth. Winter has arrived.In a world of uncertainties the one thing we can be sure of is death. While we do not know the day or the hour, it is the one appointment we cannot cancel. To dismiss the thought of death, pushing it to the back of our minds as something to be faced at a later date, is the type of foolishness Christ condemns in this gospel. If we live with no thought as to where the journey of life is taking us, we are neglecting to make elementary preparations for the coming of the kingdom. Death will catch us unaware and God will enter unexpectedly into our lives. We will be found empty inside with no oil in our spiritual lamps and the result will be disaster.

An essential part of the christian life is to cultivate a personal relationship with God, which each one must possess, work at and live because it cannot be borrowed at the last minute. We do this by developing a calm and believing attitude as we go about our normal work. There is no better way of achieving this than by using those spare moments during the day to share our thoughts, plans and worries with Christ, in prayer, telling him what's on our mind and asking him to guide us. Christ is always prepared to meet us, so we, on our part, must be prepared to meet him. He does not give us an appointment but comes as he wills into our lives. The gospel brings home the importance of being ready and prepared while we wait, by loving God and our neighbour. We are not to take the chance of going through life relying on the minimum of holiness. When the call comes, what will count are the qualities of character we have developed, not the riches we possess or the fortune we have gathered. Staying awake must be the axis around which our whole being and life rotate.

Prayers of the Faithful

In each of us there is a longing for happiness which can only be satisfied in the kingdom of God. We now pray to the Father for the grace necessary to arrive there safely.

1.   We pray for our Holy Father and the bishops of the church. May they care for the people entrusted to them with the love of Christ and keep the lamp of faith burning brightly. Lord, hear us.

2.   For a greater realisation of the closeness of God who is very near and comes to us in the brokenness of those with whom we live and work. Lord, hear us.

3.   May we live in the state of readiness for the coming of God's kingdom into our lives remaining watchful but never fearful. Lord, hear us.

4.   We pray for the sick, the aged and those wounded by rejection. May they experience the compassion of Jesus through those who comfort them. Lord, hear us.

5.   May the Lord welcome into the banquet of eternal life all who have died. Lord, hear us.

Heavenly Father, listen to the prayers we have made with sincere hearts. Help us to grow in holiness and goodness as we wait in joyful hope for the coming of your kingdom. Amen.

Thirty-third Sunday of the Year

There is a side to us which identifies with the insecurity of the man who is severely punished for his laziness in not using God's gifts. He was so wrapped up in himself and his personal concerns that he failed to face up to his responsibilities. At the end of his days he had nothing to show for his years on earth because he did not avail of the opportunities that came his way. His life was not a success story as he was mean in the service of God and showed little or no enthusiasm for christian living. On the day of reckoning the excuses put forward for his failure were feeble in the Lord's eyes and did not impress.

The gospel is forthright in reminding us of the blunt truth that the gifts of God are not ours to dispense with as we please. Neither does it suffice to hide them away, leave them unused or allow them to wither. As christians we are in the business of spreading the kingdom of God. Christ came to serve and service of others helps us to grow in his image and likeness. Whatever our gifts happen to be, and we all have a variety, we are expected to make full use of them for God's glory. This is a call to be energetic in living the gospel.

The message in this parable is to make a great deal more of life, to tackle it positively and with enthusiasm, by reaching out beyond our own selfish world and taking the risk of sharing something of ourselves with others. It's worth remembering that the times when we experience true happiness and real satisfaction are normally those which find us completely absorbed in caring for the needy or supporting a worthwhile cause. In a real sense we come closer to God when we help to further the growth of his kingdom on earth by our actions.

Failure to use our talents can be caused by a poor self-image based on the false belief that we have nothing to offer. The strains and tensions that come from the dull, monotonous routine of rearing a family, working in the kitchen and earning our daily living may not bring much personal fulfilment or make for spectacular headlines but there is no denying the sacrifice involved. The Lord will reward us for the faithful carrying out of our responsibilities in these matters. The ordinary deeds of love offered for the benefit of others may not seem to matter much but are most important in the eyes of God.

Few among us will be given the opportunity of performing the spectacular, but never forget we will be remembered for our little daily acts of decency and kindness which we regard as nothing special. Ordinary work, when done with enthusiasm and a willing heart, helps the love of God to be made visible in the dark corners of life. Our intention should be to do as well as we can whatever job we are carrying out, avoiding apathy and the 'couldn't care less' approach. In this way we can offer back to the Father the lives given to us, more fulfilled and more enriched.

Prayer of the Faithful

Gathered together as sons and daughters of God the Father who is the giver of all good gifts, we reverently make our prayer.

1. We pray for our Holy Father and the bishops of the church that, enriched by the Holy Spirit, they may direct the flock entrusted to them in the ways of truth and love. Lord, hear us.
2. For a deeper appreciation of the importance of our ordinary lives and for a realisation of how the love of God can flow from our little acts of kindness. Lord, hear us.
3. Bless all parents as they give of their best to create an atmosphere of love in the home. May their children respond with warmth and affection. Lord, hear us.
4. For doctors, nurses, home-helps and those in the caring professions who use their gifts to bring Christ's love and compassion to the poor, the lonely, the sick and the imprisoned . Lord, hear us.
5. Grant eternal rest in your kingdom to our deceased relatives and friends. Lord, hear us.

Heavenly Father, help us to remain faithful in the small things of life, so that we may be trusted with greater when we come into your kingdom. We make our prayer through Christ our Lord. Amen.

Our Lord Jesus Christ, Universal King

The feast of Christ the King brings the church's year to a close and with it comes a reminder that the cycle of our own lives here on earth will also reach its completion. The end of the year is review time and affords us the opportunity to take stock of our behaviour as members of God's household. The gospel points out very forcibly that admission into our eternal home depends on the effort we make to aid and comfort the needy. We will be assured of a place in Christ's kingdom only if we treat others as Christ treats them. This is a challenging gospel which takes on exceptional importance as it portrays a powerful image of judgement and presents us with the stark choice of being for or against Christ. There is no in between. None of us can reflect upon it without seeing areas of our lives where change and improvement are needed.

What the church is emphasising is the importance of turning our lives and hearts to Christ and trusting in his teaching, otherwise we run the danger of being rejected. God is going to judge us on the works of mercy we perform which is our response to human need. One thing is for certain – there will be no excuses accepted on the last day. No one will be granted the luxury of the sin of omission saying: 'I minded my own business and did nobody any harm. I passed by on the other side of the road.' Christ will not be deceived by appearances. He will look at nothing but the human heart, so all pretence will be wiped away, all falseness exposed and our real selves brought into light. In a glance we will be recognised as his friends, or disowned as strangers.

As the world around us is put into our hands in trust and stewardship, christianity lays great stress on involvement in the community. Jesus is still walking the earth in the guise of our neighbour who is suffering and in want. Our shortcoming as a people is that we fail to recognise this fact. He has laid it on the line that in the evening of life we shall be judged upon the love we have shown and the small acts of mercy we have performed. Often a word of encouragement, a little recognition or a friendly smile can mean more to the poor than food, clothing or shelter, as they carry the warmth of acceptance and make them feel valued. Christ becomes real to the people around us only in so far as we reach out and show concern for their welfare and commit ourselves to fostering their dignity. Whatever good or evil we do to others is done to him. Christ rules in our hearts and in the world around us when we give of our time, energy and love in performing practical acts of charity.

Prayer of the Faithful

Confident that the kingdom of God the Father is unfolding in the world, with thankful hearts we make our prayer in union with Christ the King.

1.   We pray for our Holy Father and the bishops of the church. Enable them in the carrying out of their duties to be signs of hope and beacons of light to those trapped in the darkness of sin. Lord, hear us.
2.   That leaders of governments may talk openly and face honestly the issues that divide them. Lord, hear us.
3.   For those oppressed by forces they cannot control – hostages, prisoners, the poor, the persecuted and the lonely. Lord in their weakness may they know your strength and in despair find hope. Lord, hear us.
4.   We pray for the sick. May they experience the healing power of Jesus Christ through the care and comfort of family and friends. Lord, hear us.
5.   We pray that our departed relatives and friends may enjoy the fullness of heavenly glory. Lord, hear us.

Heavenly Father help us to show your goodness, warmth and kindness to all we meet so that when we are called to render an account of our lives we may be found pleasing to you. We make our prayer through Christ our Lord. Amen.

Immaculate Conception

When we were born, we came into the world at a loss because of original sin. We were graceless in soul, blighted and disadvantaged. In contrast,. Mary from the first moment of her birth was free from the inherited guilt of original sin. She was immaculate, full of grace. In fact, the only entirely sinless person in the world. This was necessary because she was to be the mother of Jesus. God had to have a worthy dwelling place for his son so it was proper that Mary would have no hand, act or part in sin. Today on this feast just before Christmas, we think of Mary as the mother expecting her child, preparing to set out on the road to Bethlehem. It was part of her pilgrimage of faith. Like any expectant mother she had high hopes for her child, but the experience of Bethlehem was to demand much of her. Homeless and pregnant she was to walk the over-crowded streets of that city and learn what it was to be poor, helpless and completely dependent on other people. In spite of the hardship she would believe that, no matter what the circumstances, the God she turned to and trusted would always be faithful and keep his promise.

We honour her today – a tender, gentle mother, a symbol of all that is best in womanhood, without a trace of weakness. Mary is everything that makes the heart tender and the earth lovely. From her humanity she gave Christ his flesh and blood. For once, sinful human nature turned up trumps. Mary is 'tainted nature's solitary boast.' In the gospel we see her as a woman with a great mission from which nothing in the world could divert her. The privilege of the Immaculate Conception did not dispense her from doubt or from the anguish and darkness that we are all heir to. She knew how to cope with sorrow and trouble and turn it into hope and joy. At Calvary, when not even his close followers believed in him, Mary stood steadfast at the foot of the Cross, under the tree of redemption, faithful to the last.

It is the presence of Mary that allows Christ's suffering to enter and dwell in the human heart. Her life gives us comfort and great hope. We celebrate this feast as a fitting preparation for the Nativity. God calls each of us like Mary, to welcome Jesus and to make room for him in our lives. It is in saying 'yes' like Mary that we can live his word and carry his cross in a way that can change the world and bring about his kingdom.

Prayer of the Faithful

As sinners we approach God the Father, who, from all eternity, chose Mary to be the immaculate mother of his Son and confidently make our prayer.

1. We pray that the leaders of the church may never neglect to join with Mary in prayer and ask her help for the success of their work. Lord, hear us.
2. We pray that like Mary we may be courageous and willing in meeting the demands christian love puts upon us and display concern for those in need. Lord, hear us.
3. We pray that through the intercession of Mary we may overcome evil, rid ourselves of sin and make our bodies worthy resting places for her Son. Lord, hear us.
4. That the sick may experience through us the loving care of Jesus and his mother in their hour of need. Lord, hear us.
5. Grant eternal rest and perpetual light to all who have died. May they enjoy the company of Mary in the kingdom of heaven. Lord, hear us.

Heavenly Father, you have given us Mary as our mother and model to be with us at every turn on the river of life. Through her intercession make us open to change. We ask this through Christ our Lord. Amen.

St Patrick

As we are separated from St Patrick by 1500 years of history, it is no harm to remind ourselves that he was snatched from his family, deprived of his freedom at the age of 16 years by Irish raiders, and was brought, captive to our country. He spent 6 years herding swine on a bleak Antrim hillside where he experienced cold, hunger, famine and exhaustion. During that time the pain and loneliness of exile became unbearable and in his plight he turned to God and discovered the real meaning of life and the importance of prayer. In his own words, he speaks of praying as often as 100 times a day and almost as frequently at night. When the opportunity arose, he escaped to his homeland and began his studies for the priesthood.

We can hardly blame him after the ordeal of his captivity for not wanting to have anything more to do with the Irish. There were more civilised pastures in which to exercise his priestly ministry. However, one night in a dream he heard the voice of the Irish pleading with him to come back and walk amongst them once more. Answering God's call showed him to be an individual of exceptional resilience but above all a man of faith, eager to set about planting the seed of God's word.

Christianity began to take root in Ireland because Patrick was not embittered by, or resentful of the painful experiences he had undergone in slavery. Looking back on his captivity Patrick viewed it as God's way of making him realise his sinfulness. He had come to recognise that the worst slavery of all was to be bound in darkness and have no knowledge of the saving power of Jesus which can transform lives. In the history of christian missions Ireland was the first place in the West where christianity was preached outside the Roman Empire. Being a great missionary Patrick, a total outsider, adopted the language, culture and customs of the Irish, listened to their problems, attended to their needs and kindled in Ireland that vital spark of faith which has never gone out. He taught them to bring every difficulty to God and to share their sufferings with Christ. Gradually they became a people ruled by gospel values.

However, the spreading of the faith that is ours today is due to the faithfulness of succeeding generations who handed on the pearl of great price and made certain that it took a firm hold in their communities. Our faith has come down to us at a great cost. Patrick has much to teach us and many lessons to give us. His life of solid spirituality and dependence on God should serve as a model for us and help us to get our priorities right. The task of each generation is to seek new and meaningful ways of express-ing that faith and to make it active in our everyday lives in loving service to Christ as he did. As we celebrate his memory we pray that the faith of the Irish may be renewed and strengthened and that the peace of Christ will come and take possession of our land.

Prayer of the Faithful

As we honour St Patrick today, we direct our prayers to God the Father in the same spirit of faith and firm conviction which he held.

1. For the church in our country, that like Patrick it may be strong in the faith of the gospel. Lord, hear us.
2. Let us pray for Irish people throughout the world that they may be fired with the enthusiasm of St Patrick, for spreading the faith. Lord, hear us.
3. For all exiles who like Patrick must live far away from family and friends,that they may be filled with joy, trust and persever-ence in the Lord. Lord, hear us.
4. For the sick of our parish that through our caring they may be aware of God's healing and comforting presence. Lord, hear us.
5. For our deceased relatives and friends that God may bless and reward them for the sacrifices they have made for us. Lord, hear us.

Almighty Father, in your unending kindness you sent Patrick to Ireland to announce the Good News of salvation. Look on us your children, and grant that we may never lose the faith. We ask this through Christ our Lord. Amen.

Birth of St John the Baptist
(Year A, B, C. 24th June)

It was Jesus himself who said: 'Never has there appeared on earth a mother's son greater than John the Baptist.' This is a fine tribute and our appetite for heaven is sharpened with the added remark: 'Yet the least in the kingdom of heaven, is greater than he'. The birth of John the Baptist is one of the oldest feasts in the church's calendar. In the early days of the church it was difficult to mention Jesus Christ without referring to John the Baptist so much were their lives woven together. John was born in Judea, six months before Christ, of aged parents and Elizabeth his mother was a cousin of Mary. He was an unusual character, an eccentric who from his earliest years lived in the wilderness – what we would call a drop-out from normal society.

From the outset his life had all the indications of tragic greatness, steeped as it was in mystery and solitude. He looked the part of a prophet with his long hair, flashing eyes, rough camel hair coat and diet of locust and wild honey. Once he began to preach, the crowds flocked to hear him and were so fascinated by his message that many mistook him for the Messiah. He was fearless in denouncing evil and a thorn in the flesh of those who did not want to face the truth in their lives. His popularity with the people prevented King Herod from putting him to death when he condemned his adulterous marriage to Herodias, his brother's wife. Instead he had him arrested and chained up in a dark prison. For those in search of God, John's greatest desire was to point them towards Jesus. He was very clear in fulfilling his role of being a voice crying in the wilderness preparing a way for the Lord, and making straight his paths. His whole life was absorbed in being a fearless speaker for God and a supporting character to Jesus.

In every age there is a need for prophets to speak for God in the various situations of life. Everyone's life is designed for the special purpose of being a voice for God. When God's word is heard people have an opportunity to judge their actions in the proper light and in the face of such truth are challenged to repent and change. John the Baptist was born to be God's speaker and each one of us, by virtue of our baptism, was called to be one. We live our vocation properly to the extent that we allow Jesus to take over our lives while following him with our own faltering steps, and announcing him as the Lamb of God who takes away the sins of the world.

Prayer of the Faithful

On the feast of John the Baptist, we turn in prayer to God our Father and ask for all the graces necessary to bear witness to the light shining in the darkness.

1.   We pray for our Holy Father and the bishops of the church, that they may remain true to the faith entrusted to them and tend their flock with care, courage and perseverance. Lord, hear us.
2.   For those who are prophets among us speaking out like voices in the wilderness. May our hearts be open to receive their message. Lord, hear us.
3.   We pray for our families. May they never lose the faith but be messengers in spreading the Good News. Lord, hear us.
4.   For those who are sick. May they receive comfort from the consoling words of friends. Lord, hear us.
5.   We pray for the dead. May they rest in peace. Lord, hear us.

Lord God, may the life of John the Baptist inspire us to greater holiness. Fill us with his spirit as we work in the service of your people. We ask this through Christ our Lord. Amen.

Assumption

The middle of August is normally tinged with a feeling of sadness. The summer is drawing to a close and for children it's almost the end of the school holidays. In the country the farmers are busy saving the harvest, making the most of the warm weather, in anticipation of the autumn days ahead. The 15th of August the feast of the Assumption marks the end of Our Lady's earthly life. It's a feast day at the beginning of harvest time that has been celebrated for almost fourteen centuries of our church's history. And how appropriate, because Mary is the first of the great harvest gathered by her blessed Son. Where Mary has gone we hope to follow.

The Assumption means that Mary, on the completion of her earthly life, was taken up body and soul into the glory of heaven as the fulfilment of her destiny which she achieved by living a life of loving response to God's will. As a young woman she had her own plans and hopes but God put a different proposition to her when the angel Gabriel saluted her in tones of reverence. She was completely amazed. As a carpenter's wife, quite content with her lot she considered herself unworthy of special treatment. In response to the will of God she meekly said: 'I am the Lord's handmaid. Be it done to me according to your word.'

Today's feast gives us an opportunity to reflect on Mary who was the great background figure in the life of Christ, always co-operating with her son. It should not be too difficult to apply the message of Mary's life to our own because like us she is not remote from real life. She lived with the same ups and downs as we do everyday. Mary knew what suffering was as she stood by the cross with the body of Christ in her arms.

This is a very joyful feast, proclaiming for us the Good News of salvation. It's a reminder that our bodies are temples of the Holy Spirit and that like Mary we are destined for glory. In fact we believe that what happened to Mary will happen to all of us. One day we too shall enjoy the vision of God in heaven as whole people – body and soul.

Prayer of the Faithful

Conscious of our unworthiness we raise our minds and hearts, to God the Father, in prayer and place our needs before him.

1. We pray that the church may continue to grow in faith and loving commitment as it joyfully announces Mary as a sign of hope and comfort in a despairing world. Lord, hear us.

2. We pray that all mothers may seek help in times of difficulties from the Holy Mother of God. Lord, hear us.

3. May we accept the sorrows and sufferings of life that come our way and try like Mary to discover the hand of God in them. Lord, hear us.

4. We pray that the sick may find in Mary a source of strength and joy. Lord, hear us.

5. For all our deceased relatives and friends. May the Lord reward them with eternal happiness for their lives of faithful service. Lord, hear us.

Heavenly Father, you give us heart for the most difficult tasks that have to be done. May we so walk in faith and love in this life that we may join Mary in the company of Jesus your Son and live forever and ever. Amen.

All Saints

On this festival of faith, as we celebrate the glory of countless millions of people who, down through the centuries, have gone home to God, we are given a glimpse into our ultimate future. Those who are now gathered in heaven with Christ were men and women who toiled and suffered for the love of God. They took their faith seriously enough to allow it to shape their lives in order to complete the task that God had given them. Few of them held important positions and many went unnoticed in their communities. They did nothing out of the ordinary and in a short time were forgotten. The fact that their names do not appear on the church's official role of honour, reminds us that those who are canonised are only a small fraction of God's friends. We have all met men and women who lived their faith in a non-spectacular manner, as parents coping with the cares of the family and struggling to make ends meet in difficult circumstances. They got on with what they had to do and experienced the joys and disappointments of their children growing up. In the hard experience of life they managed to keep their sights on the living God, trusting that he would work all things for the good. Their outstanding quality was faithful perseverance in this long and painful task.

This gospel paints a picture of the qualities Jesus considers necessary for making a person a saint, and they differ from what constitute earthly success and honour. He lets us see the value of a humble daily life and how precious it can be if we take up our cross and follow him. That is the life all of us have pledged ourselves to follow. The saints are put before us for our imitation to show us the way and point out the path we have to travel. We need human faces and firm friends to help us in our search for God. The example of their lives encourages us and spurs us on, telling us that our future is with God because we are already his children. Our glorious future has to be worked out in loving service here on earth and we have been given the grace necessary to achieve it, announcing, as it does, that heaven is already within our grasp. All Saints' Day gives us fresh courage to renew our resolve and to thank God for giving ordinary folk like us the ability to become saints. As we honour the saints, we pray that where they are we also may one day be.

Prayer of the Faithful

Inspired and encouraged by the example of the Saints we turn to our heavenly Father and place our needs before him.

1.   That the church may be purified and renewed in holiness and be a sign of love and compassion in a broken world. Lord, hear us.
2.   Called to sainthood in our ordinary lives, we pray for ourselves that, however great our difficulties and however many our faults, we may never forget that God loves us. Lord, hear us.
3.   May we keep on trying to love and serve others even when we are insulted and injured. Lord, hear us.
4.   For the sick and especially those who bear the cross of incurable illness whether mental or physical and for the compassionate people who care for them. Lord, hear us.
5.   That the Lord will welcome into his presence those who have died, firmly hoping in the resurrection. Lord, hear us.

Heavenly Father, you have allowed us to be called your children. As we labour day by day, help us not to be discouraged by our failures but to trust in your mercy and pardon. We make our prayer through Christ our Lord. Amen.

Year B

First Sunday of Advent

The first Sunday of Advent marks the beginning of a new church year. Amidst the excitement of preparing for the Christmas festivities, the season of Advent reminds us that we have to make preparations for the deeper meaning of what Christmas is all about God's presence among his people in the person of Jesus Christ. His coming on Christmas Day fills us with hope, and gives us encouragement that amidst all life's troubles our future is secure because it is in God's hands.

There is a note of high hope about this Advent season. It proclaims the message that God has not abandoned his people. He has sent his son among us to come to our aid and free us from our sins. This holy season celebrates the abiding presence of Christ in the world and his birth in each of our hearts. It tells us about the beginning and future ending of the story of our redemption. While we look forward to Christmas and the celebration of Christ's birthday, we cast a glance into the future and to that great day when Christ will come in glory. In the meantime we are to wait in joyful hope for our Lord and Saviour to be revealed and so we pray, Maranatha – Come, Lord Jesus.

Echoed and re-echoed throughout the readings is the warning, 'Be on your guard, stay awake because you never know when the time will come.' It is a grim reminder that a day of reckoning lies ahead. To be found wanting and unworthy of the kingdom on that occasion will be painfully frustrating. The choice is Christ or catastrophe. The real challenge of Advent is to prepare ourselves in body and soul for that great moment, by letting God's presence and power get to work in our lives. Life is incomplete without God and we are useless and inadequate without his presence. He alone can satisfy our deepest longings and fill us with inner peace. Advent makes us aware of our need to turn to God in hope and humble prayer, begging him to save us. It is a time for soul searching and renewal, for becoming more conscious of our sins and asking pardon and forgiveness. If we have abandoned God, neglected prayer or broken the commandments, now is the time to make a fresh start at building a closer relationship with him. There is not much point in Christ coming into our world if he is not at home and alive in our hearts. God values our response to his love. Above all Advent is a season when as christians we reach out to the disadvantaged and bring them the joys of Christ.

We are invited to listen to the voice of God in the countless ways he speaks to us every day and recognise his love. The challenge of God in Jesus is around every corner, at work, on the street, while we are with friends or at home in the dull routine of life. There is no day when he does not knock at the door of our hearts. One way we can let him in is by availing of the opportunities to serve and be neighbourly in our community. We pass through this world but once and any good we have to do should be done now. While Advent is about waiting for God to come into our lives, it's good to remember that God has been waiting for us longer than we have been waiting for him.

Prayer of the Faithful

As we enter the holy season of Advent, we ask God our Father to help us to stay awake and make ready for the coming of Christ.

1. For all who exercise authority in the church especially the Pope, our bishops and priests that they may be alive to the presence of God in their midst. Lord, hear us.
2. We pray for our own community that amidst the hustle and bustle of preparing for Christmas the message of Jesus will not be forgotten. Lord, hear us.
3. Let us see clearly this Advent the needs of those less fortunate than ourselves. Lord, hear us.
4. For all those whose lives are filled with sorrow or sickness, that they may realise God has not abandoned them. Lord, hear us.
5. Grant eternal rest to those who have completed their earthly journey. Lord, hear us.

Heavenly Father, as we look forward to your Son's birth among us, may we live by the example he has shown us with true christian faith. We make our prayer through Christ our Lord. Amen.

Second Sunday of Advent

John the Baptist was a prophet – a chosen messenger whose role in life was to prepare the way for God's entry among his people. He came out of the desert and captured the imagination of the people who flocked to hear him, by announcing that the long awaited day of salvation was about to dawn on them. His words stung like the lash of a whip as he reprimanded his listeners for their loose lifestyles which were making them careless and apathetic. The Baptist's message was simple: 'Do penance, reform your lives by prayer and fasting for the kingdom of God is at hand.' The voice of John the Baptist speaks to us across the ages and urges us to prepare a place for the Lord in our hearts.

Advent is an invitation to conversion and John the Baptist gives us some down-to-earth advice on how to change our lives for the better. He talks about filling in valleys of prejudice, levelling down mountains of pride and straightening out the crooked paths of injustice. This morning we ask ourselves what in our lives needs a complete turning around to allow God to come close to us. There are areas and dark corners of ourselves which we do not want disturbed even though we are aware that they prevent God from entering into our innermost being. This Advent time of prayer and penance brings home to us the need to make a fresh start if only to prevent spiritual drift. Preparing a way for God in our hearts is a time-consuming and costly business. It demands listening to what God is saying to us and, if necessary, acting upon it by making changes in our behaviour. Welcoming God involves removing all blockages and obstacles which prevent him from coming close. Preparing a way for the Lord may mean walking a new path. Christ cannot save us without our co-operation. Like a true gentleman he does not force an entry into out lives but waits to be invited.

The voice of John the Baptist reminds us that we have the important task of announcing Christ to others. Our every-day life is a message telling everyone through acts of kindness, honesty and faithfulness that Christ is right here with us. We may be the only book about Christ which many people will ever read. His gospel of love is the answer to the problems of our troubled world. John the Baptist invites us to turn this Advent season into a real spiritual homecoming by making the necessary preparations for the arrival of the Saviour into our lives.

Prayer of the Faithful

Just as John the Baptist called for repentance, we ask God the Father to help us towards a genuine conversion.

1. We pray that the church may be a sign of love and forgiveness as it prepares a way for the Lord's coming. Lord, hear us.
2. That people everywhere will open their hearts to Christ by working to build on world-based honesty and repentance. Lord, hear us.
3. For peace and harmony in our homes and hearts and honesty in our dealings with one another. Lord, hear us.
4. For the sick of our community, that they will share in the hope and joy of the Advent season. Lord, hear us.
5. Let us remember especially those who have died recently ... that they may enjoy their eternal reward in heaven. Lord, hear us.

God our Father, during Advent make straight the path for us to prepare to meet you at Christmas. Through Christ our Lord. Amen.

Third Sunday of Advent

The joy of Advent shines forth with an inspiring message of hope and encouragement urging us to rejoice and be happy because the Lord is near. What is more, it tells us that joy is basic to being christian and our vocation is to radiate this joy. Experience bears it out that rejoicing is not always the hallmark of a christian. All too frequently, christianity has been associated with sadness. Many of us are more familiar with the gospel message of carrying the cross than of its abiding characteristic of joy. We tend to think of Jesus as the man of sorrows and acquainted with grief, yet as he concluded his ministry and was about to leave, he says: 'These things I have spoken to you that my joy might be in you and your joy be complete,' (John: 15:11). While there is hardship and suffering in the life of Jesus there is a joy which is compatible with pain.

We were created for happiness. It is the purpose of our whole being and we spend our lives searching and striving to attain it. Somehow this happiness seems to escape us as we go searching after it in the wrong places. Our greatest mistake is to equate joy with pleasure and to look for it in material things. We can buy pleasure and it will cost us dearly, but all the money in the world cannot purchase happiness. christian joy is something deeper and richer than the smile and laughter upon a happy face. It comes from an awareness that God is with us and produces a contentment and an inner peace that cannot be taken from us. Friendship with God is the source of christian joy. No trials can drown this joy since it is born of faith. It is a characteristic of the soul that cannot be easily described but should be evident in the life of a believer.

On the first Christmas when God came down in the person of Jesus, he filled the world with glad tidings of great joy. His life was geared towards God the Father in joy, prayer and thanksgiving. We are so caught up with our daily problems that we fail to reflect the joy of that marvellous truth: 'that God so loved the world that he gave his only Son and that whoever believes in him might not die but may have eternal life' (John 3:16). There is no greater proof of love than to give of ourselves to others. Our Christmas joy cannot be complete unless we show generosity to those who have nothing to give to us in return. We can not reflect the light who is Christ if we live by values that do not even remotely resemble those of the gospel. The happiest people are those who are doing most for others. They know from experience that it is in giving that we receive. The day will arrive when they will be greeted with the words: 'Well done good and faithful servant, come and join in your master's happiness.'

Prayer of the Faithful

As we move a step closer towards Christmas, we pray to God our Father that we may always find christian joy in our hearts.

1. For the holy church of God and all who minister in it that they will show the joy of Christ's love to all people. Lord, hear us.
2. That we will all hear the lonely voice of John the Baptist calling us to repentance and sincere sorrow for our sins. Lord, hear us.
3. We pray that we may always find time for Christ in our lives and so we may be ready to welcome him with true christian joy. Lord, hear us.
4. For those who are overburdened with life, the lonely and the sick that the joy of Advent may shine in their lives. Lord, hear us.
5. That those who have died may experience a true and lasting happiness with God in heaven. Lord, hear us.

Heavenly Father, with confidence we place before you our needs. Teach us to commit ourselves to your way of life and in so doing find our peace. Amen.

Fourth Sunday of Advent

When we reflect on childhood memories, if we are among the fortunate ones, our dear mother is there. Be she young or old, dark or fair, how else would we be here had not our mother, by her very nature, made our welfare her vocation. The relationship we share with our mother is special and is based on a bond of mutual love. It should come as no surprise that Mary is at the centre of today's gospel, which gives us a simple but moving account of the greatest message that was ever delivered. In it we are told simply and plainly that there was a young maiden, who knelt down at the angel Gabriel's mysterious message and, in the freedom of her heart, gave the total gift of herself to God, saying: 'Be it done unto me according to thy Word.'

The Annunciation was the moment when God first revealed a mystery that he kept secret for endless ages. It is true that his love for us is so great that he wants to become one of us. Mary was needed by God so that he might carry out this plan for the world and send his Son among us. She was asked to co-operate with God and be the mother of Christ. The moment she said 'Yes' to the angel, salvation dawned for mankind and she brought that salvation to birth at Bethlehem on the first Christmas Day. Mary did not say 'Yes' to God on only one occasion. She had to confirm that 'Yes' many times during her life. She had no idea that at Christ's birth every door would close in her face. She was shortly to become a refugee in Egypt and some thirty years later she was to see her son die the death of a common criminal.

Christmas is almost upon us and, on this fourth Sunday of Advent, our thoughts turn to Mary our mother, who is the model of listening and waiting for the Lord to come. As she turned over in her mind what the angel's greeting could mean she came only gradually to understand the message and mystery of Christmas. God not only wants to become one of us, but his reason in doing so is that he wants us to become like him. In listening to the Word of God, Mary shows us an aspect of our christian life which is of special importance. To be a christian is to be a person who keeps their ears open to what God is calling them to do, so that they can answer that call. We can ask her to help us have her attitude of listening and responding to God's call so that we can be as ready and as willing to bring Christ into our world as she was.

144

Mary brought Christ to birth in the stable and she wants to bring him to birth in our hearts. She built her life into a fit place for God and we must do the same. God did not keep Mary out of Christmas – neither must we.

Prayer of the Faithful

On this final Sunday of the Advent season we place our needs before God our Father and pray that, like Mary, we will be able to say, 'Let it be done according to your Word.'

1. For the leaders of our church that they will be inspired by the example of Mary our mother. Lord, hear us.
2. That, like Mary, our answer will always be 'Yes' to the will of God in our lives. Lord, hear us.
3. As Christmas is about to dawn, we pray that the community present will be ready to welcome Christ with open hearts. Lord, hear us.
4. For the old, the lonely and the sick, that, like Mary, they may be able to carry the crosses that come their way. Lord, hear us.
5. We remember especially those who have died. May they experience the joy of meeting Christ in heaven. Lord, hear us.

Father in heaven, as we await the birth of Jesus, teach us always to follow the example of Mary our mother. Through Christ our Lord. Amen.

Christmas Day

At Christmas, our attention is focused on the birth of Jesus in a humble Bethlehem cave. It was all so completely unexpected. The star which the wise men were following did not stop at a regal palace, but at a stable used for sheltering animals. We are amazed and surprised that God should come to us as a helpless and dependent child, of poor parents, who were far from home and soon to become refugees in Egypt. By choosing to be born in such a desolate place, out of the limelight, away from the world's palaces and riches, God's Son turns upside-down worldy notions of fame and success. He was giving us a clear message about the need to see grace and goodness in the very poorest of people and places. The first to share the joy of Mary and Joseph in their humble surroundings were the rough country folk, social outcasts, shepherds guarding their flocks by night. Their presence was an assurance that Christ was available to ordinary people carrying out their normal work. What's more, he was going to be on the side of the weak and disadvantaged.

Our celebration of the birth of our Lord is more than a remembrance of the happenings in Bethlehem on a stary night 2,000 years ago. It is a reminder that God loves us so much that he sent his only Son among us to save us, to forgive our sins and to show us a way to our heavenly home. In compassion, he broke the sacred barrier between creature and creator, by reaching down and presenting himself to us as a child, inspiring love rather than fear. Since that night, the new-born child is our living link with God, who is always near to those who welcome him with an open heart. As heaven comes down to earth, it carries with it timeless blessings which soften the hardest of hearts. Bitterness and grudges are dissolved by the affection of the new-born child who has raised us up to a life far beyond any human expectation.

Christmas focuses not only on what Jesus did by making his home with us, but on what we must do, as it reveals that we are part of God's family. This means that we need to reverence each human life, and that raises some tough questions about our treatment of other people.

The consequences of our daily living are truly enormous. To neglect the old, to be contemptuous of the poor, and to have no thought for the unemployed and the lonely, is to ignore those individuals with whom Christ has so closely identified. We all need to examine ourselves on the doors we close to Jesus. There is no point in being sentimental about the doors slammed by the folk in Bethlehem, when there is no room in our own hearts for the needy. The happiness and peace of Christmas comes from within, when God is born in the stable of our hearts.

Prayer of the Faithful

On this Christmas feast we pray to God our Father that we may grow in the love, joy and peace that his Son came on earth to spread.

1. We pray for the Pope, the bishops and all those who bear responsibility of leadership within the church. May they be inspired by the humble birth and life of Jesus. Lord, hear us.
2. May this time of Christmas be what it was meant to be – a true exchange of gifts between a father and a family. Lord, hear us.
3. May our celebration of the Birth of Our Lord be a celebration of the life which he has won for us. Lord, hear us.
4. Lord look with mercy on all those who are homeless, hungry or grief-stricken, or ill at this time. Lord, hear us.
5. We remember our faithful departed, especially those who spent last Christmas in our company. May they now enjoy the peace of your kingdom. Lord, hear us.

Lord, we thank you joyfully for this wonderful day which is the birthday of the Lord Jesus. Grant us a prayerful spirit, like the shepherds who saw and believed. We make our prayer through Christ our Lord. Amen.

Feast of the Holy Family

Christmas is, above all, a family feast and while our thoughts are still centred on Bethlehem and the Holy Family, the readings of this liturgy deal with various aspects of family life. Speaking about the Holy Family may be somewhat off-putting as our own home may be a far cry from this loving ideal. Let us not forget that Mary and Joseph, like any other parents, had their own problems and difficulties to face. The shadow of the cross was already beginning to form over the crib at Bethlehem when they heard Simeon's chill prophecy, that the Child Jesus was destined for the fall and rising of many in Israel and that Mary's own soul would be pierced with a sword. From the very beginning, the child they loved and cherished was a mystery to Mary and Joseph and as he grew up under their protection all they could do was to place their trust in God. We must do the same. The family is as old as humankind and has survived because it is built on the strong foundation of love. We may not be able to change many things in the world but our influence does extend over our own homes and our own family.

Like any other worthwhile project, family life, to be success-ful, has to be given time and energy to develop. It does not hap-pen automatically. Love, harmony and mutual respect, which are the basic ingredients of a happy family, have to be witnessed in action. Example teaches best. Attitudes of loving and caring, which are encouraged in the earliest days, have a deep and lasting influence. Children become, in later life, what their homes have made them, and when they have learned to give as well as receive, they develop a growing awareness of others.

This is an opportunity for young adults to reflect on the love and respect which they ought to show to their fathers and mothers, because kindness to parents is precious in the eyes of God. Sadly they may not have always lived up to the gospel expectations in this respect. Parents are often left bewildered and wondering at what is happening as they watch their children grow up and express values and beliefs different to their generation. Grand-parents must also be shown sensitive respect in their declining years and not be condemned to end their days in the pathetic isolation of a crucifying aloneness. More than anything else, the emphasis is to be at peace within our family circle. While a well

148

furnished home and a decent standard of living are important, it is good to remember that, unless the family keeps prayer and spiritual concerns in mind, things are bound to go wrong.

Family life never runs smoothly and today it is more difficult and trying than ever before. It is the raw material from which we fashion our sainthood. On this feast of the Holy Family we ask Mary and Joseph to make our families pleasing to God, to be the heart and centre of every home throughout the world and to put a new spirit into this basic unit of all society.

Prayer of the Faithful

As we celebrate the Feast of the Holy Family, let us place before our heavenly Father the needs of his family on earth.

1. For our Holy Father, the bishops, and religious, that they may always go about their daily tasks strengthened in the name of Jesus the Lord. Lord, hear us.
2. That the love of God will blend perfectly with mutual love and respect in all our families. Lord, hear us.
3. Guide all parents to show their children by example, the meaning of a good christian life. Lord, hear us.
4. For those families who are experiencing difficulties. May their tensions be eased and happiness reign in their midst. Lord, hear us.
5. We pray for widows and orphans and those who suffer as a result of unhappy marriages or broken homes. Lord, hear us.
6. For the deceased members of our own families. May we one day be reunited with them in our heavenly home. Lord, hear us.

God our Father, you have given us the experience of human love as a way of sharing your divine love. We thank you for our families and for the graces we have received through them. We make our prayer through Christ our Lord. Amen.

Epiphany of the Lord

Isn't it amazing in this sophisticated and scientific age that we are all so interested in stars, horoscopes and astrological signs. All of us are pleased when we read that something spectacular will happen. The Magi's journey across mountains and deserts, following the star, echoes in our hearts. We feel that we have our own star to follow – a yearning deep down within our being for meaning, truth and happiness – an individual path in life which we alone are called to tread. When the Magi found the child Jesus, it was highly unlikely that they saw an infant with a halo who was clearly recognisable as God's Son. I believe that they saw just another tiny child because that was all their bodily eyes could see. However, with their eyes of faith they were able to see beneath the surface of appearances and recognise, in this child, God's light which had come into the world. Ever afterwards, they were not guided by a star in the sky but by the light of this child, whom they saw as the Saviour of the world. We too have been given the eyes of faith to keep us on course as we follow Christ along the highways and by-ways of life, across desert paths of loneliness, pain, failure and illness. There is something beautiful about the story of the three Kings. Those Wise Men of yesteryear represent all of us on a spiritual adventure which goes on as long as life lasts. We are to be Wise Men for our day, making Jesus visible to the whole world as its Saviour and Redeemer. Our special role is to make Jesus known along the pathways of life by being open and receptive to his word. The Lord needs our commitment in furthering his work. The Wise Men did not come to the Lord empty-handed, but with gifts specially chosen which expressed the reason for their search, and neither must we come empty-handed. We may not have gold, frankincense or myrrh, but we can bring the gift of ourselves as human beings grafted into Christ. This gift of self is something more precious, as it never wears out.

The church wants us all to rejoice today. This is the day when we proclaim to all the world that Jesus came to save everybody and that his influence is not restricted to any one culture. Christmas is about making two journeys. The journey to Bethlehem and the way home by a different route. We are all making our journey home through life. Having found Bethlehem, let us hope that at the end of life's journey we will be met once more by Jesus and Mary.

Feast of the Epiphany

Today we remember the visit of the Magi to the stable at Bethlehem. Joining with them in adoring Christ as Lord and Saviour, we make our prayer to God the Father.

1. That the church on earth may serve as a beacon of light helping people to find Christ andto worship him in truth. Lord, hear us.
2. We pray that Christ may be the star that guides our whole life, the centre of our worship and the focus of our hope. Lord, hear us.
3. We pray that God may reveal his glory to those who are still searching, by opening their minds and hearts to the warmth of his love. Lord, hear us.
4. We pray for sick people everywhere; those who are disabled, those who are alone and those who find life meaningless. May the revelation of your power be at work through those who minister to them. Lord, hear us.
5. For our friends and relations who have died, that having reached journey's end, they may meet Jesus and his mother, Mary. Lord, hear us.

Lord God, you revealed your only-begotten Son to all the peoples of the world on this day. Lead us from the guiding star of faith, by which we know you now, to the vision of your glory. Amen.

Baptism of the Lord

It was certainly an unusual occasion for John the Baptist to be preaching repentance to the people on the banks of the river Jordan, and urging them to prepare a way for the Lord, when Jesus approached him and asked to be baptised. Jesus had no need of baptism as he himself was sinless and full of the Holy Spirit from the time he was born. By immersing himself in the waters of the Jordan he chose purposely to put himself on the side of sinners and to assume the burden of our sins. He came to share our way of life and die that we might live. This first act of his public ministry was one of humility and it launched his mission of loving service to the despised, the poor and the spiritually crippled. The seal of approval was put by God the Father upon the work which he was undertaking because as he came out of the water the heavens echoed with the acclamation, 'You are my beloved Son in whom I am well pleased.' This was the outward sign that he was appointed Saviour of the world. He was now ready for a ministry which would generate divine life in others.

The baptism of Jesus naturally makes us think of our own baptism. Christ's baptism was not just an isolated event in his own life, it was the beginning of a new era in God's relationship with mankind, and has implications for us all, as it affects each of us at the deepest and most personal level. At baptism the spirit of God takes possession of us in a very special way, to direct and guide us in the footsteps of Christ. Baptism unites us with Jesus in the most intimate manner, bringing us into the family of God with the right to call God our Father.

Even though we were baptised when we were a few days old, our baptism is not merely an event of the past, it is an ever present reality, a constant sharing in the divine life of the Risen Christ. It is a daily invitation to come closer to God and to be helpers in his work of saving the world. We are called to be servants of God in our own sphere of living and to make the world a better place. In our everyday lives we may not have the ability to do great things but we have the power to do good things. We are told that Jesus went about doing good. What a beautiful way for us to make a public statement about our faith. Through good works each of us, in our own way, completes the mission which Christ began after his baptism. It is a day to ask ourselves if we are being true to the direction in which our lives were pointed at our baptism.

Prayer of the Faithful

When Jesus prayed at his baptism, the Holy Spirit descended upon him. Let us now join in prayer to God the Father, that we too may receive the Spirit to help us live in accordance with our baptismal promises.

1. We pray for leaders of the church that, strengthened by the Spirit, they may carry out their work of being witnesses to God's love before all nations. Lord, hear us.

2. For christian parents, that they may be fully conscious of their spiritual responsibility towards their children who through baptism are reborn in Christ. Lord, hear us.

3. That we may be faithful to our own baptismal promises and further the saving work of Christ by sharing the blessings we have received with other people. Lord, hear us.

4. We pray for the sick ... that they may realise through their suffering that they are bearing witness to the life of Christ. Lord, hear us.

5. May all the recently deceased, who were baptised in Christ, share in his glory. Lord, hear us.

Eternal Father, at our baptism we were anointed to be your witnesses throughout the world. Grant that the power of the Holy Spirit may remain with us and that we may always bear witness to the faith you have given us, through Christ our Lord. Amen.

First Sunday of Lent

There is no doubt about it, Lent strikes a chord and touches something deep down in all our hearts, as it presents us with the challenge to reject sin and to be faithful to the God of love. Fasting, prayer and alms-giving have been traditionally the central elements of Lent for the christian. They are the tools which we have been taught to use, in order to edge closer to God, as we continue our journey through life. For some, Lent means giving up alcohol and going off cigarettes, while others see it as a time for giving to famine-relief and for going to church daily. Whatever type of penance we undertake, our motive is all-important. If we fast and deprive ourselves of food simply to have a slimmer figure, or if we give alms to establish a reputation as a do-gooder in the community our efforts are of little avail. We have received our reward and are no closer to God.

At the start of his public ministry, Jesus went into the desert for forty days and it is because of this that we must keep the holy season of Lent. We relive his experience in an attempt to establish a deeper bond and a closer friendship between God and ourselves. The journey we make is an inward one, into the wilderness of our innermost self, to stand before God in all sincerity and truth. This helps us to see ourselves as we really are and as we take stock of what we are doing with our time and our talents, we become more aware of our own sinfulness. The need to change and to renew the struggle against evil by prayer, fasting and penance becomes painfully obvious. The penance we perform should make us realise that the spiritual things of life are more important than the material. As we become conscious of our own faults, we realise that changes need to be made.

If we happen to be one of those people whose speciality is always to assume the worst in everyone, perhaps it's time to take a hard look at our gossiping, backbiting, and scandalmongering. A simple vow to hold our tongue might prove a useful medicine. We could make a resolution to be pleasant to the person with whom we always seem to clash and whom we just cannot stand. What would be wrong with giving up alcohol and gambling if they are the cause of friction and unhappiness in the home? Daily prayer is of importance to us all, as it is the vital life-line in our friendship with God. Our invitation to a personal relationship with Christ can not be achieved without prayer. We must give top priority to this exercise, which strengthens our faith and trust and brings us closer to him. Lent is a time for soul searching. It is a season when we are challenged to measure up to the call of God in various aspects of life and to take practical steps to face the evil of sin and selfishness within us. It is a call for a change in behaviour because our persistent sinfulness spoils our growth in the love of God. Lent is a season of grace to be taken seriously, if we intend it to be a purifying experience of vital spiritual worth. The challenge of saying 'No' to ourselves and 'Yes' to God is what constitutes the struggle.

Prayer of the Faithful

As we begin the season of Lent we come in faith and trust before God the Father, seeking his help in our struggle with the forces of evil.

1. We pray for the church throughout the world. May its proclamation that God's kingdom is at hand reach the hearts of those most in need of conversion. Lord, hear us.
2. We pray that as a community we may enter into the spirit of Lent and be generous in our efforts at prayer, fasting and almsgiving. Lord, hear us.
3. May we make an honest effort to go into the wilderness with Jesus and see ourselves as we really are. Lord, hear us.
4. We pray for all those who are carrying the cross of sickness. May they unite their pain and suffering with the passion of Jesus. Lord, hear us.
5. For all our deceased relatives and friends. May God give them peace and eternal rest. Lord, hear us.

Heavenly Father, hear our prayer which we make in faith. May you continue to show us your love as we answer your call to fast and deny ourselves. We ask this through Christ our Lord. Amen.

Second Sunday of Lent

In this liturgy we are given an extraordinary glimpse into the faith and character of Abraham. The command to kill Isaac, his only child, born to him in old age, was beyond his human way of thinking and seemed absurd. How else was God's promised blessing about being the father of many nations to be fulfilled, if not through his son Isaac? He was being asked to sacrifice his last remaining natural chance of survival and the very foundation on which his faith stood. The request was most painful but, in the greatness of his faith and trust, Abraham hastened to carry out the divine command. God must be obeyed at all costs. As he raised the knife to slaughter his son, God stopped the final blow. Abraham's hand was stayed and Isaac's life was spared.

Abraham's faith and obedience is an example to all of us. He always took God at his word and responded to his call, even when his faith was being tested beyond all limits. Like Abraham we are called to journey into the unknown and respond to God's call, especially when circumstances make faith seem unreasonable, and wholly beyond our human way of thinking. At moments of crisis, like at the death of a loved one when life is clouded with mystery, it is all-important to keep on trusting and take God at his word. We walk by faith and not by sight: (2 Cor; 5:7). When all is said and done we believe, not because we have seen, but because of the word and the power of God who is present in our lives.

The gospel story is about the transfiguration which was an amazing event in the Lord's life. The apostles were completely overcome when given a glimpse of Christ in all his glory and when it was revealed to them who their master was: 'This is my beloved Son, listen to him.' It was a blessed happening to sustain them in the darkness of Gethsemane, when they would witness Christ in agony. Moments of joy, when everything fits together, are few and far between. We are not meant to be spectators at the transfiguration but, like the apostles, we are to climb the mountain, reflect on its message, and live it out with conviction and sincerity. It was only through his passion and death that Christ came to the glory of the resurrection. If he is to transfigure our wretched bodies and make them into copies of his own glorious body, then the road we must journey is the one of suffering taken by Christ. The transfiguration speaks to us not only of our times of trial and suffering but also of the glory in store for us, provided we have faith and trust and never lose hope or stand in the way of God. Lent provides us, in the springtime of the year with an excellent opportunity to confront ourselves with the many false securities we hold dear and are unwilling to shed on our pilgrim journey. It reminds us that an unexamined life is not worth living. If this is to be a season of great blessing, helping us to grow into truthful, generous and lovable people, we must, through sacrifice and self-denial, die to the ways of the world. Few of us, like Abraham, will be asked to sacrifice an only son, but we are all called to turn away from selfishness and to refrain from words and actions which cause unease at home and poison family and community life. To overcome our sins and weaknesses, and to grow to maturity as human beings, requires patience and is the work of a lifetime because nothing that is worthwhile is ever simple or straightforward.

Prayer of the Faithful

Mindful of God the Father's call for complete trust in him, with great confidence we call upon his name in prayer.

1. We pray for our Holy Father and the bishops of the church, that they may inspire faith and trust in God amidst life's difficulties. Lord, hear us.
2. We pray that those who are struggling with problems of faith may have their doubts removed and replaced by a deep understanding of God's call. Lord, hear us.
3. That parents and teachers may, by the example of their lives, hand on the faith in the person of Jesus to the young people of our time. Lord, hear us.
4. We pray that the transfigured Christ may be a sign of encouragement to those burdened with sickness. Lord, hear us.
5. We pray for the dead. May God welcome them into his heavenly home and grant them everlasting peace. Lord, hear us.

Heavenly Father, increase our faith as we make our journey through difficult moments of life. Help us to recognise your presence in the people we live with, and your hand in everyday events. We make our prayer through Christ our Lord. Amen.

Third Sunday of Lent

Living in an age of freedom with laws thrown to the wind and people deciding for themselves what is right and wrong, we may well ask what has happened to the ten commandments. Do they really matter any more or are they a bit old fashioned? The giving of the commandments by the Lord to Moses on Mt Sinai signalled the birth of Israel as a nation. For the Jewish people, obeying the commandments in daily living was not considered as doing what was right, but was seen as living out a relationship with a real personal God. To keep the commandments, for the Jews, was to respond in love to the wisdom of God who had bound himself to his people. They viewed the commandments as the very wisdom of God shared with them as a gift – an invitation to behave like God and not just a test of their obedience. Our society is more advanced and sophisticated than was Israel at the time of Moses, but right and wrong are still the same. These ten commandments are the very roots of our faith. Any nation that does not keep to these basic guidelines produces a lifestyle that is not worth living and is doomed to crumble. We still need the ten commandments as they are the bricks and mortar, the very foundation of a stable society.

In clearing the Temple, Jesus shows great reverence for the House of the Lord and leaves us an example of how we should respect our own places of worship and look upon them as sanctuaries of genuine prayer. The temple was no better than a noisy market-place of buyers and sellers. The traders were guilty of using God's dwelling for their own selfish purposes of making money. All their commotion showed little regard for the spirit of true worship. We see Jesus re-asserting fiercely reverence for God's name and for God's house because the whole transaction had become an empty ritual, which obscured the true function of the temple.

As a community we gather here each Sunday to celebrate the eucharist and to thank God for the week that has passed. Every Lord's Day should be like a step on the way up to heaven but is it? Are we closer to God by being here this morning or has our Sunday worship degenerated into an empty ritual, a social outing or something we do because it's expected of us? The Sabbath should make us appreciate the God above us, the world he has given us and the people around us. All too often our belief is taken down from the shelf, given, as it were, a Sunday morning dusting but put back up again by half past twelve. God wants and desires us to worship him with more than words and external behaviour. Worship means saying to God: 'How great thou art.' It's our response when we recognise the goodness of God in our lives and know that, because the Lord is our shepherd, there is nothing we shall want. Worship and the way we live are not meant to be cut off from one another. As well as going to church on Sunday, we are called to be the church in our society during the week.

Prayer of the Faithful

We now call upon God the Father, who poured out on us his love and constant care, and ask him to create within our minds and hearts a willingness to obey his commandments, and so we pray.

1. For the leaders of the church, that they may teach God's people to obey the commandments out of love and not out of fear. Lord, hear us.
2. That we may be faithful to the command to love God and to love our neighbour. Lord, hear us.
3. For those who are walking in the darkness of error and sin because of a failure to live up to the demands of the ten commandments. Lord, hear us.
4. That we may never neglect the sick, the old, the lonely and all who suffer in our midst. Lord, hear us.
5. We commend to the Lord the souls of ..., who died during the week. Lord, hear us.

Heavenly Father, accept these prayers which we offer in faith. Let us know the love and peace of Jesus, your Son and our mediator, with you. We ask these and all our prayers through Christ our Lord. Amen.

Fourth Sunday of Lent

The most deeply moving truth that the church preaches is that we are forever loved by God. Christianity rests on the firm convict-ion that God's love reaches down into our sick, bruised and hurt world in the person of Jesus. For every faithful heart this is the very essence of the gospel story. No passage in scripture puts it better than the words which Jesus spoke to Nicodemus, 'God so loved the world that he sent his only son, so that whoever believes in him may not die, but may have eternal life.' Our love for others comes nowhere near the kind of love God has for us. Such is the extent of his love for the world, that he offers life to all and excludes nobody. God loves each of us as if there is nobody else to love. He is the father who wants to walk with his family as they go through life and who can not be satisfied until all his wandering children have come safely home.

We begin to realise the magnitude of God's love for us by looking at the crucifix. This portrays the image of the suffering Christ lifted upon the cross, absorbing the full brunt of the evil of our sins. All life's cruelties, hatreds and injustices are concentrated in that cross planted on the hill of Calvary. One of the amazing facts about the passion and death of Christ is that it has become the supreme proof of God's love. When all else fails, the down and out, the despairing, and the lonely are drawn towards that far off cross on the hillside, aware that there is someone to turn towards. The upright cross, once the sign of shame and humiliation, becomes a channel of healing grace. The tree of death becomes the tree of victory.

The first reading tells how Israel as a nation has been disobedient to the law of God and scorned his love. They broke the covenant and brought about the destruction of their temple and city. The many appeals to repent and mend their ways, made through the prophets, went unheeded. Yet, even in their darkest hour of exile, God never abandoned them but kept calling them back. Their history is a stark reminder of what happens when we refuse to take God's love seriously and reject it out of hand. It should bring home to us that we also are faced with the choice of accepting or rejecting God's love which is stronger than death. If we deny his loving kindness we place ourselves in danger of being separated from him. God respects our personal freedom and will not force his love on us against our wishes. We may refuse his mercy and reject his gift. It is possible for us to abandon the love of God for the darkness of sin and separate ourselves from him forever.

As we approach the half-way mark in our Lenten season it is a time to review flapping resolutions and to ask if our lives are joyful responses to God's love. Is his love finding expression in the way we live? What are we doing to bring the love of God into the lives of our friends? Lent is a call to step out of the ways of darkness into the light of Christ.

Prayer of the Faithful

With confidence we bring our cares and concerns before God the Father who loved the world so much that he gave his only son so that everyone who believes in him may not be lost but have eternal life.

1. That the church may always be a living sign of God's love and mercy in times of darkness and despair. Lord, hear us.
2. For the grace and strength to live in such a manner that the love of God may shine forth in all our actions. Lord, hear us.
3. May the love of God at the centre of creation bring peace into our hearts and harmony into our lives. Lord, hear us.
4. We ask on this day a blessing on all mothers whose love, gentleness and untiring patience is so much taken for granted. Lord, hear us.
5. That the sick and all those who are suffering may realise from the care and attention shown them that they are loved by God. Lord, hear us.
6. We remember our beloved dead. May they all share in the glory of the resurrection. Lord, hear us.

Heavenly Father, look with love on all your children and guide us safely on our pilgrim journey. We make our prayer through Christ our Lord. Amen.

Fifth Sunday of Lent

All the readings point in their different ways towards the passion and death of Christ. Jeremiah tells a shattered Jewish people, going into exile as a punishment for breaking the old covenant, that God will not forsake them. He foresees a time when God will form a new relationship with the people of Israel, based on love and personal respect. God will put a new heart and a new spirit into his people. This focuses our attention on the first Holy Thursday evening, the night before Christ died, when, raising the cup, Christ introduced the new covenant in his blood, to be shed for the forgiveness of sins.

The second reading tells us that because Jesus suffered and prayed with tears to be saved from death, he can sympathise with our sufferings and help us grow rather than be crushed by them. Jesus knows our plight, is touched by our anguish and distress and pleads with God the Father on our behalf. In the gospel Christ speaks his thoughts out loud and expresses repugnance for the terrible ordeal before him. His soul is troubled at the prospect of Calvary and he is tempted to pray for deliverance from it. However he cannot ask to be spared his agony as God's kingdom will only come through crucifixion and death. His moment of greatest influence will be when he is lifted up on the cross with arms outstretched to embrace all the world. Christ on the cross shows us the depth of evil of which we humans are capable and the heights of love to which we are called. Every christian is called to live out the passion of Jesus Christ in his own life. No one is excused or spared its agony. There are no crown-bearers in heaven who were not cross-bearers on earth. Following Christ means travelling the same road, laying down our lives, and leaving everything completely in the hands of God the Father.

To drive home this point, Jesus takes an example from the world of nature. Our lives, like Christ's, must resemble the grain of wheat that goes down into the ground to produce new life. The grain of wheat dying in the earth indicates how we must die to our selfishness before we can start living the life of Christ. One comes to a greater life only after dying to a lesser one. Never forget that we are God's grain of wheat, part of his eternal harvest. When Jesus calls he bids us come and die and put to death within ourselves what is opposed to true life. Christ shows that life and death have a place in God's plan for us. To be buried in the earth means avoiding sin, accepting suffering and living for others. In every place and in every heart the struggle between evil and good is still with us. The way of the cross begins at our own doorstep and we are challenged to follow its path. As Passiontide approaches we should renew our efforts to remove the layers of human sinfulness through which satan and the power of evil have made inroads into our lives.

Prayer of the Faithful

In the firm belief that God the Father will bring us through pain and suffering to everlasting life, w e make our prayer.

1. For the leaders of the church that they may bury personal ambition and empty their hearts of all self-seeking in order to become more wholesome servants of the gospel. Lord, hear us.
2. That we may be given the grace to empty our hearts of self-centredness in order to perform acts of generosity for the poor. Lord, hear us.
3. That we may come to realise the great truth Christ tells us, that if we want to save our life we must spent it generously in his service. Lord, hear us.
4. Lord, bless our sick relatives and friends. Help them to bear their daily sufferings with strength. Lord, hear us.
5. May all our family and friends who have died share in Christ's victory over death. Lord, hear us.

Heavenly Father, your Son tells us that he is the wheat grain which falls on the ground and dies in order to yield a rich harvest. Help us to die to our selfishness so that our lives may be open to your love. We make our prayer through Christ our Lord. Amen.

Passion Sunday

Palm Sunday is the beginning of Holy Week and is a day of glory and impending tragedy. The scene is set with Jesus making his triumphant journey from Bethany to Jerusalem, where he started that final movement, which would bring all and everything together through his death, crucified as a common criminal on a cross. The sight of Christ riding into Jerusalem on a donkey with people waving palm branches shouting 'Hosanna' and acclaiming him as a conquering King, made the visiting crowds, gathered for the festival, stop in amazement. Little did they know that the rejoicing would quickly be swept aside. Before long, as triumph turned to tragedy, those palm branches took the shape of a cross and the hosannas became jeers and calls for his death.

Holy Week is the most sacred time of the church year. It highlights the peak moments of Christ's love for us, gives us an opportunity to look at our lives and accept responsibility for our sins. The passion story spells out the last events of the life of Jesus and makes clear the price he paid for our sins. He was betrayed by Judas, denied by Peter and abandoned by all. In loneliness he reached out for companionship and support to the Father but there was nothing to comfort him: 'My God, my God, why have you forsaken me?' His death on the cross reminds us that there is a God towards whom we journey and whose friendship we seek. Every christian becomes aware that in his own life he has to meet the same fate as Jesus. He must join in Christ's suffering and death in order to share his glory. The road to eternal life will not by-pass the hill of Calvary. Our victory, like Christ's, comes only through the cross.

This final week of Lent offers us an opportunity to bring our hearts and minds into harmony with Christ. Make a special effort to attend the church ceremonies which dramatise the last agonising moments of the Saviour's life. Listen to the passion story in a spirit of prayer and embrace its message. There's no point in comforting ourselves with the thought that a group of Jews 2,000 years ago crucified Christ. Each of us had a hand in his death because the face of Christ is marred and scarred by the violence and injury which we inflict on our neighbours. If we are honest, we can see shades of ourselves in all those who put Jesus to death. Peter and Judas, Pilate and the soldiers should cause us to reflect on the treachery and evil that sleeps within us all. No-one can follow Jesus through the liturgy of Holy Week without the truth dawning anew in our hearts. The truth is that God loves us all with a love that cost him death on the cross.

Prayer of the Faithful

As we commemorate the triumphal entry of Jesus into Jerusalem, with confidence we place our requests before our heavenly Father.

1. For the church in countries where there is no freedom to worship, that it may draw comfort and strength from their close sharing in Christ's sufferings. Lord, hear us.
2. That we, like Mary, will take the road to Calvary during this most solemn week of the church year. Lord, hear us.
3. That in our own lives we may enter into the mystery of the Lord's death and rise with him to a newness of life. Lord, hear us.
4. For those who were sick, that they may unite their sufferings with Christ and be filled with inner peace. Lord, hear us.
5. We pray for all our dead, that they may be granted a place at the table in your heavenly kingdom. Lord, hear us.

Almighty Father, in you infinite wisdom and love, you have saved the world through the cross of Christ. May we always remain faithful witnesses to that cross in our daily lives. We make this prayer through Christ our Lord. Amen.

Easter Sunday

Easter Sunday is a day of faith, of joy and rejoicing. The resurrection of Christ is the cornerstone of our faith and the most extraordinary happening in human history. For christians there is not a day that compares with Easter Day. This is truly the day of the Lord. All our hopes and happiness come from what happened on that first Easter morning. It's a dream come true. By God's power, the stone was rolled back, the grave was opened and the tomb was found to be empty. Jesus Christ had risen triumphant from the dead. Nothing could ever be the same again because the pattern of human life was no longer limited by the cycle of birth to death in this world. Pain, despair and misery were pushed into second place as a whole new future, full of the hope and happiness of eternal life, was opened up for us beyond the grave. Heaven and earth rejoiced in celebrating Christ's victory over death for mankind. God had made his love for us absolutely clear.

The gospel captures the excitement of the disciples on that first Easter morning. It gives us a glimpse into their new found happiness as they hurried to spread the Good News. Their hearts were full of that joyful awareness of being God's people. The joy of the apostles on Easter Day is meant to be our joy too. A whole new dimension should enter our lives for we also have been given this bright promise of everlasting life. Easter life is about the joy of rebirth in the Spirit of God and we don't have to wait until the next life before enjoying it. Easter life is now. We rejoice as we realise that we are not walking the pathway of life alone. Christ is with us every inch of the journey as our Saviour, our Redeemer and our Healer. He is there assisting us, encouraging us and strengthening us for every task in life.

Easter is all about newness of life in Christ. The risen life of Christ is ours for the taking. The power of loving with the very love of God is within us and we can fearlessly stake our lives on it. Everyone of us is entrusted with the message of the Good News of God's love. Today's feast provides us with a fresh opportunity of facing ourselves with the issue of our own resurrection. It presents us with the challenge of spreading the light and the life of the Risen Christ. Are we alive in Christ with the Risen Lord firmly rooted in our hearts and actions, or are we still living in a selfish manner? Easter has no spiritual significance for us if Christ has emptied his tomb and we still lie in death in our own. If we

166

are truly the people of God then those who are searching for meaning in life will discover from us that Christ is the way home, the resting place for restless hearts. Lord, we are your people. Open our hearts this Easter Day and increase the gift of your life within us.

Prayer of the Faithful

On this glorious feast day, we give thanks to the Lord, for he is indeed good and his mercy extends to every age and every human being. In confidence we make our prayer to him.

1. Let us pray for the church that she may always be faithful to the teaching of Christ and a true witness to the faith which the apostles handed on to her. Lord, hear us.
2. That we who are gathered here in the name of Jesus our Risen Saviour, may be renewed in our faith and in our hope for the future. Lord, hear us.
3. For all the newly baptised, that they may find in us, their brothers and sisters, constant support and encouragement. Lord, hear us.
4. That those who are uncertain in their faith, despairing about the future, may experience confidence in the special love of the Lord Jesus. Lord, hear us.
5. For the sick and suffering in mind and body, that uniting themselves to the suffering Jesus, they may also receive the newness of life that he brings in his resurrection. Lord, hear us.
6. Let us pray for those who have died, that they may share fully in the life which Christ has won for us. Lord, hear us.

God our Father, we pray that the joy of this Easter Day may penetrate our minds and hearts and bring us closer to you. We ask this in the name of Jesus, the Risen Lord.

Second Sunday of Easter

There is an old French saying which states that 'God often visits us but most of the time we are not at home.' On the evening of the first day of the week, when the Lord appeared to the apostles while they were at prayer in the upper room, Thomas was not at home. The others tried to convince him, as best they could, that they had seen the Lord, but his continued reaction was to doubt. Good Friday and the death of Jesus on the hill of Calvary, had crushed Thomas' dream of a lifetime, and left him a deeply wounded, disillusioned and an angry man. He would not easily trust again without crystal clear proof. 'Unless I see the holes that the nails have made in his hands and can put my hand into his side, I refuse to believe.'

The story of Thomas is instructive and consoling because our path to faith in the Lord Jesus is often a slow walk through moments of doubt and times of confusion which create a rift between ourselves and God. Thomas spelt out his anger and lack of faith when he had reached rock bottom and his hopes were dashed. Is it any different from our anger and lack of faith when our life is shattered by a broken marriage, a death in the family, the loss of a job or a young person who lets the side down? Thomas stands for all of us who travel the road of doubt and at times are unsure of our belief. The loud doubts he echoes in the gospel lurk in all of us. Jesus respected Thomas' honesty and met him at the very point of his uncertainty. He understood fully his situation as he does ours in our moments of crisis and despair. Doubt for him proved to be a growing point of a faith made stronger when tested.

It's a morning for honest reflection on the depth of our own Easter faith, and a time to ask the Lord to strengthen our conviction and trust in his word. How else as christians are we linked across the centuries with the disciples of the early church if not by an unbreakable bond of faith. The bottom line of that faith is our belief in Jesus Christ as the Risen Lord. Faith is a struggle, a challenge and a battle and there is nothing comfortable about it. Living as we do in an age where there is a natural explanation for everything, it is difficult to see beyond surface appearances and to trust unreservedly in God's word.

As descendants of the first christians, mere belief in Christ as the Son of God is not enough. There must be a life in his name.

The gospel made a real impact on the lives of the first believers. They took it to heart and reached out, related and encouraged one another in a prayerful spirit of neighbourliness. For us, living a truly christian life involves putting into practice in our daily lives the faith which we profess to believe. There is no greater example of faith than to live with others in a common spirit of friendship, harmony and love. Faith is a blessing because it alone gives meaning to our lives and is a driving force to our existence. When everything else fails and our faith is needed, nothing can compensate for its absence.

Prayer of the Faithful

Confident that God the Father grants all our requests, we join now in prayer to express our needs to him.

1. That the church in our age may once more achieve a full flowering of the faith, so that its light may shine forth to all nations. Lord, hear us.
2. That, come what may, we may never lose faith in the goodness of each human being even when goodness is difficult to see. Lord, hear us.
3. That by our actions doubters will have the closed doors of their minds opened and their faith restored. Lord, hear us.
4. We pray for the sick of our community. May the strength of the Risen Christ touch their lives and bring them comfort. Lord, hear us.
5. We pray for those gone before us marked with the sign of faith … May they find in Christ's presence, light, happiness and peace. Lord, hear us.

Almighty Father, give us the faith to live all our tomorrows confidently and to meet others peacefully and joyfully. We ask this through Christ our Lord. Amen.

Third Sunday of Easter

Lent is well and truly over. We are deeply immersed in the Easter season, celebrating Christ's victory over death. Yet today's readings focus on the necessity of repentance, conversion and the avoidance of sin. As christians we must always remember that in order to share in the life of the Risen Christ we have first to share in the life of the crucified Christ. There are no shortcuts to eternal life – if there is no cross there is no crown. Death and resurrection must take place in each of our lives. We have to die to self in order to live for God. Sin must be avoided at all costs, as sin alone separates us from the love of God and the glory he has won on our behalf.

The resurrection cannot be limited to a historical fact, to an event that happened to Jesus Christ almost 2,000 years ago. It is a present reality whose light and warmth we should already be experiencing. Resurrection must take place here and now in the life of every christian. We never know what true life means until we live it in the footsteps of Jesus. This is not something we achieve overnight but is a gradual transformation that takes place within us as we turn away from deeds of darkness and live for God. Gradually we come to view the world, not with our own eyes but with a Christlike gaze.

The gospel tells us how Christ opened the minds of the disciples to the understanding of the scriptures. He explained why he had to suffer and rise from the dead on the third day. Moreover, they were to be his witnesses, preaching penance for the remission of sins, to all nations. This morning our prayer is an invitation to Jesus to come into our lives so that our minds and hearts may be opened to let in God's word. It is our turn to be witnesses to the gospel and to show forth the resurrection in our lives. The first disciples could not keep the Good News to themselves but hurried to share their great joy with anyone who had ears to listen. Likewise our relationship with Jesus requires us to communicate the good news by our attitudes, values and lifestyle. The christian message is never fully ours until we have shared it with our family, close friends and the different people we meet in life. If we are to be witnesses to Christ's gospel we must stop living in a half-hearted manner and show forth the resurrection in our lives.

Drawing close to Christ implies truly christian behaviour and being of one mind and heart with him. The risen Lord can only make an impact on the world if our words and actions combine to reveal his power. We are called upon to spend our lives without reserve in his service.

Prayer of the Faithful

As members of the church we are witnesses to God at work in the world. We ask God the Father to grant us all we need for the spread ing of the gospel.

1. We pray for the church that it may be a beacon of light helping people who are in darkness to come to know the risen Lord as the way the truth and the life. Lord, hear us.
2. May our lives be characterised by peace and joy which is real and active so that others may recognise Jesus in us. Lord, hear us.
3. For the power to forgive those who have wronged us and the grace never to hold grudges. Lord, hear us.
4. For the suffering, the oppressed and the sick that they may find support and encouragement and never lose hope. Lord, hear us.
5. For those who have died. May they share in the peace of the Risen Christ. Lord, hear us.

Heavenly Father we praise you for your gift of peace which the world cannot give. May we hold fast to it by our willingness to recognise Jesus as Lord in our lives. We ask this through Christ our Lord. Amen.

Fourth Sunday of Easter

Ever since the days when the early christians painted the picture of Christ as the Good Shepherd tending his sheep, on the walls of the catacombs in Rome, the image of Good Shepherd has been a favourite in christian circles. Generations of Christ's followers have been comforted and consoled by the picture of Christ the Good Shepherd anxiously seeking out the lost sheep and carrying it home on his shoulder. The image provides inspiration as it expresses the type of care, compassion and guidance which Christ offers to all of us. It gives us a permanent assurance that each one of us is loved as if we were the only one. Jesus is telling us that he knows us individually and thinks so much of us that he cannot let us out of his sight. The fact that we have a special place in his heart should instil hope in us and increase our confidence. Even when sin causes us to wander and stray, the Good Shepherd is there to come to our rescue. He brings us back carrying us shoulder high into the safety and companionship of the fold.

As we dwell on the closeness of the love and care God has for us in treating us as his adopted children, we can well ask ourselves how we are responding to this new and intimate relationship. Is it evident by word and example from our behaviour that Christ is the cornerstone of our life or have we kept him at a safe distance? The word of God always challenges us to declare our stance. Drawing close to Jesus demands truly Christ-like behaviour. In accepting us as his adopted children God is calling us to live the life of Jesus, which means that we in our turn have to be loving and caring and draw close to those we meet. Sometimes we deceive ourselves by keeping people at arm's length with obligations to nobody.

Today we are invited to examine how great and caring our love for our friends is. The task of every baptised person is to bring to the attention of the community the love that the Father has for us by letting us be called God's children. Caring for one another is shown by discreet acts of kindness, like writing a letter of sympathy, making a phone call, giving an understanding look or an unexpected gift – all of which say, 'I am with you always.' Caring as a good shepherd is a hidden source of sensitive communication. It offers hope to a friend, to continue on the road of life with a tiny flame of confidence in his heart. Our invitation through baptism is to have hands to help others, feet to hasten to the poor and needy, eyes to see misery and want and ears to hear the sighs of our friends in sorrow. In every age Jesus is calling men and women to care diligently for the intimate needs of their brothers and sisters. This is what being a Good Shepherd really means.

Prayer of the Faithful

Mindful of the love that God the Father has lavished on us by allowing us to be called his children, with confidence we place all our needs before him.

1. For all who are leaders in the church, that like Jesus they may be true and faithful shepherds guiding their flock on the pathway to eternal life. Lord, hear us.
2. Lord, give us the compassion to enter deeply into the joys and troubles of our neighbours and so imitate the love of the Good Shepherd. Lord, hear us.
3. That young people may have the courage and the generosity to become shepherds of the flock. Lord, hear us.
4. For those in our community who are sick, that they may experience the love of the Good Shepherd. Lord, hear us.
5. For those who have died. May they rest in peace with the risen Lord. Lord, hear us.

Heavenly Father, as we journey through life, help us to hear your voice, obey your commands, and follow in your footsteps. We make our prayer through Christ our Lord. Amen.

Fifth Sunday of Easter

While listening to a phone-in gardening programme on the radio, yesterday morning, a caller asked for advice on pruning fruit trees. Explaining how to go about it, the expert remarked that it is surprising the amount of dead wood one can shake out of a very good tree after a hard winter and the necessity of pruning and cutting back branches in order to produce fruit. The gospel is telling us that it is amazing the amount of dead wood that can be found in a good life. In ways our lives are no different from a garden. If we are to get the best out of them they will need caring and cultivation. We have to take the advice of Jesus, the master gardener, and rid ourselves of weeds and briars, which, if let go unchecked, will choke and destroy christian growth. This means cutting away what is useless and nourishing what is good. The pruning Christ is talking about is a cleansing of the whole person, body, mind and spirit.

As a christian it is not easy to stay in good spiritual shape. Even the best of lives can benefit from a little pruning. The good fruit that we are expected to bear is love of our neighbour in word and deed. This is the test of our genuineness because it has the stamp of the love of Christ imprinted in it. How wrong it is to close our hearts and turn our backs on the people next door by gossiping about them, spreading scandal, running them into the ground and taking away their good name. There is nobody without fault and even the best of people can be torn apart on their weaker side. The decision to live love has its price and we should not minimise the difficulties involved. Barriers of hatred and prejudice cannot be broken down to make way for kindness and tolerance unless we are prepared to cure our speech by pruning our tongues. The practical love of our neighbour will more than make up for a multitude of our own sins.

If Jesus is to have an effect on the world, it is through his followers, living in such a way that people will see the hand of God at work in the most ordinary situations in our lives. Christ is dependent upon us being his hands and his voice carrying the lamp of his redemption to others. The greatest contribution each one of us can make to the well-being of the church is to allow Christ's love to seep into our own life blood. If we live in Christ and he lives in us the fruit we can bear is beyond imagining. It's an occasion to reflect on the depth of our personal inward enduring commitment to the gospel because, apart from Jesus, there can be no lasting growth. God demands a lot from his children in expecting them to make the church a vibrant community by living good and fruitful lives.

Prayer of the Faithful

United as one body of worshippers in the Lord, vine and branches, we place our needs with confidence before God our Father.

1. We pray for unity within the church, that it may be a true community, producing the fruits of love and peace. Lord, hear us.
2. As branches of the vine, let us cut out what is useless and nourish what is good in our lives. Lord, hear us.
3. We pray that our love may not be words and talk but something real and active which breaks down the barriers of hatred and resentment. Lord, hear us.
4. For those in our community who are sick, lonely or rejected, that as christians we may reach out to them in the love of Christ. Lord, hear us.
5. We pray for the dead, that they may find eternal rest in God. Lord, hear us.

Heavenly Father, guide us on the path of true light. May we feel the strength of your outstretched arm as we journey on our way to you. We make our prayer through Christ our Lord. Amen.

Sixth Sunday of Easter

There is no getting away from the fact that the most important thing Jesus asks of us, and commands us to do, is to love one another. The night before he died, he gave us a simple command: to love one another, as he loved us. The model and standard for christian behaviour is this love which Christ has shown for us on the cross. The one requirement attached to receiving this gift of God's love is the undertaking that we share it with others. Love for those whom we can see, brings us as close as we can on earth into the love of God whom we cannot see. To experience Christ's love we have to root out selfishness and start thinking about others more than ourselves. When we refuse to share, we condemn ourselves to a winter of loneliness, encircling ourselves with a wall which keeps people out or at a safe distance.

As disciples we are called to be persons for others, making sacrifices for them, following the example of Jesus. Love is a form of self-sacrifice which demands us to give, not just of the things we possess but of ourselves, our time and our talents. For instance, mothers and fathers bear witness to Christ in their everyday lives by labouring tirelessly to feed their families, nursing their sick children and counselling them when they are confused. Facing up to these commitments may be hard and costly as it is a long uphill struggle with many falls and falterings, but in doing so they are guaranteed to find God and happiness. Wherever there is love, God is present. This is a message that has to be preached by word and example. The most effective way of communicating this love must surely be to treat everyone as a friend, giving them the respect they deserve.

God's love for us surpasses anything we can ever imagine. Each one of us is loved individually and intimately. 'As the Father has loved me so I have loved you.' We do not deserve God's love and we cannot earn it by ourselves. A fundamental truth is that God has declared his choice, taken us on and loved us from the beginning even before we were born. It is his love for us that led him to send his Son into the world to take away our sins. In moments of trial and stress when people are hostile and we feel the pull of bitter resentment in our hearts, it is important to remember that Christ's own love was not limited to the people he liked and we should close our minds to thoughts of revenge.

Instead let us fix our thoughts on the wonder of God's love for us which gives us an invitation to share in his divine life. Fulfilling the commandment of love draws us into the family of God. In the evening of life, we will not be judged by our weaknesses or our faults but on the amount of love we have shown. Therefore, let us love one another.

Prayer of the Faithful

Because we are God's family, we cannot say that we love God if we harm our neighbour. We now pray that our love for him may be more than mere words and may influence our behaviour.

1. We pray for our Holy Father and for the leaders of the church, that their love for their flock may be sincere and generous. Lord, hear us.
2. For all those who do not believe in God. That they may see and encounter him in the love of christians. Lord, hear us.
3. For all married couples. May they be faithful in their love for each other and so bear witness to their christian faith. Lord, hear us.
4. We pray for our sick. May they be comforted in their trials by the consolation of faith and the love of christians. Lord, hear us.
5. For those who have died and whose loving company we have shared in this life. May they enjoy lasting peace in the kingdom of God. Lord, hear us.

God our Father, hear our prayers, and fill our hearts with your love so that we may always live in a way that pleases you. We make our prayer through Christ our Lord. Amen.

Ascension of the Lord

Ascension Day speaks of mystery and of the power to reach through to another dimension. It marks the end of Christ's mission on earth and celebrates his glorious return to the Father in heaven. Although it was the last act of the cycle of Jesus's life, death and resurrection, it was not a day for sadness but an occasion for joy and renewal of hope. In ascending into heaven, Christ thrust himself out of the ordinary into the extraordinary, from the here in Galilee to the everywhere throughout the world. He ceased to limit himself to one time or one place or one group of people. Through the power of the Holy Spirit he became invisibly present and available to all who wished to be in contact with him, partake in his work and share his glory.

For the apostles it meant their period of training was over and the time had arrived for the beginning of their mission, 'to go out to the whole world and proclaim the good news to all creation.' (Mark 16:15). At the Lord's departure the disciples stood motionless, transfixed by what had happened. The sadness in their hearts was understandable as it was their second painful experience of separation from Jesus, and they felt that their lives would never be the same again. They were called back to reality by two men in white who interrupted their daydreaming, beckoning them to be about their master's business. Their mission was not to stand around looking up to heaven, waiting for something to happen. In the absence of Christ, they were to be his messengers, proclaiming the Good News to the poor, the oppressed and all people in need.

The return of Jesus, in all his glory, to the Father gives us a glimpse of the great future to which we have been called. Provided we remain faithful to his teaching, our final home will also be with the Father in heaven. Like the apostles, Christ commands us to be his witnesses in preaching the Good News to the ends of the earth. It is a daunting task but it is made tolerable by the assurance that he has not left us orphans but, through the power of the Holy Spirit, he is with us in all our endeavours.

Life is often thought of as a pilgrimage and all of us are travellers on that important roadway. Because many are weakened by the trials, suffering and disappointments of life, they lose hope and are unsure of where they are going, not knowing if there is anything at the end of the road. They find their happiness by dwelling on memories of the past. Like the apostles, on Ascension Day, they spend their time waiting aimlessly and idly gazing up to heaven. Christ's ascension assures us that there is a purpose to life and that our journey, however difficult, will take us back to the Father. Meanwhile, we live in the hope that the words of Jesus will come true for us when he said: 'Where I am, you shall be.' (John 14:3).

Prayer of the Faithful

Mindful of Christ's glorious return to his heavenly home, we make our requests to God the Father who never disappoints those who trust in his promises.

1. We pray that the church may give courageous witness and boldly proclaim Christ's message throughout the world. Lord, hear us.
2. For the grace to lead lives which are holy and in keeping with the destiny to which we have been called. Lord, hear us.
3. Grant us the spirit of humility so that we may do what is right, show kindness and never fail to give of our best. Lord, hear us.
4. We pray for the sick and the elderly. Help us to show them respect, sympathise with their needs and do all we can to assist and comfort them. Lord, hear us.
5. We pray for the dead. May they be brought into the eternal life of heaven which Christ has won for them. Lord, hear us.

Heavenly Father, we thank you for the inner strength you offer us through the power of the Holy Spirit. Help us to carry out the work of your Son so that one day we may join him, living and praying with you and the Holy Spirit for ever and ever. Amen.

Seventh Sunday of Easter

The gospel takes us back to Holy Thursday evening when Jesus, realising that his life is almost over, celebrates his farewell meal – the Last Supper – with his disciples. The following day, Good Friday, would see him suffering a most terrible death on the cross. As we listen to his prayer on the night before he died, we see that his thoughts were on how helpless his friends would be without him. He voices his concern for their welfare knowing that because of their mission they will encounter opposition and hatred in the world. He gives them assurance and prepares them to cope with life after he has gone to the Father. Jesus did not pray that they would be spared these trials and sufferings but that they would remain faithful in spite of opposition.

These parting words of Christ are meant for us just as much as they were for the apostles. We have been taken into this prayer of Jesus, as he has chosen us to share in his work and make even the smallest of our acts of compassion important. Our calling is to be missionaries dedicated to the truth of God's word, by the way we live and by our behaviour. It is not an easy pathway to travel, but God has not left us to carry out that great endeavour with our own strength. If we place our lives in his hands, he will equip us with the qualities of mind, heart and character which are necessary for the task. Often on occasions when we run into difficulties in life, we think God has abandoned us. It would be helpful in times of trouble if we could remember that God did not offer a release from problems, but the ability to cope with them, provided we turn to him for comfort and help. What we have to do is to humbly admit to him that we cannot manage on our own. Only by turning to the wounded Jesus on the cross can we properly face our problems. With his power we can turn despair into hope, sorrow into joy and hatred into love. All that matters is to be one with the living God, feeling his presence like a great reassurance and a deep calm in the heart.

The gospel ends with prayerful appeal to remain true to our christian roots – to be consecrated to the truth. This means that we are to have a value system, not dictated by the prevailing spirit of the age or the trends of society, but based on the gospel message. In this way we will know what is important and when the suffering, struggles and tragedies of life occur, as they inevitably do, we

will remain on course able to work through the situation by clinging closely to our belief. The fruit of faithfulness is a unity and a
freedom that the world cannot give. We would be selling ourselves short if we were ever prepared to ignore this call to believe
more firmly and take our mission seriously.

Prayer of the Faithful

*United with christians everywhere, with joy and confidence we make our
prayer to God the Father who never disappoints those who trust in his
name.*

1. We pray that the church may be true to its mission of promoting
peace and unity among christians. Lord, hear us.
2. We pray for ourselves, that we may be courageous in bearing
witness to the dignity and uniqueness of the poor in our society.
Lord, hear us.
3. We pray for the families of our parish. May they rise above their
differences, live in harmony and grow in wisdom and grace.
Lord, hear us.
4. We pray that the Lord may be with the sick of our community
to bring them healing and comfort. Lord, hear us.
5. We pray that our dead relations and friends may enjoy everlasting happiness in heaven. Lord, hear us.

*Heavenly Father, give us the courage to be living witnesses to our faith
and bring us to the glory of the resurrection. We ask this through Christ
our Lord. Amen.*

Pentecost

Over the past seven weeks since Easter we have been celebrating, in joyful manner, the resurrection of Jesus Christ, and recalling his many appearances to the apostles. As they recognised his presence, their hearts burned within them and they were filled with comfort, reassurance, inner peace and strength. Today is the feast of Pentecost which recalls the descent of the Holy Spirit on the apostles in the form of a roaring wind and tongues of fire. The first reading describes the spectacular baffling effect produced on the disciples by the coming of the Holy Spirit. The change in their lifestyle was startling, as the Spirit urged them to be their very best selves. They threw aside caution, were no longer afraid and rushed out to begin their mission of preaching the Good News, boldly proclaiming their faith in a crucified Christ. Suddenly there was no longer uncertainty, everything fell into place and made sense. At that moment the church was born. The spirit of God had filled the disciples with new hope and courage. They received the power and strength to set off into the world and enthusiastically continue the work which Christ had begun.

The coming of the Spirit on that first day of Pentecost was not a once and for all event, but the beginning of his permanent presence in the church. By virtue of our baptism, the Holy Spirit is closer to us than we dare imagine. Wherever there are hearts open to receive him, the Spirit of God is poured out, inspiring minds to undertake their mission as Christ's representatives. This feast brings home to us that God calls us to a deeper relationship with him and wants us to share in his life. It is an invitation to enkindle the fire of love and to stir up the grace of our baptismal calling. We do not always know when the Spirit moves us, yet we are frequently surprised by the power that drives us into action. Whenever we go beyond our own selfish indifference and reach out in genuine concern for people in trouble, then the Spirit of God is at work guiding us, giving us renewed strength to turn upside down accepted human values and the will to move along in a new direction.

As we face trials and crosses and encounter the difficulties and disappointments which can leave our daily lives in tatters, we stand in need of the help of the Holy Spirit, whose presence makes such a difference to our outlook. Christ has promised that the power of the Spirit will come if we ask for him. It's essential then that in prayer we leave the door of our hearts open to invite him in. We become different persons and changed people to the extent that we allow the Holy Spirit to disturb our complacency, uproot our mediocrity and make way for fresh growth. What the Spirit will bring into our lives if we permit him to lead us, is joy, peace and love. On this Pentecost Sunday, we thank God for the gift of the Holy Spirit who works in countless hidden ways to deepen our faith, fill us with strength and inspiration and to renew our lives.

Prayer of the Faithful

The Holy Spirit has made us one people, one family, one body in Christ Let us then make our united prayers to God the Father.

1. That the church may experience a new Pentecost every day and may realise its mission to proclaim God's goodness to the world. Lord, hear us.
2. We pray that our prejudices and sins may not block the working of the Holy Spirit in our lives. Lord, hear us.
3. Let us pray to the Holy Spirit for this parish, that we may bear example to one another and so enjoy happiness in this life and the next. Lord, hear us.
4. We pray for those who are sick, either mentally or physically. May the Spirit bring them healing and peace. Lord, hear us.
5. We pray for those who mourn the death of a loved one ... that the Spirit may console them and give them hope. Lord, hear us.

Almighty Father on this day when we celebrate the coming of the Holy Spirit to your people, send your Spirit into our hearts that we may live as your Son lived. We ask this through Christ our Lord. Amen.

Trinity Sunday

As we flick through the pages of the gospel we find that they unfold for us intimate secrets about the inner life of God. From what Jesus said and did while on earth, we can grasp bits and pieces of the mystery of God. For instance we would never have known that God is a family of three persons had it not been told by Jesus. He revealed his startling nature to us for the first time after his baptism. As he came out of the waters of the Jordan, the Holy Spirit descended on him in the form of a dove, the heavens opened and a voice said, 'This is my beloved Son in whom I am well pleased.' (Mk. 1:11.) Throughout his life on earth Christ was forever talking about God as his Father and his mission was to do the will of his Father. He referred to himself as God's only son, and we learn that the Spirit's job was to carry on and continue in the church the work he had begun.

Today's feast of the most Holy Trinity celebrates the mystery of three persons in the one God, all bonded together by love. It fills us with awe and open-eyed reverence, for we do not have a God whose limits we can define. In the Trinity our minds are brought into loving contact with the complexity and wonder of God, which no language is adequate to describe. His greatness and goodness exceed the boundary of all thought and are beyond our human attempts to comprehend. St Augustine tells us when we are speaking about God not to marvel because we don't understand, for if we did understand then he would not be God. A God without mystery would have no claim to our reverence. We should never look on the Trinity as a problem to be solved, a puzzle to be worked out or something simply to test our faith. Christ has given us this special insight into the inner nature of God to make us aware of the life we share at our baptism, when the Holy Spirit is poured into our hearts, making us adopted children of the Father. Every time we make the sign of the Cross while blessing ourselves, we express our faith, calling upon the name of the Trinity. The action accompanying the words reminds us that it is through the cross of Jesus that the life of the Trinity is open to us, and that the cross is the only means by which we can follow Christ our Saviour into eternal life.

Trinity Sunday brings home to us how intimate and personal

God's love is for us. It shows God taking an interest in every individual, as Father, redeemer and spiritual guide. After all our attempts to express wonder at the immensity of the mystery of God, who is just yet merciful, far and yet near, completely other and different from us yet loving and caring, we rightfully acknowledge that words are a poor substitute for worship and contemplation. On this feast we pray the simplest of christian prayers: 'Glory be to the Father and to the Son and to the Holy Spirit, as it was in the beginning is now and ever shall be, world without end. Amen.'

Prayer of the Faithful

Secure in the knowledge that God the Father loves us, we bring our needs before him, confident that he will listen to our prayers.

1. We pray that the church throughout the world may arouse in the hearts of all people, a deeper understanding of God as Father, Son and Holy Spirit. Lord, hear us.
2. We pray for ourselves and our families that we may reflect the unity of the Blessed Trinity in the care and concern we have for one another. Lord, hear us.
3. We pray that those who are in search of the truth may be guided to a knowledge of God who is all loving and merciful. Lord, hear us.
4. We pray for all those who are sick. May they discover the kindness and compassion of Christ from the loving hands of those who tend to their needs. Lord, hear us.
5. We pray that our departed brothers and sisters may enjoy the fullness of eternal life in God's presence.

Almighty God, pour forth your love into our hearts so that we may come to a deeper knowledge of the mystery of your life. We ask this through Christ our Lord. Amen.

Body and Blood of Christ

Today, all over the world, congregations like ours are coming together to celebrate as we are celebrating with heartfelt thanksgiving in a great act of common worship. It is nearly 2,000 years since Jesus Christ said 'Do this in memory of me.' The gospel reading tells us of the simple beginnings of the Mass, how Jesus, on the night he was to be betrayed, celebrated the eucharist, his final meal, with his disciples. He took time to eat this meal with them so that they could share in and be part of his work. He took bread, broke it, saying: 'Take it, this is my Body.' Then he took a cup and when he had given thanks said 'This is my blood, poured out for many.' From the earliest days, the church has taken the Lord at his word. By doing what Jesus himself did on that occasion we experience repeatedly his real presence among us. With the gifts of bread and wine we bring what we are and what we have as an offering to the Lord.

Corpus Christi is a festival for pondering with thanks on God's hospitality to us, the supreme and final gift of his love. The offering on the cross of our Lord is, for each one of us, fully effective. We remember with gratitude the promise he made to be with his friends and followers as their food and nourishment in their pilgrimage through life. All of us are people on a journey facing the trials and sufferings of everyday happenings. What better companion can we have for support than the presence of Jesus? Although we have not yet reached our final destination, travelling in his company is a powerful assurance that we are on the right road. He is food for our souls and the spiritual help we need to make us break off the chains that bind us to this earth. Holy Communion is the remedy for our daily faults and not the reward for sanctity attained. It is not because we are holy that we receive Jesus but because we wish to change and to become like him. What is demanded of us is that we share the eucharist with others, for we make our pilgrimage through this valley of tears as a community and not as isolated individuals.

One of the fruits of our weekly gathering should be a great increase in charity among the assembled faithful. Union with Christ in the eucharist means drawing closer to our brothers and sisters, especially the weak and the poor of our community. There should be no dissention, strife or bitterness amongst those gathered around the table of the Lord. This is the acid test of the sincerity of our belief. In our daily life we are asked to forgive, to overlook weaknesses, to understand the failure of friends and not to close our hearts when we are hurt. For God to love us we must try to be loving also. The celebration of the eucharist is the great festival of the church, the centre from which all grace flows. We bring to it all the possibilities, desires and longings of our existence. To have time for God and to give ourselves to him is an important expression of our faith.

Prayer of the Faithful

Placing our confidence in the generosity of God the Father who gave us his Son in the eucharist as food for our souls, we bring before him our needs.

1. We pray that the leaders of the church may continue to witness to Jesus Christ, who is the Bread of Life in a world which is hungry for meaning. Lord, hear us.
2. We pray that our coming together to celebrate the eucharist may be a real offering of ourselves in faith and humility. Lord, hear us.
3. That we may be actively concerned about the poverty of our brothers and sisters and do what we can to lessen it. Lord, hear us.
4. That all who are making their First Holy Communion may always stay close to Jesus who is food and nourishment for their journey through life. Lord, hear us.
5. We pray for the sick. May their sharing in the eucharist give them strength to bear their sufferings. Lord, hear us.
6. We remember our departed relatives and friends. May they enjoy eternal rest in the company of Jesus, the Bread of Life. Lord, hear us.

Heavenly Father, make us truly grateful for the gift of the eucharist which gives hope and meaning to our lives. We make our prayer through Christ our Lord. Amen.

Second Sunday of the Year

The story of God calling Samuel by name is almost magical. There's a wonderful picture of the boy lying asleep in the dark, behind the sanctuary, where only one light remains glowing. He's awakened three times by a mysterious voice calling him by name. In no way does Samuel suspect that the Lord is calling him– after all he is just a boy with no airs or graces, a mere servant of the old priest Eli. It is Eli who makes it clear that the voice he is hearing is the voice of God and directs him how to reply. With the straightforward simplicity of a child, Samuel springs to his feet in unquestioning obedience and total willingness to serve: 'Speak Lord, your servant is listening.'

The story of Samuel is our story too. He stands for all of us – people of no significance, the small print of life. We may not be important in the eyes of society but none of us is ever ignored by God. We are always in his mind and forever under his care. God is constantly calling us into a relationship with him in the circumstances of life we find ourselves in. When we were baptised our ears were symbolically opened to hear his call. In the noisy ranting world in which we live, there is a danger of God's voice being drowned out and not heard. That's why it is important to have a quiet and peaceful corner to develop pockets of silence, where we can be alone to listen to the voice of God, calling us and directing us along his pathway. God can only speak to a person who is listening. We tend to talk too much and listen too little.

The gospel speaks to us about the call of Andrew and how the disciples stood and stared as Christ passed by. Christ is forever passing by and his invitation is straightforward and open-ended. He's constantly asking us what we want out of life. If we wish to discover where he lives, he throws his life open for inspection under many different disguises. He invites us to come and see him, homeless and hungry sleeping on pavements and under doorways in the wet and cold. 'Come and see me lying in hospital beds dying of cancer or with some incurable disease.'

God's call is an on-going affair and often reaches us through the plight of a neighbour. It takes courage to open our hearts and answer that call. Sacrifices will have to be made and a comfortable lifestyle disturbed. If we are to be the people God wants us to be and to do the job he intends us to do, we must give ourselves willingly to Jesus who has already given himself to us. Openness to others combined with real sensitivity to their needs and a willingness to share our time and material goods, are essential qualities for us to develop if we are to share fully in Christ's vocation. 'Here I am Lord, I come to do your will.'

Prayer of the Faithful

It was in the silence of the night and of the desert that Samuel and John heard the voice of God. Let us too, in the silence of our hearts listen and respond to your voice.

1. For the church, that all believers may be aware of the presence of Christ and of his grace at work in their midst. Lord, hear us.
2. We pray for those who are called to be christians in their places of employment and among their work-mates. Through their example may others come to hear the voice of Christ more clearly. Lord, hear us.
3. We pray for those who feel useless and a burden to society. May they know that they have a unique place in God's heart. Lord, hear us.
4. We pray for those who are old, lonely or sick and we mention by name ... that they may be conscious that God's work is being done in the circumstances of their lives. Lord, hear us.
5. We pray for the dead, especially ... May they rest in peace in the kingdom of heaven. Lord, hear us.

God our Father, speaking through the prophets in a long unending line you have revealed your love for us. We ask you to listen to our prayers and to give us the grace to live as you would want us. Through Christ Our Lord. Amen.

Third Sunday of the Year

The readings of this liturgy are especially chosen to highlight the theme of repentance. Jonah, a reluctant Jewish prophet, was sent to preach repentance to the Ninevites, the sworn enemies of Israel. As a fervent patriot he had no enthusiasm for the job and begrudged God squandering his mercy on non-Jews. He would have preferred to see the city of Nineveh destroyed rather than its people converted, but God thought otherwise. These people were important to him and worth calling to repentance. To Jonah's intense annoyance, when he preached, the people mended their ways and their city was spared. God's call to repentance is based on his love and respect for us. It's an affirmation of our basic worth and pre-supposes that we are valuable. Unless we are gripped by this feeling of being worthwhile objects of God's love, we have missed the point of the gospel's call to repentance.

What was striking about the apostles' response to the call of Jesus was their realisation that something better was on offer. They sensed that Jesus was inviting them to a higher way of life and they saw themselves, not as they were, but as they could be. To such an invitation there could only be one response: to repent and believe the Good News. Repentance is not as easy as it appears. There's more to it than saying extra prayers, doing a stint of fasting and being sorry for past sins. The gospel gives us a picture of what is involved in the process. Leaving our nets and disentangling ourselves from worldly pursuits in order to follow Jesus is not a one-off decision. It is an on-going battle and the challenge of a lifetime. We have to constantly look at our sinfulness, re-assess our behaviour in the light of the gospel and, if need be, make a fresh start. There are no half measures in following Christ, no gloating over earthly possessions, no hankering after material rewards.

We need to repent and change our ways no less than the people of Nineveh. The story of Jonah speaks to us about our own closed minds, hardened attitudes and bigotry. It shatters any illusions we may have about being a tolerant people. The thorns and briars of hatred and prejudice are deeply ingrained in our being, and can only be rooted out by repentance, and a change of heart. Deep down we know that we are not yet the people God is calling us to be. Jonah's message holds out hope for all of us. If the pagan people of Nineveh, could place their faith in the preaching of a

Jewish prophet and change their lives accordingly, can we be less generous to Christ who died to save us? The Good News is that God's loving mercy is available to all who repent, whoever they are, wherever they live and whatever they have done. By choosing to repent we can change our lives.

Prayer of the Faithful

Jonah discovered that there is no getting away from the Lord. We turn now in prayer to God the Father for the grace to change our lives and believe firmly in Christ's call to repentance.

1. That the leaders of the church may work tirelessly in bringing Christ's message of repentance to those who seek the Lord with a sincere heart. Lord, hear us.
2. As sinners may we come to a deeper realisation of the love and mercy which God has for all who turn to him with a humble and contrite spirit. Lord, hear us.
3. Time is short and this world is passing away. We pray for the grace never to lose ourselves in the pursuit of material goods. Lord, hear us.
4. For the sick of our community whose pathway is long and painful. May they rest secure in our love and care. Lord, hear us.
5. We pray for the dead, especially friends who were recently with us. May they find peace and happiness in the kingdom of God. Lord, hear us.

O Lord, guard us all the days of this troubled life, until the shadows lengthen, the evening comes, the busy world is hushed, the fever of life is over and our work is done. Then, Lord, in your mercy, grant us a safe lodging, a holy rest and your blessed peace at last. All this we ask through Christ, our Lord. Amen.

Fourth Sunday of the Year

Occasionally when public figures speak, we refuse to take them seriously because they convey the impression that they are not sincere and are merely voicing the party line. The term 'credibility gap' is one way of expressing our suspicion that there is no depth to their fine words. The most fundamental criticism we can make of any person is to say that they are not one of their word. Every age has its true and false prophets. In today's gospel we are told that Christ spoke with authority and conviction; he never was a dictator, yet because he spoke with authority and conviction; he was nailed to the cross. His preaching had a great impact on all open-minded people who were listening. Its effects were staggering because he spoke from the heart and was fired with enthusiasm for the truth. As a leader Jesus had no political pull, or military clout, and yet people were spellbound and challenged to the core of their being by the compelling power of what he was saying.

The crowds weren't captivated by him just because he was a gifted preacher who told them what they wanted to hear. When he spoke, everyone detected a ring of truth in his every word. They sensed that somehow or other he was different; this was the word of God. We do not have to know the gospel by heart to realise that Jesus speaks on every aspect of human life – and he does not offer what he has to say as a personal opinion, or a studied conclusion, but as rooted in reality and truth. Jesus makes it clear that he is the sole voice of God in the world, speaking the final word from God the Father. He emphasises that what he says is the standard expected of us and the test we must pass if we are to reach heaven.

In a rebellious age, the whole notion of talking about authority seems quaintly out of fashion. Thinking about authority can send shivers up our spines as we recall how badly we have been treated by parents, teachers, and those we are working with. Jesus uses his authority to call forth the best in each one of us and to draw each person towards God. That is why the words of Jesus are so precious – they are about how to be saved and should be heeded. They provide us with the answers to proper living. The real reason for authority in the church is to keep the Lord's word alive in the world and to keep us reminded of what he says and speaks to us, because we are prone to laziness, to the lowering of our ideals and the watering down of the commandments.

The word of God will always challenge us to the depth of our being. Today it is asking us how honest and authentic we really are as we face the problems of living the christian message amid a questioning world. If we follow it and live it we are speaking with authority in our own right and pointing people to God.

Prayer of the Faithful

In prayer we now approach God the Father, who has power and authority over all things and unload the burdens that weigh us down.

1. For our Holy Father, bishops and all those who exercise authority in the church; that they may be filled with gentleness and love. Lord, hear us.
2. That parents may be more anxious to be loved and respected by their children than to create an atmosphere which breeds suspicion and fear. Lord, hear us.
3. That those who exercise authority in our local community may be sensitive to the needs of their people and show them genuine concern. Lord, hear us.
4. We remember the sick of the community at home and in hospital. May we be alert to their needs and care for them with willing hearts. Lord, hear us.
5. We now ask that our dead be brought safely home to the company of the risen Christ. Lord, hear us.

Heavenly Father, we rejoice in your abundant love for us, establish your authority within us and be our companion on the road of life. We make our prayer through Christ our Lord. Amen.

Fifth Sunday of the Year

We would have to be living the life of a hermit to close our eyes to the pain and misery of life about us. Our hearts would be of stone not to be moved by a friend's marriage on the rocks, a neighbour's child with a nervous breakdown and the suffering and heartbreak which is the common lot of so many in daily life. The grim pictures on TV of war, famine and children dying of starvation are calculated to shake even the faith of a saint. No wonder many people are forced to the conclusion that it is a punishment from God or that there is no God at all. There is no understanding why good-living people are asked to suffer and carry such heavy crosses. Nothing threatens our confidence in a caring God more that the sight of suffering.

The Book of Job is an attempt to come to grips with the problem of human suffering in a brutally direct way. Job, a good-living religious man is put to the test by God. He is stripped of his wife, family and all his possessions, and is finally struck down with ill-health. He is so overcome that he feels there is nothing to live for but misery. For all his deliberations as to why he has to suffer or why God has put his hand down so heavily upon him, Job doesn't come up with any convincing answer to the meaning of his present distress. The truth is that there is no easy answer. Job was not the first person, nor the last to be baffled by the problem of suffering. Illness and death can be the most trying and important times of our life. Often we neglect God until we are struck down in such a crisis with ill-health and have inactivity thrust upon us. When we rise above our despair we go to him looking for his healing grace. We are driven to trust him totally, for there is no other way to face suffering than to realise that it must be part of God's mysterious plan. Sickness forces us to put aside the feverish activity of daily living and focus instead on the home which is offered us by our heavenly Father. These are the occasions which are especially critical, when we have to face up to the hopes and disappointments of life. There is no point in thinking what we might do if our circumstances were different.

In the gospel passage Jesus comes to Simon's mother-in-law, stretches out his hand and cures her. Christ gives us no answer about suffering nor does he try to explain why people have to suffer but he showed us the importance of turning suffering into joy. By identifying himself with the sick and the dying even to dying himself on the Cross, Jesus clearly revealed that suffering is part of God's mysterious plan. It all depends on how we shoulder our cross, for, by uniting our trials with Christ's we can enjoy his victory. Whatever happens to us, all things will work together for those who love God and share in the passion of Christ. The gospel does not guarantee our freedom from suffering but gives us the assurance that God is with us however great our suffering may be.

Prayer of the Faithful

Like the people who brought to Jesus all who were sick or possessed with demons, we place before our heavenly Father all who are filled with pain and sorrow, and in need of his healing love.

1. For the church, that her people may always rely on the Lord in trials and difficulties. Lord, hear us.
2. That the Lord may give hope and encouragement to the starving of the world who are unjustly deprived of food, clothing or freedom. Lord, hear us.
3. May all those who suffer from depression and anxiety find in Christ a sure anchor as the way, the truth and the life. Lord, hear us.
4. For those suffering through illness, for whom life has become an intolerable burden, that they may see meaning in their trials. Lord, hear us.
5. We pray for our dead, and for those who mourn their loss. May the resurrection of Jesus bring them hope and comfort in their grief. Lord, hear us.

Almighty Father, watch over your family, protect us and keep us in your care for all our hope is in you. Through Christ our Lord. Amen.

Sixth Sunday of the Year

The disease most dreaded by the Jews of old was leprosy. It was an infectious plague which struck fear and horror into its victims because there was no hope of a cure. The fate of the leper was truly pathetic. As soon as the first signs of the disease appeared, the afflicted person was debarred from all social life and forced to withdraw from society. This meant bidding farewell to his family, leaving behind his way of life, his trade, everything and everybody he had known and loved. It was a farewell as final as death. The mental anguish and heartbreak of being completely banished from the local community, was utterly devastating. In every sense the leper was an outcast, with no hope of enjoying human companionship or receiving love. The victim was reduced to the status of a non-person, scavenging for food on the town dump, with a warning bell slung around his neck. Moreover, it was taken for granted that the disease was a punishment for sin and a sign of separation from the life-giving power of God. The prophet Isaiah used leprosy as a symbol of how diseased God's people were when they were unfaithful to him.

The gospel shows us how Christ was moved to compassion when he met the leper. He was not afraid to reach out and touch the infected man. This is only one of many personal encounters between Jesus and sick people, where his compassion is so evident. It says something profound about the healer, as a font of mercy, and gives us an insight into God's caring approach to physical and spiritual sickness. Spiritual leprosy is a reality in every age. It's a sickness of the soul which cuts us off from God and is much more serious because it remains invisible and goes unnoticed for a much longer time. The really good news for all of us is that just as Jesus reached out to touch and cure the leper, he stretches out his healing hand to bind up the wounds of all our sins.

It's a day to be mindful in our prayers of people who are victims of Aids, that modern plague which threatens the health and lives of thousands. The Aids generation has come of age and they are the social lepers of our times. What is often forgotten is that they are still people. As yet, there is no cure or vaccine to prevent the infection. Anyone who makes self-righteous statements with deep conviction like 'Aids is the wrath of God' or 'Serves them right, they have made their bed, let them lie on it,' does not have the heart and mind of Christ. By the very nature of our discipleship, the Lord sends us out to heal, reconcile and love unconditionally. God's power is in its kindness which reaches hearts in ways beyond explaining. While we might feel a pang of moral outrage at the treatment received by lepers in the time of Christ, if the need arose could we be counted upon to bring his healing and compassion to a friend threatened by the dreaded disease of Aids?

Prayer of the Faithful

Like the leper in the gospel who cried out for healing, we now approach our heavenly Father with the assurance that our prayers will be answered.

1. We pray that the church may never fail in its duty of welcoming the marginalised and those excluded from society. Lord, hear us.
2. We pray for the success of the efforts of those involved in medical research into eliminating incurable diseases. Lord, hear us.
3. That our parish community may reach out with love and care to the rejects and untouchables of our own neighbourhood. Lord, hear us.
4. We pray for the sick, the deprived and the lonely. May we never fail them in their hour of need. Lord, hear us.
5. We pray for those who have died in Christ. May the Lord receive them with love and mercy into his kingdom. Lord, hear us.

Almighty Father, help us to follow your example by reaching out to those we ignore. Increase our faith and accept our prayers in the name of your son Jesus Christ our Lord. Amen.

Seventh Sunday of the Year

During the course of a day we use thousands of words and take them for granted, without giving much thought to the gift of speech. In this gospel we see the power of the word of God at work in a memorable scene, when four men arrive with their paralytic friend whom they lower to the feet of Jesus through an opening in the roof. This man had been a burden to his neighbours and Jesus sensed the deep distress behind the faith of those who carried the stretcher. When he uttered the healing words: 'Your sins are forgiven,' God's power flowed through the paralytic, freeing him of spiritual paralysis as well as bodily sickness. There was a moment of supreme suspense as the man rose to his feet, picked up his mat and walked outside. The cure of his illness was the sign that his sins had been truly pardoned. The scribes, who were spokespersons for traditional Jewish belief, stated that only God was capable of forgiving sin and questioned what Jesus had done.

In an age when it has become fashionable to ignore the reality of sin as an offence against God, our sins are ever before us, placing a barrier between Christ and ourselves. Like the sick man in the gospel we are in need of Jesus' healing words, to free us from the burdens of our past and to enable us to live in a new way. His words heal the sickness of our souls and restore fullness of life to our personalities, crippled and blunted as a result of past wrongdoings. We should not be surprised to find forgiveness of sin at the heart of Christ's ministry, for his mission is to bring the peace of God and wipe out the tyranny of evil. Sin is a form of paralysis that effects us all.

It places a barrier between God and ourselves. However, Jesus understands our weakness as sinners and is concerned about curing our spiritual illness. His aim is to set us free, to walk in friendship with God. Despite our ingratitude, he persists in loving us and wants us to stop looking back and clinging to the memory of past sins. He makes it quite clear that he does not want to imprison us in our past or close us up in our failures.

Forgiveness is a wonderful thing and the most profound healing a person can experience. One of the greatest gifts Christ gave to his church was the power to forgive sin, which is available through the ministry of any priest. The words of forgiveness spoken to the paralytic are with us in the sacrament of reconciliation. All of us are crippled by some type of sin and are more in need of the healing words of Jesus than we would care to admit. We would be foolish to remain spiritually paralysed through sin because of our fear of approaching the priest. Our return to grace is always eagerly awaited by the Lord.

Prayer of the Faithful

The distance created between God and humankind is caused by sin which is an illness of the soul. Aware of our need for healing, we now approach the Father and ask for his love.

1. We pray that the church of God may be constantly at work carrying out Christ's saving mission through the forgiveness of sins. Lord, hear us.
2. That priests who celebrate the sacrament of reconciliation may always show compassion and understanding to penitents. Lord, hear us.
3. May we always be ready to forgive others, realising that this is the shared duty of all who follow Christ. Lord, hear us.
4. We pray for the sick and the handicapped. May the Lord bring them comfort and hope in their sufferings. Lord, hear us.
5. We commend to the Lord all those who have died. May they rest in peace. Lord, hear us.

Heavenly Father, we thank you for the forgiveness shown to us by your Son. May we in our turn show forgiveness to all who have offended us. We make our prayer through Christ our Lord. Amen.

Eighth Sunday of the Year

It was not surprising that the Jewish religious leaders objected to Jesus, for he disturbed them by teaching a religion of happiness and love. They criticised his disciples for feasting while the disciples of John were fasting. In reply Jesus pointed out that a marriage feast was no time for mourning; and fasting would be wholly out of place on such an occasion. He stated that the love of God for his people was so warm as to be comparable to the relationship between a husband and wife. The new age that he had come to introduce was nothing less than a wedding between heaven and earth. He came to move beyond the old frontiers of human experience and to offer a new vision of life. He appealed to his listeners to open their eyes to see what was happening and welcome the message of God's saving power. A completely new attitude was called for, because the old form of religion was being replaced by a worship that came from the heart.

In any walk of life, a change is no easy matter and there is a trauma in letting go because our minds become fixed and settled in their ways, and are unable to accept new teaching. There is a sense of security, living with old values,which makes it difficult to cast off comfortable and cherished attitudes. As we become pre-occupied with self preservation we tend to cling to systems from which we got support rather than launch out into new methods. There is always a sense of loss when we move from one way of thinking to another. It is not easy to take a risk, enter the unknown and adopt a new approach. We do our best to put off such decisions and postpone them to a later and more convenient time, because complacency rules our way of doing things. Newness poses a definite threat. Change is challenging but the alternative to change is standing still.

Opening a new chapter means closing an old and with the changes brought about in church worship by Vatican II many complain that our religion is not what it used to be and that it has lost its sense of mystery. There are those, with closed minds, who can find nothing good in the new liturgy and those who can barely tolerate the old. Neither are prepared to admit that the basic truths of christianity have not changed. We are shaped and defined by our past and any church of the future must respect and reflect that aspect of history. What has changed is the language and images each generation uses to understand and express these wonderful truths. Our task is to rediscover personally and communally our christian faith in each generation, in fidelity to the past and with equal openness to the present.

For those who believe in an ever-creative God, new beginnings are always possible. They afford the opportunity of looking ahead in hope and of moving beyond old boundaries towards new horizons. Without a vision, worship can sink into meaningless ritual. The most important thing is that we hold onto the vision and keep it alive as best we can. Without a vision, the people will perish (Proverbs 29:18).

Prayer of the Faithful

We now make our prayer to the wise and loving God who, in the midst of the shifting sands of time, guides and protects us.

1. We pray that the church may joyfully proclaim the Good News of the gospel in words and in worship which are meaningful and expressive to the particular age. Lord, hear us.
2. For the realisation that opening our hearts to God's saving power in Christ is much more important than observing an ancient religious practice. Lord, hear us.
3. May we remember that the miracle of change is always possible for those who seek Christ's help in attaining it. Lord, hear us.
4. We pray for the sick. Make us channels of the Lord's caring hands in showing them his love and concern. Lord, hear us.
5. We pray for the dead. May they find eternal rest in the company of the Risen Christ. Lord, hear us.

Heavenly Father, look lovingly on our changing world and keep us safe amid the uncertainties that darken our days and cloud our nights. We make our prayer through Christ our Lord. Amen.

Ninth Sunday of the Year

As a christian community we hold Sunday to be holy and a day when we remember our risen Lord, by recalling and celebrating his resurrection. Although every day of the week belongs to the Lord, on Sunday we stop work, slow things down and call a halt to our feverish weekly activities in order to take care of the most important aspects of life. We need to take time out from the grinding demands of our daily labours to see where our lives are going, and reflect on why we are here in the first place. Otherwise our stay on earth may amount to no more than a meaningless succession of days. Sunday provides an opportunity to remind ourselves that we belong to the Lord and that here on earth we are pilgrims on the move journeying to our final destination, which is the kingdom of God the Father. We are social beings who need to express our love of God in the company of family, friends, those with whom we have worked alongside and other worshipping believers. When we assemble in church to listen to God's word and take part in the eucharist, we bring to the altar the joys and heartbreaks of our tattered and broken lives and ask God to give us healing and new strength to face the difficulties of the week ahead. Celebrating the memory of the Lord's resurrection on Sunday puts a definite spiritual pulse into our lives.

While going to Mass is of utmost importance and the high point of the day, there are other dimensions of Sunday observance which must not be neglected if God is to have the first place in our lives. During the week we can find ourselves being very busy, with so many things to do that we have precious little time to spend with other people. A conscious laying aside of work, prevents us from living solely in the material dimension at the expense of our spiritual well-being. Sunday gives us that opportunity. It is a day for involvement in parish life and for family togetherness which deepens the bonds of love and companionship within our own homes.We can see from the controversy in which Jesus was embroiled, that what creates a sacred atmosphere on the Sabbath is not as clear-cut and as easily definable as might appear at first glance. In defending the action of the disciples who pulled some grains off the stalks in the field on the Sabbath because they were hungry, he makes it clear that the spiritual

202

quality of people's lives is not be be judged on holding strictly to niggling rules which assume more importance than the values they were meant to protect. To be of real worth, the Sabbath observance must be an outward expression of a desire, within the heart, to give back time to God in praise and thanksgiving.

While there is no need to be puritanical about the Sabbath, the marked tendency to turn Sunday into a full trading day gives cause for grave concern. Sunday was intended by God to be different from the rest of the week. We need a regular day of rest to ponder on the real meaning of life. This is an occasion for renewing our commitment to making Sunday that special day when we avoid unnecessary work and join the people of our parish around the eucharistic table, making it truly the Lord's Day.

Prayer of the Faithful

Assembled for the breaking of bread, we confidently make our prayer to God the Father who has commanded us to keep the Sabbath holy.

1. We pray that the leaders of the church may stress the importance of letting the sacredness of Sunday overflow into weekday activities. Lord, hear us.
2. We pray that our Sunday worship may not be mere lip-service but a lamp for our steps and a light for our path. Lord, hear us.
3. That those assembled for the eucharist may realise that strife and bitterness make a mockery of their celebrations. Lord, hear us.
4. We pray that the sick and those in hospital may never be lonely and without friends to comfort them on the Sabbath day. Lord, hear us.
5. We pray that the dead may now rest in the company of God. Lord, hear us.

Heavenly Father, listen to our prayer and strengthen us in our resolve to keep the Sabbath as a special day for appreciating you, the world you have given us and the people around us. We make our prayer through Christ our Lord. Amen.

Tenth Sunday of the Year

The mysterious beginnings of evil in the world and its consequences are poetically described in the familiar story of Adam
and Eve's fall from grace in the garden of Eden. It's a striking
account of the way in which sin corrodes the relationship between
God and people. God called out to Adam: 'Where are you?' Adam
hid because he was guilty and felt ashamed and embarrassed for
what he had done in eating the forbidden fruit. Instinctively he
shifted the blame onto Eve, saying: 'It was the woman you put
with me: she gave me the fruit and I ate it.' When Eve was confronted she accused the serpent. The whole sorry episode is typi-
cal of the way we, as human beings, go about things and try to
avoid accepting responsibility for our actions. We have an urge to
shift the blame and profess our own innocence because we feel
ashamed of our actions and don't want to own up to them.

Sin, as we all know, is an offence against God. It's our doing,
and it distances us from him. When sin is uncovered it sits uncom-
fortably on our shoulders. Deep down there is an unwillingness
to admit that we are wrong and to express penitence for our
offence. The consequence of not admitting our sin is that we cannot
receive God's forgiveness. Like Adam and Eve, we hide. Even
though Adam and Eve sinned, God, we are told, continued to
walk in the garden, which means that he did not reject them.
Though fallen from grace they did not remain beyond the reach of
his mercy. God's forgiveness is there for us also, but unless we
reach out to him in sorrow and admit our guilty behaviour our
sins remain unforgiven. The ability to say sorry in words and actions is an integral part of any relationship. It is important to have
a sense of sin and a realisation of its consequences so that we can
reach out for forgiveness.

To have a clear vision of what our present life means, God's
call 'where are you,' must echo in our own hearts. Otherwise life
becomes a hiding game of avoiding responsibility for our actions,
and for the persons we are. The conflict between good and evil
will continue for as long as humans live on the earth. Many of us
do go into hiding throughout life because of sin. We lack the courage to face our situation and to admit honestly that we are drifting
and lost, naked in the sight of God.

The gospel paints a picture of our Blessed Lord offering us healing, strength, forgiveness and a way out of our difficulties. The entire life and mission of Jesus was a renewal of the dialogue between God and his people. So, let us not be afraid to turn to him for help in our lives. If we confess our sins with sorrow, we will know with faith that we are forgiven, and travel on life's journey with our minds and hearts set on heaven.

Prayer of the Faithful

As descendants of Adam and Eve, the struggle between good and evil is at work in our lives. With this in mind, we pray to God the Father to deliver us from temptation.

1. We pray that the church may be renewed and give faithful witness to the proper values of life and so help restore a fallen world. Lord, hear us.
2. That we may give whole-hearted support in upholding the truth and in opposing the subtle influences of evil. Lord, hear us.
3. We pray that our young people may be sensitive to the goodness of those who care for them and may they look to the future with hope. Lord, hear us.
4. We pray for the sick, especially those who are handicapped, mentally or physically. May they receive the comfort of God's love from those engaged in caring for them. Lord, hear us.
5. For those who have died. Receive them, Lord, into the fullness of your love in heaven. Lord, hear us.

Heavenly Father, your love for us never changes or fades away. Give us the courage to walk in your presence all the days of our life. Through Christ our Lord. Amen.

Eleventh Sunday of the Year

As we travel in the countryside at this time of year, we see the miracle of growth taking place all around us in flowers, trees, plants and shrubs. Words cannot capture the magnificence of the scene as the cycle of nature blossoms forth in all its beauty. It is fascinating and a sure sign that harvest time is approaching. We don't have to be professional gardeners to appreciate that growth is a gradual process. It has its origins in tiny seeds being buried in the earth and demands time, tender care and patience for it to blossom and produce fruit.

The readings are concerned with growth, not physical growth but spiritual growth. They speak of the importance of us coming to God in prayer and good works in order to grow in God's favour and friendship. God is at work in every age and in each of our lives. The seed of his word was first planted in our hearts at baptism. Our task is to water and tenderly care for it so that it can work powerfully within us. As most of us were baptised as infants, parents have a vital role in nurturing the seed of God's word in their children. The example they set by prayer and good christian living in the home will go a long way in determining their children's attitude to life and to God.

The mustard tree reminds us of an important truth of the christian life: the seed of God's life within us grows slowly and invisibly. We cannot rush the growth of seed in the earth and neither can we rush God's growth in our hearts. There is nothing we can do to hurry it. Because our path to perfection seems so frustratingly slow we often lose heart. Many of us have the uneasy feeling that after years of struggling with the christian life, we are no nearer to God. There appears to be no mastering of our personal shortcomings. The same old sins keep recurring preventing our progress on the roadway to perfection. Patient endurance and unbounded hope are virtues we need to develop. How easily we forget that God rewards our efforts, our ability to keep trying and not our excellence. We fail to realise that his grace can work through our human weaknesses and limitations and can accomplish what is beyond our dreams. We are not going to be able to measure it but can be certain that it will happen provided we play our part and are intent on pleasing God.

We tend the seed of the Word of God that has been planted in our hearts by prayer and the sacraments, which dispose us to perform good works and acts of loving kindness. In this way we make ready the earth in which the seed of God's word can blossom. There is no age at which we cannot grow in God's grace. So let us realise that life is but a passing shadow and the few years given to us here below are for soul-making. If we do not grow in moral and spiritual stature while on earth, there will be lots of growing up to be done in purgatory.

Prayer of the Faithful

Full of hope and confidence we make our prayer to God the Father anxious for an increase of his presence in our life.

1. We pray that the church may continue to grow and be a symbol of justice, love and truth in the world. Lord, hear us.
2. We pray that as a community we may continue to grow in wisdom, strength and in the love of God. Lord, hear us.
3. We pray for our families, especially our children that they may grow in the ways of grace and mature into Christlike people. Lord, hear us.
4. May all of those who are sick in our community experience comfort through our care and concern. Lord, hear us.
5. We remember our beloved dead and we thank you for the blessings they brought into our lives. May they now enjoy the peace of your kingdom. Lord, hear us.

Heavenly Father, help us grasp the importance of the time in which we are living. Open our hearts to your word so that we may always bear fruit. We ask this through Christ our Lord. Amen.

Twelfth Sunday of the Year

It's an un-nerving experience to be caught out in a small boat when, without warning, the sea suddenly changes from peaceful blue waters to angry mountainous waves. The power of a stormy sea is so overwhelming that it can become a frightening ordeal. We all have experienced fear, so we can appreciate the plight of the apostles in the storm-tossed boat. In desperation they turn to Jesus who is asleep in the boat, seemingly unaware of the danger, and indifferent to their peril. With angry shouts they awaken him: 'Master, do you not care that we are going down?'

This story has a thoroughly modern ring to it. We can easily make a connection between the storm at sea and the trials and sufferings of our own lives. Troubles, disappointments and misfortunes come our way from time to time and severely test our faith. Although we will not readily admit it, sometimes we feel disappointed with God when set-backs bring sadness and anxiety into our homes. As parents, it's hard to stand by and watch our children make a mess of their lives, especially when we have done our best to set a good example and bring them up according to true christian values. We are tempted to react angrily with God and ask: 'Why don't you intervene and stop all this heartbreak?' Feelings such as these are deeply human, very understandable and nothing of which to be ashamed. Our reactions are no different to the apostles: 'Lord, do you not care?'

When God does not give an immediate answer to our prayer, we lose heart, panic and have a frightening sense of drowning beneath the waves of despair. The truth is, ours is a stormy world and God does not give any ready answers that satisfy our human questioning. We want him to justify himself for what he does or fails to do, to account to us for his creation. There are mysteries in nature beyond our solving and suffering is one of them. Remember, God did not take away suffering and death, even from his own Son. There can be no answer to these questions except one inspired by faith and faith is what we lack.

Today's gospel should give us hope. It shows us that Jesus is always near, hidden in the heart of suffering. It calls on us to have faith and to take Jesus seriously because he alone can give us courage and inner peace which casts out fear on the stormy voyage of life. If only we realise that the almighty God is with us we have the power to dispel all the fears that come our way.

Prayer of the Faithful

Conscious that God the Father can bring peace to our troubled world, we now pray that with his help we may be able to weather the various storms that threaten us.

1. We pray for the church, the barque of Peter; guide it safely through the stormy waters that threaten to engulf it. Lord, hear us.
2. We pray for the leaders of troubled nations, that they may work tirelessly to bring peace with justice to their unsettled countries. Lord, hear us.
3. We pray for sailors, fishermen and all those who earn a living from the sea that they may be preserved from every danger. Lord, hear us.
4. We pray for the disabled and those suffering from long illnesses. May they find inward peace in Christ's healing power. Lord, hear us.
5. We pray for the dead. May they experience the ever-lasting peace of Christ. Lord, hear us.

Heavenly Father, may the trials and troubles of life's storm-tossed waters purify us and bring lasting peace to our souls. We make our prayer through Christ our Lord. Amen.

Thirteenth Sunday of the Year

The gospel portrays an example of the healing power of Christ in an uncommonly moving scene. Jairus, a respected synagogue official, has a little daughter who is seriously ill, on the point of death. In desperation he seeks out Jesus and begs him to come to his house, to lay his hands on his daughter and cure her. Jesus responds without hesitation, but on the way news comes that the little girl is dead. To continue further would be useless, but with calm authority Jesus calls for faith and proceeds to the house. In the quiet of the sick room, speaking just two words, he restores the child to full health.

The heart of Jesus could never resist a hand outstretched in need or an appeal for help made in faith. Healing was at the centre of his public ministry and a point worthy of note is that his healing activity extended to both body and soul. In his lifetime he went around the whole of Galilee curing whatever illness or infirmity was among the people and filling them with the life-giving presence of God. The healing acts of Jesus were themselves a message, that he had come to set men free.

The mission of the church in every age is to continue the healing work which Jesus began through his miracles. Every christian is called to this ministry in one way or another. The unique healing power of Jesus was in his willingness to show compassion. Nailed to the cross on the hill of Calvary, he pardoned the good thief even though he did not remove him from his agony. There can be no doubt that his sins were forgiven, that he was spiritually healed. Real healing so often takes place in doing the simple ordinary things of life, that are so often neglected or taken for granted.

All of us are called to represent God by Christ-like actions and nobody can be excused from caring because our vocation is to be healers. When a friend of ours is terminally ill, medical knowledge and skill together can not make them well again. What they need more than anything else in this situation, is that the love of God be made real for them, through the actual experience of care and concern shown by the people around them. Just by being there, even though we are powerless, we can make faith in God real for them, for we are following the Lord in his compassion. Today's Mass reminds us of the generosity of Our Lord, who became poor for our sake. We have received the richness of his many blessings and now we are asked to go out and share that same richness with others.

Prayer of the Faithful

Confident that when we pray with faith to God the Father he will respond to our request with open-hearted generosity, we now place before him our needs.

1. That the church throughout the world may be a symbol of Christ's healing work by its care for those who are sick in body, mind and spirit. Lord, hear us.
2. For doctors and nurses and all those who care for the sick. That they may show the compassion and gentleness of Jesus in caring for the least of his brethren. Lord, hear us.
3. That we may bind up hearts that are broken by our kind deeds and encouraging words. Lord, hear us.
4. We put before you our own personal needs and invite your healing power to come into our lives. Lord, hear us.
5. For the sick and the suffering. May they receive comfort and support from their families, friends and neighbours. Lord, hear us.
6. For our beloved dead, that they may enjoy forever the reward of their faith in the new life of Christ. Lord, hear us.

Heavenly Father, help us to go on trusting you and to have faith in the healing power of your Son who binds up all our wounds. We ask this through Christ our Lord. Amen.

Fourteenth Sunday of the Year

When we read this gospel we can shake our heads in disgust and wonder what sort of a community the people of Nazareth were to have turned their back on Jesus. And yet, when we do this, we miss the whole point of the gospel story. We fail to see that every day we can be guilty of this type of behaviour. We imitate the people of Nazareth when we turn our backs on the local prophets who are the presence of God in our midst. Lack of trust limits their ministry also. The problem about God and Nazareth was that God came to Nazareth in the form of a local, one of the villagers, and the community could not come to terms with the situation. They did not recognise the obvious – that God is present among people – the truth was staring them in the face but it was too familiar for them to recognise . Christ's family circumstances were too well known among the villagers and they felt because he was a native that he had nothing to offer. After all, he was only one of themselves . The unkindest cut of all – they knew him too well to be able to recognise the finger of God in their midst.

Life in many ways, is about searching for God but many of us go looking for him in the far-off hills and in obscure places. We pleasantly forget the obvious, that God moves in mysterious ways, and is most likely to be present in our nearest and dearest, and in our neighbours. God is present in the ordinary bits and pieces of life and shows up more often than we think. He is not apart from the world, nor is he confined or controlled by religious ritual and language. We meet him in every person, place and moment that comes our way. The trouble with us is that, because we stand so close to one another, we only see the faults and take for granted the great gifts of goodness which we all possess. We become a community of knockers and begrudgers once we allow ourselves to be blinded by jealousy and family prejudice. If we can put a bad word or interpretation on a neighbour's act of kindness we won't miss the opportunity to comment.

This gospel is asking us to say thanks and to give honour and recognition to the prophets of God's goodness in our midst. So express some appreciation today for the person you married, a word of praise for the lady who cooks the dinner, for the wage earner, for the neighbour who chats to you over the garden fence and for the friends who gave you time, support and attention during a recent bereavement. Let us not take for granted the presence of God among us as evidenced in the goodness shown by family and friends.

Prayer of the Faithful

Mindful that God the Father speaks to us in various circumstances, we pray that we may hear his voice and listen to his message.

1. We pray for the leaders of the church that they may speak the word of God with courage and live it with conviction. Lord, hear us.
2. We pray for christian parents that they may be strengthened to follow Christ, who is the way, the truth and the Life. Lord, hear us.
3. We pray for our families, our friends and our neighbours who have blessed our lives. Lord, keep them always in your love. Lord, hear us.
4. For all who are sick or who find life difficult. May they know God cares for them through the concern of their families. Lord, hear us.
5. Let us pray for our dead who are in your company, freed from the anxieties of life. May they enjoy everlasting peace. Lord, hear us.

Almighty Father, help us in everything we undertake this week. May the words we speak and the work we carry out be a source of inspiration for all who come into contact with us. We ask this through Christ our Lord. Amen.

Fifteenth Sunday of the Year

There is something very moving about this gospel passage of Jesus sending out twelve ordinary men, after a brief apprentice-ship, to preach the message of God's word, which they did not fully understand. They were to have a simple lifestyle, to be poor as he was poor and not to worry too much about their physical needs, nor become upset if their message was not welcome at every door. It was no surprise that their mission was highly successful. The secret of their fruitfulness was that they benefitted from the living example of Jesus and the time spent in his company.

The sending out of the twelve apostles was but the beginning of the church's mission to the world. Down the centuries ordinary people have been called in the same way, to win souls for Christ and to gather them into his church. If the word of God is to reach all people then everyone who hears it must make it known. The Good News of salvation is not intended to be guarded jealously but to be spread around and handed down. Every baptised christian is called to accomplish this work of spreading the gospel. The message of salvation is offered to all but it is not forced on anyone, for it is a personal choice to accept or reject the call of God. Today we have the privilege of responding to Christ's invitation to be fruitful bearers of his Good News. Becoming a servant of God in a society where selfishness is part of the foundation structure, is indeed a tall order. This invitation to a more dedicated life is very challenging and demands that we have a caring heart. Many of us are left with the feeling that we have nothing much to offer to the furthering of his kingdom. Parents should remember that one of the most effective proclamations of the gospel can be carried out without going over their own doorsteps: by rearing their children in the faith and upholding christian values in their homes. This is work all families can do, and it involves no small effort.

Another effective way of proclaiming the gospel is by the silent witness of a simple life-style. Many of us clutter our hearts and minds with worldly goods, which prevent us from attending to what is most important in life. So much of what we accumulate in life is left unused and wasted. We forget that the only luggage we can take with us as we leave this world is charity. Christ's work demands total commitment in small things done daily. He wants all of us to be part of his saving mission. We are his hands by the work we do, his tongue by the words we speak, and his feet by the places and people we visit.

Prayer of the Faithful

God the Father has invited us to be his ministers, to spread the Good News of the gospel. We pray now for the grace to recognise the dignity of our mission and the necessary strength to carry it out.

1. We pray that the pilgrim church may inspire people to renew their lives by faithfully bearing witness to Christ in word and deed. Lord, hear us.
2. We pray for missionaries in foreign lands that their good work in fostering the faith may be rewarded with an abundant harvest. Lord, hear us.
3. We pray for parents in our own parish community. May the words of Jesus find a home in their hearts and may they be given the strength to persevere in their vocation of handing on the faith to their children. Lord, hear us.
4. For the sick, the handicapped and those who are old, lonely or brokenhearted. May the love of Christ and the care of friends be their sure hope. Lord, hear us.
5. We pray for all those who have died; especially … Freed from the troubles of this world, may they enjoy everlasting peace in your presence. Lord, hear us.

Heavenly Father, guide our faltering steps as we walk on your pathway. Help us in our struggle, encourage us in our doubts, comfort us in our pain. We ask this through our Lord Jesus Christ your Son, who lives and reigns forever and ever. Amen.

Sixteenth Sunday of the Year

Some of the earliest christian images painted on the walls of the catacombs in Rome are of Christ as a young beardless shepherd, holding a sheep on his shoulders. This very ancient theme of early christian art is expressed in today's gospel where Christ took pity on the crowd who were like sheep without a shepherd. The setting is the apostles returning from their first experience of missionary work. They are tired and in need of a rest. Christ knows how they feel so he takes them off to a quiet place where they can relax and spend some time in prayer. But it didn't work out like that. The crowd spotted the place where they were going and arrived there before them. One might have expected Christ to tell them to go home, that he had done enough that day, but he did not turn his back on the situation. Their state was deplorable and he was alert to their needs.

We can all draw a lesson from the open-hearted behaviour of Christ in placing the needs of others before his own. If there is no rest for Jesus, there can be no rest for his followers either. By virtue of our baptismal calling, all of us have christian responsibilities and a certain amount of shepherding to do. At times there seems to be no let up especially in family life. If growing children are not cared for and given the proper direction, they are going to be lost and wander aimlessly through life with no purpose. Being the Good Shepherd that Christ wants us to be is a hard line of business. The pathway he wishes us to tread is the straight and narrow one of the Ten Commandments. Unless we are continually linked to Christ through prayer, we run the danger of wandering off and finding other pathways more attractive.

The gospel speaks of the importance of finding a quiet spot in our lives where we can be alone with Christ in prayer. Like Christ, we need to get away at times from the constant calls upon us and from the pressures that bear down on us to listen to the healing voice of God and refresh ourselves spiritually. God's voice is heard best in moments of stillness. If only we allow Jesus to make his home in our hearts, there is open to us the power and the strength of God to assist us in our living. Silent prayer alone with God is one of our greatest needs. Alone in his presence, we should ask ourselves where we are going and what we are trying to achieve. If we don't make space for God in our lives, we are

216

wasting our time and are not seeing beyond our present activity. All of our life is sacred but we will never understand this unless we accept our Lord's loving invitation to come apart and rest a while.

Prayer of the Faithful

Aware of the need to escape from the demanding activity of life in order to strengthen and restore our inner spirit, we approach God the Father in humble prayer.

1. We pray for the Pope, the bishops and all who exercise a ministry of leadership in the church, that the Lord will keep their commitment alive in the preaching of the gospel. Lord, hear us.
2. We pray for vocations to the priesthood and religious life. May our young people be generous in their response to the voice of the Good Shepherd. Lord, hear us.
3. We pray for those who have abandoned the faith and are walking in other pathways. May they be guided back to the family of God. Lord, hear us.
4. We remember the sick especially...May they experience the loving touch of the Good Shepherd through the care and concern of their friends. Lord, hear us.
5. We pray for the faithful departed. May they dwell in the Lord's own house forever. Lord, hear us.

Almighty Father, in sending your Son Jesus, you have opened up a way to eternal life. May we always follow him, the Good Shepherd, and live and work for the glory of your name. We make our prayer through Christ our Lord. Amen.

Seventeenth Sunday of the Year

The crowd have come a long way to hear Jesus and now find themselves in a deserted area without food and are feeling the pangs of hunger. In his compassion, Jesus inquires about the food supply on hand and discovers all that is available is five barley loaves and two fishes in the possession of a boy. We can easily picture this youth's bewilderment when asked to give up all that he has, to part with the only food that is available. However, his sacrifice is well rewarded when he sees Jesus feed the multitude with the food he has provided. Through the power and prayer of the Lord, the impossible becomes possible. What is given to Jesus as a sacrifice is given back by him totally transformed. The crowd is fed, symbolising that Jesus has come to give life to all people.

One message to be taken to heart from the miraculous feeding of the crowd is the importance of sharing what we have with those who are less well off, especially those who are starving. The Lord asks us to give ourselves and our resources generously to him, to place what we have and are at his disposal. Not many of us have experienced the pangs of real hunger which darkens the mind and forces an honest man to become a thief. Our problem is that we have too much food. The inclination to selfishness is strong in all of us. The more we have the more we want. There is food enough in the world for the needs of all people but not enough for people's greed.

The hungry multitude is still with us, crying out for the basic necessities of life. The sheer size of the problem may make us wonder what we have to offer. Like the apostle Andrew, we say; 'What is that among so many?' We can draw inspiration from the generosity of the young boy. The Lord did not dismiss his offering, and he won't dismiss ours either. It is in using our little efforts that God chooses to produce his greatest miracles. Our barley loaf and fish may be the small amount we set aside as a family every Lent for the poor of the Third World. On its own, the contribution may seem insignificant but multiplied around a parish or a caring community it can become a small miracle.

In the gospel, we hear now Jesus took some loaves and gave thanks to his Father. Thankfulness for what we have got, can be a beginning. Every day we live in this world is a miracle of God's divine providence, much greater than the feeding of the multitude, but because it happens with such regularity we give it no thought. This story should make us think about thanking God not only for our food but for the many blessings and benefits that come our way and which we take so much for granted.

Prayer of the Faithful

We now turn to God our Father who gives us our daily bread and cares for our every need.

1. That the leaders of the church may imitate the generosity of the young boy and share what they possess with the under-privileged. Lord, hear us.
2. That we may be conscious of our responsibility for the hungry, the neglected and the less fortunate members of society. Lord, hear us.
3. We remember those in our community who are troubled or worried. We ask you to give them strength and courage in their anxieties. Lord, hear us.
4. We pray for those who are sick and are faced with pain, suffering and loneliness. May they be strengthened by the support of their friends. Lord, hear us.
5. We pray for the dead. May their hunger for eternal life be satisfied in the presence of God. Lord, hear us.

Heavenly Father, we thank you for listening to us. We trust in your concern for the welfare of your creation. We are confident that you will give us your peace and grant what we ask, through Christ our Lord. Amen.

Eighteenth Sunday of the Year

On the day following the miracle of the loaves and fishes, our Lord had an eager audience. The people, obviously impressed with what happened, are back following him. They think that he can supply them with food and fulfil their material hopes and ambitions, without any effort on their own part. The deeper meaning of the event – its spiritual significance – escapes them completely. They don't understand what he is talking about and fail to realise that Jesus is the sign of God's presence, in their midst. Jesus reprimands them saying: 'You are not looking for me because you have seen the signs, but because you have had all the bread you wanted to eat.' This hunger for food was the starting point for Jesus to begin his teaching about the deep hunger all of us have for something more than physical sustenance.

We are all living in a world desperately wondering what has gone wrong with its dreams. All around us there is a preoccupation with hunger for material goods. The media assure us that the longings of the heart can be satisfied by the artificial securities and delights of the consumer society. Satisfaction is short lived however. New needs are created as soon as old ones are accomplished, emptiness sets in and the search for happiness begins all over again.

As we listen to the words of Jesus in this morning's gospel we come to realise that food is but basic fodder and that if we are really to live, something more is required. There is another kind of nourishment needed by the human heart, because there are other hungers that we need to satisfy. Deep down within each of us there is a hunger to love and be loved, to be listened to and to be appreciated and above all to know that there is a meaning and an eternal value to our lives. These are the hungers of the heart and the yearnings of the spirit of which Jesus wants us to be conscious and which he alone can satisfy. At this depth is our hunger for God.

You and I are in this story as it touches our personal lives. Swayed as we are by material needs, we are in constant danger of losing our taste for the food that will strengthen our souls. Jesus speaks to us and asks us, do we hunger and thirst for what he has to offer? Where do our interests and true desires rest? He calls us to work as hard to receive that bread which he is, as we normally work for the bread which does not last. Otherwise, we will never know what we are striving for, and die without realising our spiritual greatness. 'Our hearts are made for you, O God, and they cannot rest until they rest in you.' The world is full of people who spend their lives aimlessly seeking joy and happiness in the wrong ways.

Prayer of the Faithful

Only God the Father can satisfy the hunger of the heart and of the spirit, so we place our needs before him.

1. We pray for the church, that it may awaken within its members a hunger and thirst for the bread of eternal life. Lord, hear us.
2. That we may realise that the longings of the heart cannot be satisfied by the pursuit of worldly success or material comfort. Lord, hear us.
3. We pray for all those who spend their time uselessly searching for joy and happiness in the wrong way. Help them to find a real purpose in life. Lord, hear us.
4. Lord, show your special care for the sick and handicapped. Give their parents and friends support and consolation. Lord, hear us.
5. We pray for all who have died that they may be united with Christ in the new life of the resurrection. Lord, hear us.

Almighty Father, you have given us the bread from heaven, as food for our pilgrim journey. Guide our steps in the way of justice and peace. We make this prayer through Christ our Lord. Amen.

Nineteenth Sunday of the Year

We know what Elijah is talking about when he says: 'Lord, I've had enough.' Broken and dispirited on his journey in the wilderness, he has reached the end of his tether. At his lowest ebb, an angel of God comes to his rescue and feeds him with miraculous food – a hearth cake and a jug of water. His flagging hope is restored by this bread from heaven and he continues his journey to the holy mountain of Horeb, where he receives a new vision of God in the form of a gentle breeze. This gives him renewed courage and faith to march on and face the challenge of another day.

Many a time in our bleak moments we feel like saying with Elijah, 'Lord, we've had enough.' Christian life is by no means plain sailing and we often find ourselves broken and crushed by circumstances that come our way. Left to our own resources we can find no light at the end of the tunnel. To keep going we need an assurance that we are not alone in our lives and that God is with us helping us to carry our crosses, rescuing us from every predicament that befalls us. The gospel points out that we have such a help in Jesus who is the Bread of Life. He brings each of us just what we need to sustain us on our pilgrim journey to God. Jesus is heavenly bread, medicine for the sick soul, nourishment for a wounded spirit, light and strength for a weary mind, the source of new and eternal life, whose presence and power strengthens us. He is the living Bread which has come down for heaven, the unique source of life.

We can look at our lives and ask ourselves are we hungering for Christ who is the Bread of life? Coming to Christ requires far more than a weekly walk up to the altar to receive Holy Communion. If Jesus makes himself available to us then we have to make ourselves present to him. To approach the altar complaining, or with a heart full of bitterness because of hurts inflicted on us, is not a true sharing in the eucharist. There is no way we can offer ourselves to God and not try and love our neighbour who has let us down in some way during the week. In our daily round we are asked to be forgiving, to overcome faults, to understand the failure of friends, and not to close our hearts when we are offended.

In the eucharist we meet the bigness of God who has forgiven us and who asks us in our turn to give as freely as we have received. The eucharist is an opportunity for reconciliation, for wounds and old sores to be bound up and forgiveness to be shown. For God to love us we must try and be loving also.

Prayer of the Faithful

We turn now in prayer to God the Father who from the generosity of his heart has sent us his Son Jesus the Bread of Life.

1. We pray for the church throughout the world, that it may strive to bring Christ's love to everyone who is hungry for the Bread of Life. Lord, hear us.
2. That we may realise that Christ's presence in the eucharist is a constant call for us to share our lives with those we meet. Lord, hear us.
3. We pray for those who have no faith, that they may draw inspiration from the goodness which they find in those who believe in Jesus as the Bread of Life. Lord, hear us.
4. We pray for those who are sick. That they may draw strength from receiving the eucharist. Lord, hear us.
5. For those who died recently that they may share in the fullness of life everlasting. Lord, hear us.

Father in heaven, guide us on our journey and help us to walk the pathway of your Son Jesus who is the Bread of Life. We ask this through Christ our Lord. Amen.

Twentieth Sunday of the Year

We can make the mistake of thinking that the only important part of a meal is the food which sustains our flesh and bones, but there is a deeper significance to the occasion than that. What really binds people together is the chat and the fun while eating, which refreshes the heart and also creates friendship. It was no different with Jesus. At the Last Supper his love and his friendship overflowed as he showed his apostles how to be brothers to one another. Every time we come to celebrate the eucharist we relive that event. We meet Jesus as our brother and Saviour and receive the shared life of God himself. Today's gospel tells us clearly that Jesus offers us his Body and Blood as necessary spiritual food for our journey through life and he warns us of the consequences of not accepting the gift. 'If you do not eat the flesh of the Son of Man and drink his blood you will not have life in you.'

We are reminded this morning of the closeness of the union to which Christ calls us in every celebration of the eucharist. It is a union which reaches its fulfilment in eternity. Jesus is offering us a life that will not grow old but will go on forever. In the eucharist we are offered the life that Jesus shares with God the Father. Christ is not present on our altars simply for our adoration and admiration. He is present so that we can be united with him perfectly. Our celebration and reception of the eucharist can be an empty pageant if it is confined to one hour in the church on a Sunday morning and doesn't flow into the rest of our lives. Unless we are very much part of what we are doing and have our hearts set on drawing closer and becoming more like Christ we can end up leading a pagan life tinged with certain christian practices. Receiving the eucharist is meaningless and profitless if we fail to live what we celebrate. We must take our religion out of the church with us and bring it into the market place. For instance there is not much point in speaking about love without making an effort to spread it.

At the end of Mass we are sent out to serve the Lord where we live and work as Christ-bearers living his life, making Jesus present in a world that would otherwise conceal him. Today, we thank God in a special way for the great gift of his Son who is with us leading us to God our Father. Every act, every word, every thought placed on the altar of Christ benefits our world. Without frequent return to the Bread of Life, we are unable to keep the Spirit of Christ alive in our hearts.

Prayer of the Faithful

We now direct our prayer to God the Father who strengthens our lives in the person of his Son Jesus Christ, the living bread come down from heaven.

1. We pray for the church that the eucharist may unite all its members in a brotherhood of service. Lord, hear us.

2. That through the worthy reception of Christ in Communion we may deepen our love for the people of our neighbourhood. Lord, hear us.

3. That we may never fail to share our earthly bread with those in need, and so become like the self-giving Christ. Lord, hear us.

4. That those who are sick in mind or body may be strengthened by the reception of the body and blood of Christ in the eucharist. Lord, hear us.

5. For our recently deceased. That they may share in the eucharistic banquet which they believed in, while on earth. Lord, hear us.

Almighty Father, grant that by receiving your Son Jesus we may come to share his life with others and break down the walls of separation among us. We make our prayer through Christ our Lord. Amen.

Twenty-first Sunday of the Year

The declaration of Jesus that he was the living Bread come down from heaven and the source of eternal life, proved too much for some of his followers. They could not believe in such a claim and started to drift away. This was intolerable language and they were no longer prepared to walk with him. Neither surprised nor disappointed at their reaction, Jesus did not take back anything he had said nor try to make his teaching more acceptable. It was the parting of the ways. He turned to his disciples and said: 'Will you also walk away?' This was a moment of crisis, of standing up and being counted. What Christ was demanding of them was not understanding, but faith in himself. There was no way they could avoid making a choice of being for or against Jesus. Peter spoke for everyone: 'Lord, where else shall we go? You have the message of eternal life and we believe.'

What happened then, still happens. We, in our generation are faced with a decision to make about following our Lord – do we stay or do we go away? This is the drastic choice that faces all who come in contact with Jesus. Whether they will follow him without conditions or not, nobody is forced because Jesus respects our freedom. Our baptismal promises likewise put this question to us. Whom do we want to serve? It's not just a matter of accepting that certain beliefs are true but it involves a personal commitment at the level of the heart and of the mind to live by the values of Christ. The personal option to belong to Jesus regardless of where life may lead us is at the centre of our faith; and is an ongoing struggle. It is so easy for us to compromise and pick and choose from Christ's teaching what suits ourselves; God does not always correspond to our idea of him or to what we would like him to be. Christ invites us to surrender and entrust ourselves to him and to follow him on the way to the Father. This means learning to rely on God rather than on ourselves when the road ahead is uncertain and the light is dim.

Most of us, of course, have doubts and face difficulties about our faith but, like Peter, we would be lost without it. At this Mass, Christ once again invites us to be his faithful followers and to share his work among men. So let us repeat Peter's response from the depths of our hearts: 'Lord, where else will we go? We believe you have the message of eternal life.'

Prayers of the Faithful

Let us make our needs known to God the Father who guides our lives and cares for us in all our anxieties.

1. That the leaders of the church may follow the Lord with all their heart, with all their strength and with all their might. Lord, hear us.
2. We ask our Lord to strengthen our faith and help us practise it daily. Lord, hear us.
3. That we may realise that God gives us the greatest proof of his love in the abiding presence of the Blessed Sacrament. Lord, hear us.
4. For the sick of our community that in their suffering they may rely more than ever on Jesus. Lord, hear us.
5. For those who died recently … that they may have the eternal life promised by Christ. Lord, hear us.

Heavenly Father, in your great mercy and love hear our humble prayers and help us to trust in you always, however dim the light or stormy the seas. We ask this through Christ our Lord. Amen.

Twenty-second Sunday of the Year

Let us not look down too haughtily on the Pharisees who clashed with Jesus over what constituted true worship with God. The majority of them were the best of people, who devoted their lives completely to guiding souls to God. It would be easy and comforting to simply dismiss them as a group of pious hypocrites. We should assume their sincerity in being shocked and outraged at the way Jesus departed from Jewish tradition. To make matters worse he told them they had missed the whole point of religion, which was to worship God with a sincere heart. Because they had made external observance, the supreme test of goodness, their religion had sunk to the level of mere lip-service. Their worship was worthless, an empty shell, nothing more than a bundle of pious practises.

Our Lord is pointing out something he wants us to notice. Christ's words to the Pharisees are a challenge and we can hardly deny that they apply to us also. The attitude of the Pharisee lurks within all of us, so a warning about it is never out of place. Jesus is appealing to us to be on our guard against merely external compliance with ritual. If we are to keep our worship of God in true focus we must call attention to what we are doing. Jesus is telling us that while man looks to appearances, God looks to the heart and cannot be deceived. He is demanding that our innermost thoughts as well as our outward actions stand up to God's scrutiny. We are to be continually searching out what God wants of us, purifying the way we live, and practising our religion. It is surprisingly easy for our prayers and Mass-going to sink into an empty ceremony, for our worship to become heartless and without love.

The big temptation is to leave ourselves out of this sermon and not to ask what our motives behind coming to Mass this morning were – to fulfil our Sunday obligation, to be seen, to parade our latest style or to worship the Lord with real devotion in our hearts? Could we be among those who take down a belief every Sunday morning but have it tucked away carefully as soon as we come home from church. There's no denying that some members of every Sunday congregation fall into the category of mere spectators. Remember, going to Holy Communion is good provided we are striving to become more Christ-like in our daily lives, which receiving the Lord is all about.

228

Wearing a religious medal or going on pilgrimage does not necessarily make us good Catholics. Joined hands are no substitutes for sincere prayer, coming from the heart.It is very easy to depart from God's will and appear religious at the same time, but lip-service, however well performed, falls short of worship. To be more than Sunday christians, the love of God must flow into our daily lives and into our work place.

Prayers of the Faithful

Our worship is meaningless unless it proceeds from a sincere heart. We pray now to God the Father to create within us a clean heart and a steadfast spirit.

1. We pray for the leaders of the church that they may always be guided by the light of the gospel and not seek security in structures. Lord, hear us.
2. For our parish community that we may not close our eyes to the real human needs of the poor who are in our midst. Lord, hear us.
3. May we realise that the real test of how we are carrying out God's will is to be found in the way we treat others. Lord, hear us.
4. As our young people return to school for another academic year, be with them to guide and help them in their studies. Lord, hear us.
5. We pray for the sick. May our caring be a source of strength in their weakness. Lord, hear us.
6. We remember our dead who have gone before us marked with the sign of faith. May they rest in peace. Lord, hear us.

Heavenly Father, create within us sincerity of heart so that we may love and respect others as you treasure them. We make our prayer through Christ our Lord. Amen.

Twenty-third Sunday of the Year

Spending time in the company of people who are deaf and dumb makes us realise how precious the gifts of speech and hearing are. Unlike us, they are cut off completely from the world of sound and have no experience of the conversation of friends, the laughter of children and the joy of listening to music. While our sympathy and pity are with the man in today's story, nevertheless, we regard him as one of the lucky ones, to have met Jesus who cured him, gave him a break in life and made him like the rest of us. We take for granted our ability to hear and speak, but both gifts are meant for a purpose even greater than human communication. They are also our means of listening to God and speaking his word. This is something we should never forget. What we hear and what we say determine to a great extent what we do and they make us the persons we are.

This is an occasion to express our concern and care for those who live lonely lives on the margins of society because of hearing and speech handicaps. However, it is good to remember that the deaf mute is not an historical figure from first century Israel. He resembles the whole human race. His plight is ours in so far as we refuse to listen to what God is saying to us and act upon it. We all need the healing hand of Christ to make us hear and speak the message of God properly. Jesus is the one who can remove deafness and dumbness from our being so that we can make full use of these faculties. Is it possible that we are like this man because of our refusal to give a listening ear to the lonely, the troubled, and the worried? How many times have we failed to utter a word of encouragement, of hope and thanks, or have kept a discreet silence when we should have spoken the truth? Then there are the problems we have in speaking to our partner or neighbours, because of a long standing row or simply out of jealousy, envy or pride.

What Jesus is saying to us is that the greatest tragedy of all is not to be born deaf and dumb, but to have ears and fail to hear and to have tongues and fail to speak. We are the deaf and dumb who need to be brought to Jesus for his healing touch, which brings communication where there are silences, companionship where there is loneliness, and encouragement where there is despair.

Prayer of the Faithful

We have heard in the gospel how Jesus responded to the needs of the deaf man. With confidence we pray to God the Father to fulfil our needs.

1. We pray for the church that the Holy Spirit will enlighten all its members and make them receptive to the healing message of the gospel. Lord, hear us.
2. We pray for those who are poor and neglected in our society. Help us to be more conscious of them as persons who are our equals in the sight of God. Lord, hear us.
3. That we may always use the gift of speech to proclaim the glory of God. Lord, hear us.
4. We pray for the sick and the handicapped. May they realise through our caring that they have a special role to play in the saving of souls. Lord, hear us.
5. We remember the young people of our community who have started a new school year. We pray that they may discover all that is good in life as they grow in the ways of faith. Lord, hear us.
6. We pray for the dead. May they rest in peace and may those who mourn them be comforted. Lord, hear us.

Eternal Father, heal our selfishness and open our hearts to receive the good news of salvation. We make this prayer through Christ our Lord. Amen.

Twenty-fourth Sunday of the Year

The shadow of Calvary falls across today's readings and stretches into our lives with the announcement by Jesus that unless we take up our cross and follow him we are unworthy of his company. This is a reminder of something we would rather forget because nobody wants to suffer. We find it off-putting and prefer to avoid the hard things of life. All of us are very much children of this world in the way we crave for pleasure, comfort and soft times. Peter spoke for everyone when he objected to what Christ said about suffering, rejection and death – it ran as contrary to his expectations as it does to ours.

The age old problem of why people suffer has puzzled thinking minds down the centuries and has never been satisfactorily resolved. Jesus never explained why we have to suffer, nor did he rid the world of suffering. What he did was to give suffering meaning and value by filling it with his presence. In his life he showed us the proper approach to suffering and how to put the crosses that come our way to good use.

In a world gone wrong, sooner or later we are all involved in suffering. It may take the form of a disgrace that is public, an addiction that forever threatens, nights of despair or years of loneliness. We need to name these afflictions for what they are – crosses. Our Lord suffered so much himself that he has sympathy for us in the trials that beset us on our earthly pilgrimage. He encourages us to shoulder our crosses and follow in his footsteps. The only sure promise we have is that every cross, no matter how difficult and burdensome, if united with Christ's cross, becomes meaningful and a source of salvation for ourselves and each other. Crosses are ladders that lead to heaven.

Jesus makes it crystal clear about the high cost involved in being one of his people and never at any time pretends that it is less than demanding. Suffering is the blood, sweat and tears of life. The cross, which is planted in the centre of christian living, is not an invitation to lead a miserable life but is a call to hope in the face of those sufferings, which are the normal part of human existence. We must accept that God's ways of doing things run contrary to our expectations. Our Lord's teaching is for real life and real life can be very difficult.

Prayer of the Faithful

As we are gathered to celebrate the mystery of our salvation, let us turn to God the Father with confidence and implore his mercy.

1. We pray that the church may be a beacon of light and a sign of hope in the world for all who are suffering. Lord, hear us.
2. That christians may follow in the footsteps of Christ by accepting their daily crosses in imitation of the sufferings of Jesus. Lord, hear us.
3. That God may comfort and console those who are finding their crosses heavy and burdensome. Lord, hear us.
4. For the sick of our community that, they may see in their illness a splinter of the cross of Christ. Lord, hear us.
5. For our relatives and friends who have gone before us in faith. May they be in the presence of Christ who triumphed over suffering and death. Lord, hear us.

Heavenly Father, hear the prayers of your people and help us to embrace the daily challenge of the cross. We make our prayer through Christ our Lord. Amen.

Twenty-fifth Sunday of the Year

The disciples never cease to amaze us. At the very moment when Jesus is telling them about his coming passion and death, they are not even listening. They are so immersed in a quarrel, squabbling over who is the greatest among them, that what he says does not even register with them. Somehow we would really expect better from his close followers. When asked by Christ what were they arguing about they were anything but proud of their discussion. In fact they were clearly embarrassed and remained silent.

Jesus uses this occasion to put them right and to point out to them what constitutes true greatness in God's eyes. True greatness, he says, does not come from having power and influence over people but consists in humble service. He tells his ambitious disciples that everyone is important and that greatness comes from being available to all people even down to little children. Children are close to the heart of Jesus because they are innocent, wear no masks and are uncontaminated by the selfish ways of the world.

This is a very basic instruction on the kind of followers Jesus wants us all to be and challenges us to turn our worldly value-system upside down. Isn't it true that we are rather like the apostles arguing on the road about which of them was the greatest? We are full of selfish ambition; always putting ourselves first, wanting the best of everything. It is easy for us to think of what we have as completely ours, no thanks to anyone else. We fail to remember that we are stewards of the many precious gifts which God entrusts us with and which he intends to be used in his service. Being available and meeting the needs of others means being present in a hundred and one ways. People need to be listened to, understood and appreciated.

Christ' teaching is certainly no formula for worldly success as it involves constant drudgery and ingratitude. This was the pattern of service Jesus set for us when he washed the feet of the disciples at the Last Supper. We are called to do the Lord's work so that Jesus can give his love to others through us. Every life gives opportunities to serve those around. A mother is at her loving best and pleasing to God when she is rearing her children properly, as is a home-help who puts her heart and soul into caring

234

for an elderly person. To be a disciple means being open to what God may ask of us at any given moment, even in very small things. If the lifestyle of the christian is suffering service in the footsteps of Jesus, then the service that counts is the service that costs.

Prayer of the Faithful

As children we come now to God our Father, searching for a deeper faith in order to understand the meaning of suffering in our lives.

1. We pray for the leaders of the church, that they may keep before us a clear vision of patient endurance in the turmoils of our time. Lord, hear us.
2. We pray that parents may inspire their children with the love of Christ. Lord, hear us.
3. That we may realise that true greatness is not a matter of power and respectability but is to be found only in the service of others. Lord, hear us.
4. We pray for the sick that they may unite their sufferings with those of Jesus on the cross. Lord, hear us.
5. We pray for the dead who have gone before us marked with the sign of faith. May they be freed from their sins. Lord, hear us.

Heavenly Father, give us the courage to accept whatever suffering may come our way on the path of life. Lead us into the fullness of joy in your presence. We make our prayer through Christ our Lord. Amen.

Twenty-sixth Sunday of the Year

The apostles were anything but pleased when they witnessed an outsider casting out demons in the name of Jesus. They resented his intrusion, were jealous and felt threatened, because he was doing their work and yet was not part of their group. He had no right to be using the name of the Saviour, so John made a complaint in the hope of having this unlicenced preacher silenced. John must have been surprised that Jesus refused to stop the man from doing good work in his name. Jesus made it clear that all good comes from God the Father and that doing charitable work was not the exclusive right of his followers. God moves where he wills and chooses whom he wills. His spirit is at work beyond the confines of established religion.

With the best will in the world, we can all fall prey to the type of thinking and misguided notion that only the church can contain truth and only its members can perform spiritual works. It is a temptation we all have. When we think along these lines we are inclined to turn the church in on herself and deny that great works can be achieved outside her influence. We forget that an action can be good and Godly without being performed by a christian. Goodness in the world comes from God and not from men. Even within the church there is the temptation to form our own select groupings; to promote the club mentality which is basically about being in and keeping other people out. We've all witnessed unhealthy rivalry between different church organisations, different parishes and yet the aim of all is about furthering the kingdom of God. Charitable organisations, with the same objective for alleviating poverty or helping senior citizens, can be at logger-heads with one another about who is to collect, where to collect and when to collect. Their cause is very worthwhile but their tactics can sometimes be anything but edifying, giving the impression that goodness is a closed shop in their name and not in the name of Christ.

The gospel tells us that any person of goodwill doing their best to follow Christ's footsteps graces the world. Every good deed contributes towards the battle against evil, so downgrading the motives behind someone's charitable gestures amounts to spiritual begrudgery. God's action is not limited to any class of people. He may be sending his message to us in the most unexpected and tragic events that befall us. Goodness is where we find it.

Prayer of the Faithful

We pray now to God the Father for enlightenment as we bring the needs of our broken and divided world before him.

1. We pray for peace and harmony in the church, so that the gospel may be preached more effectively. Lord, hear us.
2. For the gift of forgiveness and reconciliation and the healing of hurts caused by division and bickering. Lord, hear us.
3. For a greater appreciation of the goodness of people as a channel of God's spirit at work in the world. Lord, hear us.
4. We pray for the old, the lonely, the handicapped and the sick. We ask God to strengthen them with the warmth of his presence. Lord, hear us.
5. For all our friends who have died and have gone before us. May they share in the peace and happiness of God's kingdom. Lord, hear us.

Heavenly Father, help us to see all people through your eyes. Grant us the breadth of mind and generosity of heart to accept what is good from whatever source. We make our prayer through Christ our Lord. Amen.

Twenty-seventh Sunday of the Year

What Jesus was being asked by the Pharisees was where he stood concerning marriage and divorce. He left them in no doubt about his position, emphasising that marriage is a state of life created by God himself, a lifelong union between one man and one woman kept together by a pledge of love and loyalty made in the presence of God. It's a union that cannot be undone, so when a couple marry there is no power on earth, short of death, that can free them to remarry. 'What God has joined together man must not separate.' We are called this morning to reflect on the dignity of marriage and on the permanence of the marriage commitment. This is a question that is surfacing more and more in today's church as christians are bombarded from all sides with the worldly view that life-long marriage is unacceptable. Few beliefs set us so much apart from the world as Christ's teaching on marriage, which directs us to obey God and not man.

Life could be described as a journey, and marriage is two people making that journey together in partnership. The wedding day is but the starting point when the church blesses the couple and family and friends gather to celebrate their departure and to wish them good luck for the road ahead. The sight of newly-weds pledging themselves to each other stirs something deep within us. It's an acknowledgement to the community that their lives have taken a new direction through the power of love, which demands mutual respect and trust of each other. Together they go forward to meet the rough and smooth of life and to weather the storms that even true love cannot escape. The church's blessing and family smiles are no magic wand to smooth the way for instant happiness.

A good marriage must be created. It's not so much about finding the right partner as being the right person. In marriage the little things are the most important, like speaking words of appreciation and demonstrating gratitude in thoughtful ways. It's having the capacity to forgive and to forget which means never going to sleep angry. A married couple cannot stand together and face the world unless their union is based on love. Love is what cements and binds that relationship together for life. It's a hope and a trust that has to be lived down the years through good times and bad times. Love can be easily reneged upon and then marriage fades away and dies. The solemn pledge, made at the altar of God, to love each other for better or for worse, should not trip lightly off any tongue.

Prayer of the Faithful

With confidence we come and present our needs to God our Father, who loves all his children.

1. We pray for the leaders of the church, that they may keep before its members the true dignity of marriage and so help couples stay together, in their sacred calling. Lord, hear us.
2. We pray for married couples, that they may be sensitive to each other's needs and find true happiness in their lives together. Lord, hear us.
3. We pray for those experiencing difficulties in their marriage. May they receive the grace to persevere in their commitment. Lord, hear us.
4. For the old, the lonely and the sick, that they may find love and support within the community. Lord, hear us.
5. We ask the Lord to give all those who have died a place in his eternal kingdom. Lord, hear us.

Almighty Father, you have given us marriage as a sign of your love. Help us to live in harmony with one another. We make our prayer through Christ our Lord. Amen.

Twenty-eighth Sunday of the Year

In an age when many of us find it difficult to make ends meet, contemporary society bombards us with a set of values based on the need for material security. It judges our success by the size of our bank account, the extent of our possessions and the exclusiveness of the area in which we live. But the wisdom that comes from God measures differently and ranks power and riches as nothing. There is more to life than what is immediately apparent and spiritual values run deeper than worldly standards. We are told this morning that we can't buy our way into heaven. Wealth mixes with worship of God just about as well as oil with water.

The rich young man prided himself on his goodness. He was the essence of respectability; a stickler for going to church and observing the commandments. He had his act together and was assertive enough to come forward and to ask Christ a fundamental question: 'What must I do to inherit eternal life?' The answer he got was more than he bargained for. His big boast was that he had done nothing wrong in his life, but Jesus was not all that impressed that he had kept out of harm's way. Christ was more interested in the use he had made of his life, in the good he had done and whether he was prepared to go out of his way to help others. He looked him straight in the eyes and invited him to sell all he had and to come follow him. Here was a young man brimming with life, yet the peace that he sought was placed beyond his reach, because his vision was limited to his possessions. He went away saddened because he was unable to make the sacrifice. Far from regarding him as a model to be imitated, Jesus singles him out as a warning.

Being rich and having lots of money may not be our problem but all of us are invited to answer God's call: 'Come follow me.' Jesus is asking us the same question: 'Am I worth following?' He is not asking us to admire his way of life but to live it fully and not as part-time followers. Discipleship is always costly and following Jesus makes very stark demands on our lifestyle. Our following Christ means making the best use of our present situation and placing our lives in his hands. We have only one life and Christ is inviting us to leave the world a better place for our presence than we found it. We achieve this by helping others and not by grasping everything for ourselves.

Prayer of the Faithful

We now pray to God our Father for the strength to overcome the temptations placed in our way by the lure of wealth and security.

1. We pray for the church that she may continually show concern and support for the neglected and down-trodden of the Third World. Lord, hear us.
2. For all who call themselves disciples of Christ that they may see what really matters in life is concern for others less fortunate than themselves. Lord, hear us.
3. For the wisdom to always seek first the kingdom of God and to spend our lives in its service. Lord, hear us.
4. We pray for the sick that they may be consoled and strengthened by Christ. Lord, hear us.
5. We remember our deceased relatives and friends. May they enjoy the victory of Christ in the kingdom of heaven. Lord, hear us.

Heavenly Father, give us the courage to remain poor in spirit and to follow the example of Christ, who became poor so that we could become rich. We ask this through Christ Our Lord. Amen .

Twenty-ninth Sunday of the Year

Society, at any age, can never get away from the problems posed by status and rank. It was no different in the time of Jesus. The old controversy about who was the greatest surfaces once again amongst the apostles. This time James and John are requesting favoured treatment from Jesus. It was no small honour they were demanding while over-looking the suffering involved in Christ's passion and death. With an eye to the future they were aiming at being part of Christ's inner circle, sitting beside him at his right and left hand in glory.

After calming the indignation of the other apostles created by James' and John's naked bid for promotion over their heads, Jesus clearly spells out a new standard of greatness and status, stating that success in his kingdom is not measured by worldly standards. There is no place in his community for ambitious power-hungry men who are motivated solely by self-interest. Jesus wants his followers to think in terms of service rather than of authority. In any community he wants those who have authority to be seen at the service of those under their guidance. Christ lived what he preached. His whole life, from working as a carpenter in Nazareth, to dying on the cross at Calvary set the example of such service. At the last supper, when he got up from the table, took a towel and basin and washed the feet of the apostles, he highlighted in dramatic form the importance of service. In so doing he was calling on his followers to share in spreading his gospel by giving themselves completely to his way of life.

We serve God best by helping one another. As adults we are all involved in the exercise of authority in some shape or form, whether at home or in our place of work. In leading the way we should be the first to obey the laws that we lay down. There is to be no lording it over those in our care because authority is not for the controlling of people but for the proper guidance of the community. To exercise it properly, a great help is never to lose sight of the importance of service and availability to those under our control – for this is a reflection of the life of Jesus in our own particular circumstances.

When Christ warned his disciples not to set up worldly power-structures within the christian community, he was very

242

much aware of our human failings. We are all inclined to be self-ish and to live for ourselves without showing much concern for others. The attitude of 'What's in it for me?' runs deep in all our hearts. The standard of greatness in his kingdom is the standard of the cross. That's why we must never lose sight of the character of service.

Prayer of the Faithful

Mindful of the words of Jesus, that the greatest is the one who serves, we pray to God our Father for a true spirit of service among all people.

1. We pray that the leaders of the church may be true servants, act-ing with the same concern that Christ showed for his followers. Lord, hear us.
2. We pray that leaders of governments may exercise their power for the good of their people and avoid discord and distrust. Lord, hear us.
3. That we may realise that success in God's eyes is not measured by the standards of the world but by the respect we give to our neighbour. Lord, hear us.
4. That those who are sick may realise that their suffering, under-taken in union with Christ, can be turned into a great blessing. Lord, hear us.
5. We pray for the dead, that they may reap the rewards of their earthly sufferings in eternal life. Lord, hear us.

Heavenly Father, help us to serve each other by imitating your Son who laid down his life for us. We make our prayer through Christ our Lord. Amen.

Thirtieth Sunday of the Year

The blind Bartimaeus is an example of what our faith and trust in Jesus ought to be. He has firm confidence in the person of Jesus and is not put off by the abuse of the crowd, who regard him as a nobody, telling him to keep quiet. Shouting and waving his arms in the air he persists with the plea, 'Son of David, have pity on me.' This cry of desperation from his heart, made in complete trust, attracts the attention of Jesus. When asked by Jesus what he wants, there is no doubt about his request. Life for him without sight has been one long night full of darkness. His prayer is: 'Lord, that I may see.' With the healing touch of Jesus, a whole new world opens up as he is ushered into the light of day. Although Bartimaeus may have been a beggar, he is a person of gratitude because on receiving his sight he immediately follows Jesus.

The fact that we have eyes does not mean that we always see what is most important in life. There is more to sight than merely seeing the light of day. Eyes are of little use if we fail to see the hand of God at work in our lives. At times we all experience such darkness and are sorely in need of the light of God. In caring for the blind Bartimaeus, Christ is telling us that there is an even worse state of blindness than physical blindness. We all suffer from spiritual blindness and Jesus is letting us know that he can cure this illness and prevent us from groping around in darkness.

There are so many ways in which we lack spiritual vision; hatred, pride and jealousy can prevent us from seeing goodness in our neighbours. Refusal to pay our debts or to do an honest week's work for the wages we are collecting means we are blinded to a sense of justice. Never being satisfied with what we have and always wanting more material goods is an indication that we are blinded by greed. We are all victims of some sort of blindness but to become aware of it and to have the scales removed from our eyes, we must be continually searching and praying for more light. Only prayer and trust in Jesus, who is the light of the world, can dispel such darkness and restore our true spiritual vision. The closer we are to Jesus, the more light there is in our lives. The cry of the blind man, 'Lord, that I may see,' is a prayer that should constantly be on our lips.

Prayer of the Faithful

We ask God the Father to open our eyes so that we may follow him whole-heartedly.

1. We pray for the church, that it may be a beacon of light communicating the message of Jesus to all people. Lord, hear us.
2. That through acts of kindness we may always seek out those who are despised, rejected or unloved in our society. Lord, hear us.
3. That like Bartimaeus we may have firm confidence in Jesus and follow him on the pathway of life. Lord, hear us.
4. For those who are sick and suffering, that by uniting themselves with Christ's suffering they may share in his glory. Lord, hear us.
5. We remember our deceased relatives and friends. Grant them eternal rest and perpetual light. Lord, hear us.

Father in heaven, fill us with your love and dispel the darkness from our lives so that we may work in the light of Christ your Son. We make our prayer through Christ our Lord. Amen.

Thirty-first Sunday of the Year

To those willing to listen, Jesus goes straight to the heart of what constitutes true worship and spells out clearly the guidelines for good christian living. He tells us God's commandments can be reduced to two: love of God and love of our neighbour. We are to love God with all we have got and, as if that is not enough, we are to love our neighbour as ourselves. This is the total and complete commitment of love that Jesus is talking about and calling upon us to practice. It is easily defined but presents us with a difficult challenge as it is far removed from the way in which most of us live. A moment's reflection will reveal that the person we care most for and look after best is our self.

Religion is about going up to God and out to our neighbour at the same time. Love of God is so interwoven with love of our neighbour that it is a difficult balance to achieve. If we don't strike the happy medium we can easily separate religion from life. To say our prayers and attend Sunday Mass, while ignoring our neighbour, is a mere half-hearted response to God's love, which presents no challenge. It amounts to slicing the commandments down the middle and living with half the gospel. Worshipping God in isolation makes a mockery of religion; likewise love of our neighbour, which has no reference to and does not proceed from the love of God, comes to nothing more than a form of refined self-love.

The biting question to be faced is whether the love of God is evident in the love we have for our neighbour. Take home-life for example: as the years pass it's so easy to slip into the habit of taking our partner for granted, looking upon her as a provider of meals, a maker of beds and a housekeeper, while failing to respect her as a person in her own right. The same can be true of the children; prized possessions, no doubt, but my property.Perhaps it's time to become a bit more conscious of those we have ignored and failed to treat as people and to see the faces of those who desperately need our love. We show our love for God through definite and deliberate works of love for the sick, the old and the lonely because we meet God in their lives. Christian love is about getting out of ourselves and reaching towards the needy. The kingdom of God is continually proclaimed when the love of God and the love of our neighbour are evident in the community.

Prayer of the Faithful

Needing the love of God our Father above all things, we now open our hearts and turn to him in prayer.

1. We pray that the church may radiate the warmth of the love of Christ and so contribute to the peace of the world. Lord, hear us.
2. We pray for our own community. Help us to appreciate one another and become more sensitive to the needs of the poor. Lord, hear us.
3. We pray that our homes may be places full of your peaceful presence where we are taught to care and respect others as children of God. Lord, hear us.
4. We commend to your loving care all who are sick in mind and body. May they be given the strength to face their difficulties. Lord, hear us.
5. We pray for those who died in the hope of resurrection. Grant them eternal rest. Lord, hear us.

Heavenly Father, make us worthy of your call. Give us the grace to live out this commandment of love in word and deed. We ask this through Christ our Lord. Amen.

Thirty-second Sunday of the Year

We have all heard the saying 'It's the thought that counts, it's the self giving in the gift which expresses love' – and that is what Jesus is telling us in the story of the widow's mite. What makes her gift valuable and important is not its size but the heart and the sacrifice behind it. In the eyes of the passers-by, the widow's offering is virtually worthless but in the sight of God it is most precious. After throwing her last two coins in the box, she is able to say: 'This is the best I can do for it's all that I have got.' What wins her the Lord's favour and earns his commendation, is the fact that she keeps nothing back for herself. Her small gift is her all. In a way she is making an offering of her total life to God.

This little incident outside the temple is worth recalling because it draws our attention to the manner in which Jesus weighs us up and judges us. While we are content to be guided by appearances, to judge people by what they possess and to value presents by how much they cost, Christ measures us in a totally different way. His searching eyes penetrate into our souls and reveal the inner motives and the hidden intentions behind our actions. He is concerned with the sacrifices we are making, how much of our lives are surrendered to him and whether we are taking his demands seriously.

The hidden value of the widow's offering teaches us that material goods are not the most important factor in the world. The issue being discussed in this gospel is discipleship: generosity of spirit, not money, for we all have something more precious than money to offer God. What God is looking for is our lives. He wants our hearts and not our possessions. So often our giving and contributions to worthy causes are conscience solvers. They amount to a fulfilling of the externals without indicating any real compassion of heart. We can all use them as an excuse to avoid personal involvement and dedicated service to the marginalised of our area. What is hardest to give is ourselves in love and concern, because it costs more than reaching for our purses. Our Christmas presents are another case in point.

Learning to give generously to God is a difficult lesson to master and yet there is no true following of Christ without such self-denial. This gospel story invites us to live in a way that hurts and does not count the cost, for it is in giving that we receive. Our life story can easily be one of non-response to the needs of others, indicating how little we really give of ourselves to God. There is an immense gap between what we are and what we should be. The life-giving sacrifice of Jesus, who gave up everything for us on the cross, can inspire us to bridge that gap.

Prayer of the Faithful

Our hearts go out in prayer to God the Father who gives bread to the hungry and who upholds the rights of the widow and the orphan.

1. We pray for our Holy Father and bishops of the church. May they never waver in working for those who are poor and heavily burdened. Lord, hear us.
2. May the Lord strengthen and comfort those who have lost their life's partner and are now deprived of their supportive love. Lord, hear us.
3. For single parents and those who are living in irregular unions. May they grow in holiness of life and be blessed with God's love. Lord, hear us.
4. We pray for the sick, for whom it is our duty and privilege to care, that they may join their suffering to that of Christ. Lord, hear us.
5. Let us ask our heavenly Father to welcome into his eternal home our friends and relatives who died recently. Lord, hear us.

Heavenly Father, open our hearts to those around us so that we may recognise your presence in neighbours and friends and discover the happiness of sharing with them. We make our prayer through Christ our Lord. Amen.

Thirty-third Sunday of the Year

As Autumn leaves signal the end of another season and the approach of Winter, the church, on this Sunday every November, invites us to pause momentarily for serious thought. It directs our attention to the end of the world, the last judgement and the Lord's coming in glory. Every age has its share of false prophets, scare-mongering, predicting doom and calamity, so we may not take easily to such a message. It's apt to release, within our minds, great surges of fear about punishment, destruction and death. Yet scripture is not meant to frighten or threaten but to give consolation, hope and encouragement in life's difficulties. The great truth of the gospel is that God's love has triumphed over the power of evil and will put all things right. God is on our side and will see us through our present troubles.

The readings aim to focus our minds on an overall view of life's purpose so as to encourage us to live on a more spiritual level. We are on an earthly pilgrimage and have within us deep-seated longings for a better world. At journey's end we are hoping for an everlasting happiness, for a bright dawn to emerge out of our present darkness. What is important to remember is that our own death spells the end of our particular world. At that moment, life's mission is accomplished and we go forward to meet Christ face to face. It may happen at any time and we've got to be prepared for the encounter. While we cannot avoid a sudden death, we can take steps against an unprepared death by living each day carefully as if it is our last and by keeping God ever in our sights.

Nowadays we seldom hear talk of hell. It has become a forbidden conversational topic and yet the reality of it all is, Christ states that it is possible for us to shipwreck our lives, turn our backs on him and not be called into his company on the last day. Hell means eternal separation from God who is love; a calm and deliberate rejection of his mercy. It will be a sad parting, a missed opportunity, but God will always respect our freedom. We will have no-one to blame but ourselves for preventing God from drawing us to eternal life. Where we will stand when Christ comes, will depend on the way we are trying to live now. Being his friend at the moment of death will not be a matter of luck. We are what we are doing. Christ comes to us each day offering us his life and inviting us to his side. The call he makes at death is only the final in a series of approaches. Judgement is happening all the time.

If we are carrying God in our hearts wherever we go, heaven will not come as a surprise, but as a full blossoming of the world we have been building for ourselves. It makes sense to pause and to do some spiritual stock-taking. We can all check what our relationship with God is like and where our hearts and values lie. Have we put our confidence in the way he has shown us? We are people with a glorious future so let's not spoil it by refusing to live upright lives.

Prayer of the Faithful

Having taken to heart the saving words of scripture, encouraging us towards final perseverance, we now approach God the Father in prayer.

1. We pray for our Holy Father and the bishops of the church. May they attract all nations towards the way of salvation by the effective witness of their own lives. Lord, hear us.
2. We pray for those who live their lives in the fear of persecution. May they have the strength to persevere in spite of all difficulties. Lord, hear us.
3. We pray for ourselves that we may prepare for the coming of the kingdom by daily lives of truth, honesty and goodness. Lord, hear us.
4. We pray for those who are bearing the burden of sickness. May they experience your love in our concern for them. Lord, hear us.
5. We pray for our dead. May you bring them into your kingdom of light, happiness and peace. Lord, hear us.

Heavenly Father, you are always near to us. You know our needs better than we do ourselves. Grant that we may live this life with our hearts open to your forgiving love. We ask this through Christ our Lord. Amen.

Our Lord Jesus Christ, Universal King

Today the church year draws to a close on a sombre note with a gospel scene from Good Friday. Jesus stands on trial before Pilate accused of being a king. With death staring him in the face his reply is crystal clear. He admits to being a king, but not in a recognisable worldly manner of kingship, as his horizons are not limited to earthly life. Christ is a spiritual leader who rules by truth and love. He is out to touch the hearts and minds of all people and claim their souls for God. His mission on earth is to unfold a vision of this new world, to announce the Good News that God counts us as family, regards us as his children and in return seeks our allegiance.

By the way we live, we declare where our loyalties lie. Christ tells us to stand firmly by service of our neighbour, forgiveness, love and solidarity with the poor. In his own life we have a model of how to put these values into practice. Down the centuries his followers have imitated his example and laid down their lives for the sake of his kingdom. We know the standards to build our lives around. If we take his call seriously, he will be there to meet us in the end.

The Feast of Christ the King provides an excellent opportunity to review the quality of our christian commitment. What effort have we been making to allow Christ's kingdom to come alive in our hearts and in our community? Jesus is calling us to rise above the basic instincts of selfishness, bitterness and pride and to pledge our lives in his service, because it is God's world although we might not think so now. In our better moments we realise Christ is the way. The effort involved in rising above a worldly level of behaviour does not come easily and brings us no end of trouble and frustration.

The dilemma confronting Pilate, when he finds himself face to face with Jesus, has parallels in our own lives. Pilate is obviously disturbed, clearly under pressure, a victim of indecision but anxious to avoid trouble. He is convinced Jesus is innocent yet does not want to lose face by offending his powerful accusers. He fails to follow his conscience and washes his hands of Jesus. It is the same story for so many of us. We too wash our hands of our christian responsibilities. Within our family, at work or in the neighbourhood, how often do we take the easy way out and let christian standards go by the board? There is no denying that christian values are not popular. We need not expect an easy passage through life if we are standing for what we believe. The cross and suffering will become our throne also. Today's feast calls us to make room for Christ in our hearts by imitating his life however imperfectly.

Prayer of the Faithful

Encouraged by the word of God we turn now with grateful hearts to the Father and thank him for the work of reconciliation achieved through his Son, Jesus Christ, on the cross.

1. We pray for the leaders of the church. May they always give witness to the values of Christ's kingdom in the preaching of the gospel. Lord, hear us.
2. We pray for all peoples that they may come to recognise Christ as their King and Saviour. May they help spread his kingdom through the promotion of justice, comradeship, forgiveness and love. Lord, hear us.
3. We pray for all families, that they may be united in harmony and live in God's love. Lord, hear us.
4. We pray for all who are seriously ill in hospital, for the housebound and all who are in need of Christ's healing. Lord, hear us.
5. We pray for our dead. May they enter into Christ's heavenly kingdom and enjoy forever the lasting peace of paradise. Lord, hear us.

Heavenly Father, you have called us to be part of your kingdom. Help us to build on earth a home which bears the imprint of heaven. We make our prayer through Jesus Christ. Amen.

Immaculate Conception

Most of us occasionally enjoy recalling the times of our childhood. We love looking back on those carefree moments of yesteryear, when we knew nothing about responsibility, and insecurity was not our lot. In those days we had our mother and although we were not able to appreciate her then, we now realise that it was her loving presence which made us happy and secure. Deep down in our hearts we have an affection for our mother which nothing on earth can take away.

On this feast, just before Christmas, we read the gospel story of the annunciation which describes the way God prepared a worthy dwelling place for his Son in the midst of the human race. Motherhood was furtherest from Mary's thoughts when the Angel Gabriel appeared to her and announced that she was to conceive and bear a Son and name him Jesus. Her reaction was one of complete surprise because she was unaware of the exceptional relationship that existed between herself and God. She could not imagine why an ordinary girl, destined for a commonplace life, should enjoy such special favour. Nevertheless she humbly surrendered her thoughts and heart to God and accepted what she did not understand. This was the most important decision that ever touched the human race because at that moment Jesus Christ rested in her womb. God made man came into our world and began dismantling the reign of darkness which started with the sin of Adam and Eve. Through Mary's freely uttered 'Yes' God's plan was fully realised. She had nothing to offer but herself. Yet from her humanity she bore the Saviour who overcame sin and death.

We are celebrating an outpouring of grace, lavished on a frail young girl, whom we honour as the heroine of God's people. Mary stands before us as the finest example of what it means to be a disciple walking here and now in the footsteps of Christ. She is everything God wishes a human being to be; a beautiful person unscarred by sin and fashioned from the first moment of her existence in the image and likeness of her creator. God invites each one of us to continue Mary's 'Yes' by welcoming Jesus and making room for him in our lives. She is an example of what God can accomplish within us if we allow ourselves to be moulded and shaped by his hands, because what God wills for Mary he wills for us also.

As we struggle with our own sinfulness and find ourselves in situations where we are unwilling to immediately say 'Yes' to the Lord, Mary is in a unique position to help. She looks at us with a motherly love and draws us gently to herself. Mary is our spiritual mother to whom we can turn in our troubles. With a motherly love she guides and encourages us to walk in the way of Christ, which is the way of light. On this feast day, we ask Mary to share her privilege with us and make our bodies worthy resting places for her Son.

Prayer of the Faithful

Following the example of Mary, we praise and thank God the Father who out of the abundance of his generosity gave us his only Son as our Saviour and redeemer.

1. We pray for our Holy Father and the bishops of the church that like Mary they may listen to the word of God and spare no effort in spreading it. Lord, hear us.
2. We pray for mothers of families that in moments of trial and suffering they may look to Mary for encouragement and help. Lord, hear us.
3. We pray for those who have strayed from the practice of the faith. May they find in Mary a true refuge and a source of hope. Lord, hear us.
4. We pray that the sick, through the intercession of Mary, may experience the healing hand of Christ laid upon them. Lord, hear us.
5. We pray that the dead may be welcomed into the company of the saints and join with Mary in the eternal praise of God. Lord, hear us.

Heavenly Father, you have called us to do your will. Give us the help we need each day to be faithful to you. We make our prayer through Christ our Lord. Amen.

Saint Patrick

We pause on our Lenten journey to honour the patron saint of our nation. Patrick is remembered, not alone in Ireland, but world-wide on his feast day. Unlike the majority of Celtic saints from the Island of Saints and Scholars, he was not Irish born, but an outsider. Patrick came from Roman Britain of christian parents,but at the age of sixteen was captured and sold into slavery by Irish pirate raiders plundering the Welsh coast. Deprived of his freedom in his mid-teens, Patrick's life in captivity was grim, difficult and painful. We are told that he spent six years shepherding swine and living roughly on a bleak Antrim hillside. During that time when he constantly experienced cold, hunger and exhaustion, not only did he learn the language and the customs of his captors, but in the silence and loneliness which surrounded him, he discovered God and the real meaning of prayer. It was a desert experience and a painful process which built up Patrick's robust faith and solid spirituality. Eventually he made his escape, was re-united with his family and began his studies for the priesthood. All the time a dream about Ireland kept haunting Patrick and in it the call from God rang clear. He knew that he had to return there and preach the gospel to those people who had deprived him of his freedom.

Patrick's work in bringing christianity to Ireland was not easy but he continued to preach the faith, ready for death at any time amidst personal danger. In spite of fierce opposition and persecution he set up monasteries and convents and worked to abolish paganism by adapting ancient Irish celebrations into christian feasts. By his way of life, he proclaimed that Christ's love and friendship were more powerful than any passing trial.

When Patrick died there was a great sorrow throughout the land. All who had found inspiration in his preaching and teaching mourned the news of his passing. On arrival in Ireland he had encountered a barbarous people, ignorant of God and worshipping idols. At his death he had left behind a society which, by a miracle of grace, was truly converted to christianity. While this feast day is an occasion for joy and celebration, we must not overlook its central figure who has become the symbol of our identity as a christian people. Having inherited a religious tradition from an honoured past, it could happen that familiarity with the faith has bred contempt within us and that we are no longer open to the mystery of Jesus. The voice of Patrick speaks in every generation with the invitation to share the faith he brought by living lives of loving service. The completeness of his commitment to God was lived out in day-to-day trials, sufferings and failures. His brand of holiness is open to all who are striving to love God and are dedicated to doing his will.

Prayer of the Faithful

United with one another, and with the generations of believers that have gone before us in the faith of St Patrick, we make our prayer to God the Father.

1. That the church may be filled with the spirit of obedience to God's will which was so evident in the life of St Patrick. Lord, hear us.
2. We remember in a very special way Irish people who have made their homes in other countries. May we all be reunited in our heavenly home. Lord, hear us.
3. For perseverance in the faith which St Patrick brought to our country at so great a cost. Lord, hear us.
4. That all who are sick may experience God's healing and comforting presence. Lord, hear us.
5. We pray for all the dead, that the Lord may receive them into his kingdom. Lord, hear us.

Heavenly Father, keep us true to the faith to which St Patrick dedicated his life. Support us and make us aware of your presence in our lives. We ask this through Christ our Lord. Amen.

Assumption

There are times when the monotony of daily living and the drudgery of dull routine sap all our energy and eat into our souls. It usually results in a weakening of our conviction that the Lord is present and at work in our lives. We may even go so far as to doubt the possibility of a hereafter. At such moments we are crying out for the kind of reassurance and comfort that this feast day brings, for in contrast to such despair, Mary's Assumption helps lift our minds and hearts above the encircling gloom. It reminds us of our final homecoming by assuring us that there is another dimension to our existence and that death has not the final say.

This gospel opens a window on Mary's life. We get a glimpse of her as a young woman full of joy, hope and happiness, setting out in haste over the hill country to visit her cousin Elizabeth. Both women had great news to share. Although well on in years, Elizabeth was soon to give birth to John the Baptist while Mary was carrying the Saviour of the world in her womb. Their conversation was an outpouring of joy. Mary experienced happy times but she was not spared any of the trials of a mother rearing her child. There was nothing grand about the home of this faithful mother, living within the confines of the small village of Nazareth. Mary was a good wife to Joseph the carpenter. She knew the humdrum routine of ordinary housework and was open to the uncertainties of what tomorrow would bring. The sword of sorrow promised by Simeon at the presentation of the infant Jesus in the temple, continually cut through her heart and made its presence felt from time to time. There were many things in life she did not understand, much that she found painful to accept and still through all not knowing what lay before her, Mary never took back the 'Yes' she had answered to the angel. Jesus was always at the centre of her existence.

All lives must end, but the details of Mary's death are lost in the haze of history. Having completed her earthly pilgrimage, she was assumed, body and soul, into heavenly glory. It was the final flowering and crowning grace of Mary's friendship with God. Mary's Assumption reinforces hope in our own future because she points forward to our final homecoming. Where she has gone we hope to follow. This feast is a reminder that our bodies are temples of the Holy Spirit, and that the joys of eternal life are what

God wishes to share with all his adopted sons and daughters. In the meantime our chief concern is to become more like Jesus, by allowing our lives to be influenced by Mary, who has so much to teach us about her son.

Prayer of the Faithful

As we celebrate Mary's Assumption we unite our prayers with her and confidently place our needs before God the Father.

1. We pray that the leaders of the church may be encouraged, strengthened and renewed in their service of God, through the intercession of Mary. Lord, hear us.
2. We pray that, following the example of Mary, all mothers may make their homes dwelling places of love and holiness. Lord, hear us.
3. That those who have lost their way in life may turn for refuge to Mary the Mother of Mercies. Lord, hear us.
4. That those who are sick and in sorrow may find comfort and assurance in praying to Mary. Lord, hear us.
5. We pray that our dead may enjoy eternal happiness in the company of Mary and all the saints. Lord, hear us.

Heavenly Father, fill our hearts with gladness on this feast of the Assumption. Give us courage and strength to accept the crosses which come our way and guide us safely to eternal happiness. We ask this through Christ our Lord. Amen.

All Saints

The hour went back last weekend, the darkness has closed in around us and it has made the nights very long. We are inclined to look on November with a touch of despair; fallen leaves, rain, dampness and fog with little else ahead but the dismal winter. The church has traditionally associated the end of the year with the end of life. The festival of All Saints is meant to be a ray of sunshine at the beginning of these dark days. All Saint's Day brings to mind the ordinary people down the ages who were friends of God. Few of them held important positions in life and their names do not appear on the church's official role of honour. They are not canonised saints. God alone remembers them and the good works they have performed. They are the common folk from all walks of life who in their day tried to live the christian life to the full. Like ourselves they experienced the trials of growing up, the tensions of living with others and all the normal difficulties and uncertainties of life. They had to cope with their own personal problems and weaknesses. However great their difficulties and faults, they accepted that God loved them and relied on the strength of that love more than anything else.

Today's feast should give us fresh courage to continue taking up our cross daily and to follow Christ. It tells us that even now we must start living as children of God. Heaven is within our reach. It reminds us that holiness of life is not for the privileged few but what God expects of all of us. We don't have to step outside the doors of our homes to start growing in holiness. Holiness is about bringing the spirit of Christ into our lives. The command of Jesus, 'Be perfect as your heavenly Father is perfect,' is addressed to everyone. We are called to reflect something of the holiness of God himself.

The saints are very close to Christ. They are God's gift to his church. The example of their lives encourages us, spurs us on and keeps us from settling for the mediocre or second rate. They are our friends in heaven and we should not hesitate to pray to them so that something of their spirit may rest on us. At the present moment all of us are saints in the making so we should be conscious of our dignity and high calling as christians.

All Saints' Day gives us a glimpse into our own glorious future, our eternal destiny which has to be worked out in love and service here on earth. As we honour the vast army of God's friends, in the same breath we ask God's favour, that where they are now, we too may be in the future. We pray that one day this will be our feast as well.

Prayer of the Faithful

As we commemorate all the saints who have gone to glory we ask our heavenly Father for the help and support we need on our journey of faith.

1. We pray that our Holy Father and the bishops of the church may grow in holiness and enrich the lives of those to whom they minister. Lord, hear us.
2. For a greater awareness of the fact that our individual call to sainthood comes through the day-to-day ordinariness of our own lives. Lord, hear us.
3. Give courage and confidence to parents and teachers who guide young people in the way of holiness. Lord, hear us.
4. For those in our community who are sick, that they may experience peace and inner healing. Lord, hear us.
5. For our friends who have died. May they enjoy eternal rest with the saints in heaven. Lord, hear us.

Heavenly Father, look lovingly on us your children. Keep us safe in your care as we make our pilgrim way towards your kingdom. We ask this through Christ our Lord. Amen.

Year C

First Sunday of Advent

The first Sunday of Advent is with us again, a curtain raiser, ushering in the new year of the church. The season has a twofold character. It is a preparation for celebrating Christ's birth among us and a reminder of his second coming in glory, at the end of time. When Christ was born, his arrival into our world went unnoticed but for Mary and a faithful few who were prayerfully waiting for the Messiah to come among them. They had read the signs of the times correctly. The readings contain some valuable pointers warning us to be ready and prepared for his second coming. Let nobody be fooled, one fact remains true and pertinent: all roads in life lead to the Day of the Lord. During the run-up to Christmas we can benefit from giving some consideration to who we are, what we are doing with our lives and how we are approaching the one great test that really matters – our personal meeting with the Lord on judgement day. Our future very much depends on the way we are living at this moment. We are the masters of our own destiny.

As a pilgrim people we celebrate in our Sunday eucharist Christ's presence among us until he comes in glory. What type of a welcome are we giving Christ in our hearts if we are neglecting prayer, squandering money, bickering in the family or drinking to excess? Are we not a bit off target and failing to make progress in good christian living? Unless we are imitating gospel standards there is no room to congratulate ourselves cosily on the birth of Christ at Bethlehem because he is not born into our hearts. His presence has had no influence on us as we haven't wakened up to our need for a Saviour to free us from our sins.

During Advent the church makes an appeal for an improvement in our lives and for a new depth of sincerity to our religion. It calls on us to make a fresh start at building a closer relationship with Christ. Prayer, penance and works of mercy are necessary preparations for the coming of the Lord.

Advent provides an opportunity to look around at what needs to be put right, to see how we have failed, and to assess the ways in which we can do better. If prayer has been neglected, now is the chance to begin anew. Whatever our past, God is only too willing to look lovingly upon us. His arms are always outstretched to welcome us home. There are so many ways in which all of us can improve. It's remarkable how easily we settle for idleness, carelessness and indifference. Our fallen nature is our slump factor, pulling us down and leading us to sin.

Advent is above all a time to deepen our friendship with God by thinking of his great love for us in sending his Son as our Saviour. It's only fitting that in return we should show our love for him. If we do so our vision of Christ will become clearer and a driving force in our lives.

Prayer of the Faithful

As we begin the new church year, we pray to God our Father to help us prepare for the coming of the Lord into our world and into our lives.

1. We pray for our Holy Father, for our bishop and priests that they may be renewed in this season of Advent. Lord, hear us.
2. That as a community we may not fail to recognise the coming of Christ in those whom we meet in the course of our day. Lord, hear us.
3. As we look forward to the Christmas celebration of Christ's birthday may we, by our willingness, share the hardships and trials of those who are experiencing difficulties in their lives. Lord, hear us.
4. For the old, the lonely and the sick, that they may feel the healing presence of Christ. Lord, hear us.
5. We pray for those who have died … that they will meet Christ on their heavenly journey. Lord, hear us.

Lord God, during this Advent season give us a new vision as we wait in joyful hope for the coming of your son Jesus Christ. Amen.

Second Sunday of Advent

If Christmas is going to be a deeply religious experience and not just a pagan festival of merriment, the holy season of Advent has got to be taken seriously and not robbed of its meaning. These days leading up to the celebration of Christ's birth are a time of hope and renewal. They provide us with an opportunity for strengthening and deepening our union with Christ. The Lord is close at hand but his presence cannot be felt in our lives unless we open our hearts fully and make room for him through prayer and repentance.

The repentance for which John the Baptist calls goes beyond a simple confession of wrongdoings. It involves a profound change of the whole person and demands turning our backs on old self-centred habits. John gives us some down to earth advice on how to smooth a passageway for Christ coming into our lives, by pointing out obstacles and barriers at the door of our hearts that need to be removed. Among the valleys to be filled in, are, no doubt, the many gaping sins of omission (the good we meant to do and never got round to doing), our neglect of family and neighbours, those wasted opportunities in life for helping others and for soul-making. The mountains of our pride can only be levelled out by the daily practice of the virtue of humility.

John's words leave their sting behind and are a bitter pill to swallow. They hurt because there is so much in our lives to be set right. He is speaking an uncomfortable truth, challenging us about our sinful behaviour, which we would rather not discuss. He's telling us that there is a wrong way to live and a right way. If we are to make a clear pathway for God to come into our hearts we have to turn away from sin, resolve to conduct ourselves better and humbly ask Jesus to give us his light instead.

There are pockets of silence every day, moments when we are alone and can turn to God in silent prayer. Time spent in prayer helps us to acknowledge our failings and gives us great courage in grappling with the shadow side of life. Prayer sharpens our ability to hear God's word and helps us come to terms with our inner emptiness which cries out for consolation. Through prayer we come to know God and enjoy the blessings that he wants to pour out upon us.

We are waiting for our God standing on the door-step of

eternity. He is calling us home, offering us salvation in the person of his Son. On the first Christmas Day, he entered our world and opened the door to eternal life. This Advent let us ask the Spirit to lead us by prayer and repentance through that doorway. Then on his arrival we will be found without stain of sin and at peace.

Prayer of the Faithful

God our Father, as we prepare in a deep way for the feast of Christmas in confidence we place before you our needs.

1. For the leaders of the church, that they may follow closely in the footsteps of the Lord. Lord, hear us.
2. For ourselves, that our celebration of Advent may heal our bitterness and leave us prepared to greet the Christ child. Lord, hear us.
3. For families divided by misunderstanding or mistrust, that they may experience a renewal of love with each other. Lord, hear us.
4. May all those in prison, in hospital or who are sick be renewed in spirit during this time of preparation. Lord, hear us.
5. Let us pray for the members of our community who have completed Christ's work in this life, that they may see the salvation of God. Lord, hear us.

Heavenly Father, guide us towards Christmas with strength and grace so that when the Lord comes he will find us prepared to meet him. We make our prayer through Christ our Lord. Amen.

Third Sunday of Advent

There is no mistaking the theme which rings out loud and clear in today's liturgy – it's a message of hope and rejoicing. The dawn is beginning to break and the Lord is very near, closer to us than we realise. Christ's nearness is the strength which touches all our lives for he is now working with us and in us. This call to rejoice, lift up our hearts and be happy, presents us with a challenge and requires some soul-searching in the face of the problems confronting us at any given moment. Sadness is so much part of the fabric of our lives that we are inclined to ask – what have I got to rejoice about, with an alcoholic husband, with a wife who has cancer, with a severely handicapped child or a with a bereavement in the family? If times were better it might be easier to feel joyful.

The dreadful happenings of the world around us give little cause for rejoicing. While we continue this earthly journey we experience a bitter sweet mixture of joy and sorrow. Christian joy does not come from the absence of sorrow, pain or trouble but from an awareness of the presence of Christ within our souls. Paul was in prison when he made his call to the Philippians to be happy and rejoice in the Lord; Zephaniah was rejoicing at the height of the Jewish exile when things could not have been worse politically and the nation was at a moral low point. Both their plights were more disastrous than ours yet they did not allow personal circumstances to rob them of this joy. They had it because they were grounded in the peace of God.

How are we to attain this spiritual joy which should be rightfully ours? We ask the same question as John was asked by the people. He replies in uncompromising language that the secret is to commit ourselves to God's way and in so doing find our peace. Happiness comes from doing good, being honourable and showing concern for those in need. Experience shows that the giving of what we have will certainly make demands on us. Sharing made demands on Christ who came into our world and pilgrimaged with us from the cradle to the grave. The joy which stems from our faith means that whether playing or praying, laughing or weeping, walking or dancing, Christ shines forth from us. No one who has ever experienced this joy would exchange it for all the pleasures and comforts of this world.

If the gospel is Good News, could this conclusion be reached from the expression on our faces? We should be a joyful people constantly experiencing an abiding feeling of happiness because things of great value have been promised to us. The test of christianity in troubled waters is not to be over-alarmed at what is happening but to face the world with hope and confidence. The purpose of our whole being is happiness.

Prayer of the Faithful

With prayer and thanksgiving, we place our needs before God our Father.

1. Give courage and strength Lord to our Holy Father, our bishops and priests, so that they may radiate joy in proclaiming the Good News. Lord, hear us.
2. That we may be sincere in recognising the needs of the poor and marginalised in our community. Lord, hear us.
3. That the dreadful happenings of the world around us may not prevent us from rejoicing in the Lord's coming. Lord, hear us.
4. May all who are sick discover the strong and loving presence of Jesus. Lord, hear us.
5. That those who have died may enter into the joy of the Lord. Lord, hear us.

God our Father, may the coming of the redeemer stir up the joy within us through prayer and the practice of virtue. We make our prayer through Christ our Lord. Amen.

Fourth Sunday of Advent

With Christmas just around the corner, the days of Advent waiting are almost over. On this fourth Sunday the scripture readings
are alive with excitement about the Saviour who is coming very
soon. It is no surprise that the spotlight is focused on Mary because no one can help us to understand the meaning of Christmas
better than Mary. The visitation to her cousin Elizabeth is more
than a happy exchange of support between two women sharing
the joys of childbearing. It's a story of faith as well as friendship
and human love. Elizabeth clearly recognises that Mary is carrying Jesus the image of the unseen God when she says: 'Why
should I be honoured with a visit from the mother of my Lord?'
What a warm welcome the unborn Christ child received at Elizabeth's home in contrast to the cool welcome he would receive in
Bethlehem when there was no room for them in the inn.

Mary reveals in living colour how all christians are to await
Christ. She was carrying him as a gift to a world in need and we
are to do likewise. We are signs of his presence when we give ourselves to others – and what better time than at Christmas, when
we meet family and friends with warmth and added feeling. It's a
social celebration of family, food and fun and its joy should not be
spoiled by somebody being left out because they are not grand
enough to take part in our festivities. At Christmas everybody
ought to feel an insider, but society doesn't work that way and a
lot of people feel more outside then than they have ever been in
their lives. Let's not forget the humble origins of Jesus, born into
our world of pain and sorrow, in a stable on the very bottom rung
of the social ladder.

All our celebrations are an empty sham if Jesus is not born
into our hearts. Good things need to be done at a deeper level out
of love and affection and a spirit of generosity. The gifts that we
give have no purpose unless God is part of the giving and unless
we make Christmas a pattern to be followed in everyday living.

Like Mary we are all invited in our own lives to do the will
of God. Perhaps this year a neighbour or an old friend has to
spend Christmas in hospital away from the security of family. It
could be that old age has taken its toll and the Lord has called
someone home leaving a vacant chair by the fireside down the
road.

A visit made there in the spirit of Mary to Elizabeth will always be appreciated and will bring loving warmth and badly needed company. It's one sure way of offering the perfect Christmas gift of saying to God as Mary did, 'Here I am Lord, I've come to do your will.'

Prayer of the Faithful

As we prepare to celebrate the birth of Christ our Saviour, we ask God our Father to make our hearts a worthy dwelling place as Mary did.

1. We pray for the church that like Mary it may carry the word of God faithfully to the world. Lord, hear us.
2. Let us pray that at this Christmas celebration Christ may fill us with his peace in a new way. Lord, hear us.
3. May the visit of Mary to her cousin Elizabeth inspire us to call upon our friends who are lonely and in need of company. Lord, hear us.
4. That the members of our community who will be away from home at Christmas may be comforted by our prayers and an awareness of our love for them. Lord, hear us.
5. For those who live in the shadowland of sickness, that they may experience the saving power of Christ our Saviour. Lord, hear us.
6. That the dead who trusted in God's promise may receive eternal life. Lord, hear us.

All powerful Father, giver of the breath of life, prepare our hearts so that like Mary they may be worthy dwelling places, for your Son Jesus, who lives and reigns with you. Amen.

Christmas Day

There is always an appealing freshness about the Christmas story. We never tire of hearing how the infant Jesus lay in swaddling clothes in a manger at Bethlehem. The shepherds guarding their flocks on the nearby hillside were filled with awe as the chorus of angels broke the silence of the night with their joyous song of praise: 'Glory to God in the highest and peace to his people on earth.' The great feast of the nativity celebrates the closeness of God to us, born into our ordinary life. It's a mystery which stretches our minds beyond their limits moving us towards that horizon where time touches eternity. The new-born child is our living link with God. We are amazed and surprised that God should come among us in such humble circumstances. The simplicity of it all challenges us to get rid of falseness and pretence, otherwise we will never realise our need for a Saviour who will open a door and give us a fresh start with glorious possibilities. To make this new beginning we need to rediscover our lost innocence and acknowledge our dependence on God.

Christmas is the promise that we are not alone in our struggles. Christ did not remove himself from the brokenness of our human condition but experienced our poverty. From his birth in a stable as one who was homeless to his death on the cross as a common criminal, Jesus always identified with the spiritually, physically and materially poor of this world. The child who drew his first breath on a covering of straw in Bethlehem was the Christ of Calvary who gave his life that we might have everlasting happiness. Many of us are disappointed because in our search we tend to look for God in the spectacular, but the Christmas story tells us that God is to be found right before our eyes in the ordinary, in the people and the situations we take for granted. Above all, we can experience his presence in our hearts, provided we make room for him by removing the barriers and obstacles that get in his way. God often visits us but most of the time we are not at home. If the glory of God that comes to us as a child in the manger is not to be lost, we must ask the Lord for the grace in this short life of ours to do things his way. By softening our hearts and sharing what we have with the poor and the needy we lessen the gap between what we are and what we should be.

Forgiveness is the hallmark of Christmas. As well as expressing sorrow for our sins we must rid ourselves of bitterness and open the doors of forgiveness to those with whom we need to be reconciled. This is a time for healing rifts, for mending broken friendships and letting bygones be bygones. Spare a thought for those who have been bereaved during the past year. The pain of loss always surfaces during this feast of the family. Whatever we do out of love for the Lord will not be lost and the joyful peace of Christmas which descends on us will never be taken away.

Prayer of the Faithful

United as the family of God in celebrating the birth of Jesus, we pray to the Father with thanks in our hearts for sending us so great a Saviour.

1. We pray for the holy church of God throughout the world. May it spread Christ's message of peace and be a light of hope to those dwelling in darkness. Lord, hear us.
2. Guide the world's leaders into the paths of peace and grant them wisdom to see where they walk. Lord, hear us.
3. We pray for ourselves that at home and among our friends we will share the joy and wonder that comes from God being in our midst. Lord, hear us.
4. For the poor, the sick, the bereaved, the lonely and those unable to be with their families during this festive season. Touch their lives with your comforting peace. Lord, hear us.
5. Look with mercy Lord upon all who have died during the past year and bring them safely home to your kingdom. Lord, hear us.

Heavenly Father, you sent Jesus into the world to be our Saviour. We thank you for your loving kindness and ask for the grace to walk every day in your presence. We make this our prayer through Christ our Lord. Amen.

Feast of the Holy Family

Today's gospel outlines the heartbreaking experience of Mary and Joseph when they were quite certain they had lost Jesus. He slipped away from the family circle without informing his parents and went off on his own to the Temple. Even Mary and Joseph did not escape the tensions, anxieties and worries which are the ordinary ups and downs of family life. Their joy in finding Jesus was dampened by his sharp words, 'Don't you realise that I must be about my Father's business.' It was difficult for them to realise that he was growing up, coming of age and asserting himself outside his immediate family circle. All parents can easily identify with this happening because it rings so true of our own age with its generation gap, teen culture and lack of communication.

Which young person has not wondered at times if parents will ever understand the things that are so obviously important to them? Parents for their part learn painfully that rearing children is a test of their own growth as adults. If they fail to keep growing as adults they will never understand their children growing up. Children, of necessity, have a life of their own which parents must not stifle by attempting to turn them into carbon-copies of themselves. They must be ready to place faith in their children, striking that delicate balance of slacking control gradually. The time will come when they have to let go altogether, as their children begin to assert independence and launch out on their own.

This goes to show that family life is a full time job and a difficult one for everyone concerned. Living together, rubbing shoulders with one another demands love, loyalty, respect, reverence, self-denial and generosity. Few are born to do the great work of the world, but the work that all can do is to make a small home circle brighter and better. A happy home is not made out of bricks and mortar nor luxury carpets, but has its foundations in Christ – who is love. The family at Nazareth was the ideal family because of the presence of Jesus there. The same can be true of our family. God can make it a channel of grace if we spend time as a family in prayer. If prayer has not been part of the fabric of home life, or if it has been neglected, the new year is an ideal time for a fresh start. If we enter the new year determined to improve the quality of our family life, we will have taken something valuable from our recent celebration of the birth of Jesus Christ. Today the Holy Family at Nazareth is set before us as a model and as an inspiration. If we follow in their footsteps we will begin to perceive the mystery of godliness at the heart of our lives and especially at the centre of our families.

Prayer of the Faithful

Recalling the joys and sorrows of the Holy Family at Nazareth, we turn to God the Father and ask his blessing on all our needs.

1. We pray that the family of the church throughout the world may be an example and guide to the nations of the world in their search for harmony and peace. Lord, hear us.
2. For health and happiness in our own families and a greater appreciation of those members whose love we take for granted. Lord, hear us.
3. For parents who are separated and children who are neglected. May the tensions and pain of their present situation be eased to give way to reconciliation and peace. Lord, hear us.
4. We pray for the sick of our community, that the warmth of the love which they receive from family members be a comfort to them in their illness. Lord, hear us.
5. Grant eternal rest and perpetual light to those members of the christian family who have departed from this world. Lord, hear us.

Heavenly Father, clothe us in kindness and patience. As we grow in age, may we increase in maturity and become more like your Son. We make our prayer through Christ our Lord. Amen.

Second Sunday of Christmas

The church is at pains to make us reflect a little more deeply on the real message of Christmas, which is the feast of the great beginning of our salvation, while she still has our seasonal attention and mood. The gospel, which is profoundly beautiful in its message, presents us with God's plan of salvation. The gift of God's life has been given to us in the person of Jesus, who has come to earth to meet us in our humanity and made himself available to all. In Christ we have a brother who loves us to the extent that he came among us as a man, and shared not only our life, but our death as well, because his purpose was to be our Redeemer and Saviour.

Jesus, first and foremost, is God joining himself to us in the flesh. He would walk in our shoes, share our kind of living, celebrate in our joys, weep in our tears, suffer in our sorrows and give thanks in our accomplishments. As a result we are called to be his adopted children and heirs to God's heavenly kingdom. Christmas at its deepest level means we are part of the family of God.

The turn of the year presents us with an opportunity to dwell on our christian identity. If God has become man for our sakes we must ourselves become more fully human and treat others as persons. To live life to the full we have got to be alert to all the possibilities of our humanity and understand the real purpose of our existence. Jesus frees us from the shackles of sin which cling so easily and indeed from death itself.

We are a new creation because God is truly one of us. Our mission is to accept Christ as revealed to us in our quarrelsome battered human family and become involved in his saving plan for the world. In his own time many failed to welcome him; doors were slammed and there was no room for his message, because hearts were cold. There are those in every age who do not accept him and choose to live in the darkness. It would be a pity to prevent the light of God from shining in our lives by our failure to remove selfishness, hatred and bitterness from our hearts. Unless we keep that firmly in our minds Christmas will only be a sentimental pause at the end of a year and the challenge of Bethlehem will be lost completely.

Prayer of the Faithful

Called out of the darkness of sin into the wonderful light of God, we confidently place our needs before the Father.

1. We pray that the church may joyfully preach the Good News and give hope and encouragement to all peoples. Lord, hear us.
2. We ask your blessing on the work of missionaries who are devoting their lives to teaching and preaching the word of God in foreign parts. Lord, hear us.
3. We pray for everyone in our parish community. May they grow in your love and live in your peace. Lord, hear us.
4. For those who are sick or in hospital. May they be consoled through the love and care shown them. Lord, hear us.
5. We remember all who have died. Grant them eternal rest in your kingdom. Lord, hear us.

Heavenly Father, enlighten our hearts and open our minds to the values and qualities of life which your son has brought us. We ask this through Christ our Lord. Amen.

Epiphany of the Lord

Our Christmas celebration began with the shepherds on the hill country going over to Bethlehem to visit the new born King and ends with the arrival there of the Magi, in all their splendour. What attracts our attention is that they made their journey, guided by a mysterious star, which stopped at an out-of-the-way place with no visible signs of royalty, and they worship in simplicity and joy at the feet of the child, offering gold, frankincense and myrrh. Life was never the same after that discovery. Christ made all the difference to them, transforming their souls, calling them out of darkness into his own wonderful light.

The story has a relevance and holds true in every age. It symbolises the religious journey of all people who are seeking God, using a glimmer of faith to point the way forward. The search for the truth always involves leaving the comfort and security of previously held positions and views and facing the unknown. It requires courage, determination and hope as the journey will be long and the pathway lined with failure, doubt and confusion. Deep down in our lives there is an uneasiness and a yearning after freedom and happiness which can only be fulfilled when we experience the presence of God.

Like the Magi we are called to search and to discover the presence of Christ in our lives. It's an on-going relationship which cannot be programmed, labelled or packaged. What's important is to be open and receptive in order to read the signs of the times. Christ is being born every day in our lives. Nevertheless, although God has come to us we shall find him only if we search for him and discover him, only if we set out on a journey to meet him.

Christ is to be encountered in the most unusual and varied of places. He can be found in the smile of a child, in the painful expression of a person sick in bed, in the bitter tears of a poor person and in the happiness of newly-weds. Whenever we look into the eyes of another person we are gazing into the eyes of Christ. The same is true of our shared communications. When we meet other people we may not have gold, frankincense or myrrh to bring them but we can offer the priceless treasure of the presence of Christ in us. It's hardly right then to come before people empty-handed, and with no gifts of encouragement to offer them, on their pilgrim way. We are christians, not for our own sakes, but for others. This feast teaches that the faith is for sharing. God has called and given us the task of showing his Son to everyone we meet.

Prayer of the Faithful

We make our prayer to God our Father in the same spirit of faith as the Magi who knelt in humble adoration before the child Jesus.

1. We pray that the church may show Christ to the world in simplicity and humility. Lord, hear us.
2. Lord, give us hearts that are open so that we may find Jesus in our daily lives, in our homes and work places. Lord, hear us.
3. Lord, we have no gold to offer, but we bring you the gift of ourselves and we ask you to be Lord of our lives. Lord, hear us.
4. We pray that the light of Christ will shine on all those who are old, lonely or sick. Lord, hear us.
5. For those whose earthly pilgrimage is over. Let us pray that like the wise men they too have found the Lord. Lord, hear us.

God, our Father, you sent your Son among us, as Saviour to make us into one people. May we walk in the path of goodness and come to the light that shines forever. Amen.

Baptism of the Lord

Baptism was the way in which Jesus presented himself to his people at the outset of his mission. By the banks of the Jordan we see him, who was sinless, joining the crowds of sinners, taking his place in the long procession of people who were turning towards God through the pathway of repentance. That marked the beginning of his public ministry and the start of his life as a travelling preacher. By identifying with us he took upon his shoulders the tremendous burden and responsibility of our sins and began gathering all people into the one family of God. It was such an important moment that the Spirit of God took possession of him in a very special way and the heavens rang out with approval: 'This is my beloved Son in whom I am well pleased.' The baptism of the Lord was the event to which mankind had been looking forward because it brought God's light into a world of shadows and opened up the possibility of a new relationship for people with their creator. It so intimately united us with Christ that we too can be called God's children.

Today's feast reminds us of our own baptism and presents us with an opportunity to reflect on the implications of leading the life of a christian. It's a time of special importance because it marks our spiritual birth – the beginning of the Lord reaching down, touching our lives, claiming us for his own and adopting us as his children. Our parents and godparents were speaking on our behalf when they introduced us into God's family as infants – but as adults we have to ratify, act out and personalise that deeply religious decision. Through baptism Jesus introduces himself into our lives with the message that we are free from the debt of original sin which we inherited from our first parents – that we are restored and reconciled with God whose love is for us. We are now part of his family and can call God our Father.

Belonging to God's family involves obligations to be undertaken and decisions to be made about how we are to lead our lives. By our baptism we are invited to answer Jesus' call to do good, to follow in his footsteps by being honest in our dealings and kindly in our conversation. This requires strength of character as it often calls upon us to stand apart and be counted. But a committed follower of Christ will lead a worthy life and make the world a better place for his presence. Only when we are doing God's will are we behaving as beloved sons in whom the Father is pleased.

Prayer of the Faithful

At his baptism in the river Jordan Our Lord began his public ministry of preaching and teaching strengthened by his Father's love. Placing our trust in that same love we make our prayer.

1. That the church may guide all christians joined with your Son through baptism, to understand one another better and work together for the salvation of all peoples. Lord, hear us.
2. Let us pray for all baptised christians, that we may be anointed with the spirit and empowered to live as children of God. Lord, hear us.
3. For all those who will be baptised during the coming year, that they may walk always as children of the light keeping the flame of faith alive in their hearts. Lord, hear us.
4. For the lonely, the poor and the sick that they may know the Good News of Christ's presence in the way we help them. Lord, hear us.
5. May our departed family and friends come to the fullness of eternal life promised them in the sacraments. Lord, hear us.

Almighty God, send your spirit into the hearts of your children that we may remain faithful to our baptismal calling. We ask this through Christ our Lord. Amen.

First Sunday of Lent

At the beginning of Lent the church places us before an open doorway and invites us to embark on a journey of spiritual growth. Like Jesus in the wilderness, we are being led by the Spirit into a forty-day period of prayer and fasting, to help us reflect on the direction our lives are taking. It's an honest and frank attempt by the church to make us come to terms with the harsh reality of the hard slog for salvation.

In the desert Jesus is confronted by the forces of evil on three occasions and is subjected to severe temptations in the depth of his soul. The devil meets him face to face and in an effort to turn him away from God's plan of redemption, offers him false happiness with enticements of security, power and fame. None of these temptations got the better of him and he emerges victorious but only after a prolonged struggle. Temptation is a real test and the worst thing about it is that it is always an attraction. When tired and hungry, it would have been so easy for Jesus to turn stones into bread but he refused to use his power for his own comfort and allow his feelings to influence his actions. The temptations of Christ are those faced by christians of all ages. They are a testing of our faith as they force us to make decisions for or against God. As followers of Christ, we must be ready to stand and be counted as we are constantly at risk from the evil one. Because Jesus experienced temptation himself, he understands us in our weaknesses and is there to give us hope and encouragement.

Lent is a time for us to get back to basics, to replenish the soil in which our christian faith grows by curbing our selfishness and our pride. Pampered by creature comforts, we fall into the trap of thinking that material things will bring happiness and so we spend time having our wants and wishes satisfied. The truth is otherwise. Instead of helping us on the road to heaven, so often they turn out to be false escapes that lead us into unhappiness and frustration, raising us up for a great let-down. All of us experience these tendencies within ourselves, but the gospel states that there is more to life than the satisfaction of our appetites.

In the desert our Lord turned his back on all that stood in the way of doing his Father's will. Lent is a time of quiet and purposeful reflection which helps us to discover the will of God.

Fasting and self-denial, backed up by prayer and alms-giving, keep us growing in friendship with God. Let us make this Lent a time for beginning all over again by renewing our trust in Jesus who was tempted and triumphed over the evil one. Our prayer ought to be, 'Be with me Lord, when I am in temptation.'

Prayer of the Faithful

As we recall the forty days our Lord spent in the desert in conflict with the powers of evil we ask our heavenly Father to listen to our prayers as we begin our Lenten journey.

1. For the church throughout the world, especially in those countries undergoing the severe trial of persecution, that it may stand firm and never lose heart. Lord, hear us.
2. That this season will be a time of reconciliation and growth for our community, our family and our friends. Lord, hear us.
3. For those undergoing instruction in the faith, that the word of God may be engraved in their hearts. Lord, hear us.
4. For the sick and the housebound, that they may not lose faith but may they see the goodness of God in the tender hands of those who care for them. Lord, hear us.
5. We recall our friends who have gone ahead of us sealed with the sign of the cross and commend them to God's loving care. Lord, hear us.

God our Father, we have begun our Lenten journey of prayer, fasting and almsgiving. Stay with us in our trials and temptations and deliver us from the evil one. We make our prayer through Christ our Lord. Amen.

Second Sunday of Lent

There came a point in the ministry of Jesus when events took a turn for the worse and a decision had to be made regarding its future direction. Accompanied by three of his closest associates, Peter, James and John, Jesus retired up the mountain to seek the guidance of God the Father in quiet prayer. As he prayed, he seemed to be fully taken up into another world. His face was bathed in light and at his side were Moses the law-giver and Elijah the prophet. Deep in conversation with them he was made aware of the full extent of his suffering and death. It was only through the passion and cross that he would come to the glory of the resurrection. In the midst of this severe message the apostles were enveloped by a cloud and experienced a radiant glimpse of God's presence. Shielding their eyes they saw Jesus transformed by a dazzling splendour and heard the voice of God the Father in heaven declare: 'This is my Son, the Chosen One, listen to him.' The vision passed and the moment of insight into Christ's real personality was over. All was peace and quiet, and they went back to face the harsh realities of life.

The purpose of the transfiguration on the mountain was to make the apostles aware of the divine presence in the man with whom they walked and talked and to establish beyond all doubt in their minds that Jesus was the Son of God. It revealed to the disciples who their master really was and by giving them a taste of future glory, prepared them for the humiliation of the passion. When they first cast their lot to follow Jesus, little did Peter, James and John realise the price they would be asked to pay on the journey. Now they discovered that it would involve huge sacrifices. Christ was inviting them to crawl up the hill of Calvary and carve their names on the foot of the cross.

Experience teaches us that nothing worthwhile in life is ever simple or straight-forward. The message of the transfiguration is that there is a connection between suffering and death and the resurrection and glory. When things are difficult and the haul is very long it is good to remember that there is no short cut to glory. Real happiness and peace of mind only come after Calvary because the cross and suffering are inescapable.

The transfiguration speaks of the gradual process of change that takes place in our lives when, like the apostles, we accompany

Christ on the road to Calvary. We become so taken up with the everyday concerns of living that we often lose sight of the end to which we have been called. At times we are dragged down with feelings of failure and worthlessness but suddenly a piece of good news, a spark of joy, hope or love changes our outlook and we see our lives in a new and better light.

Lent affords an opportunity, through prayer and fasting, for putting the house of our soul in spiritual shape. It teaches us that the road to heaven is by the sweat of our brow through the daily chores of work and putting up with the frustrations and disappointments of family living. By rooting out prejudice, selfishness, and hatred we are better able to meet all people with love, understanding and compassion. The gospel tells us that a successful relationship with Jesus can improve us, and make a difference to our lives. Jesus does not change the world but he can transform our hearts if we let him. We all grow brighter the more we are tuned into the God-like image we are meant to reflect. The transfiguration is about letting the glory of God shine through us so that others can catch a glimpse of that glory.

Prayer of the Faithful

On Mount Tabor the Father said to Jesus: 'This is my beloved Son, listen to Him'. As his beloved sons and daughters we confidently place our needs before him.

1. We pray that our church leaders may continue to radiate the loving presence of Christ in the world by the example of their lives. Lord, hear us.
2. We pray that during this Lent we may show forth the glory of God in our kind actions and generous alms-giving. Lord, hear us.
3. We pray that those who are in real danger of losing their way in life because of feelings of failure and worthlessness, may realise that God has promised them a share in his glory. Lord, hear us.
4. We pray for all the sick and the handicapped that they may bear their crosses with courage and strength. Lord, hear us.
5. We pray for our beloved dead, that they may share in the splendour of the risen Christ. Lord, hear us.

God our Father, accept these prayers which we offer in faith. Fill our hearts with your love and keep us faithful to the gospel of Christ. We make our prayer through Christ our Lord. Amen.

Third Sunday of Lent

We tend to think of Lent as a time for stepping up acts of personal devotion and piety without giving much thought to its real purpose, which is an invitation to repent, be converted and return to the Lord our God. Like the Jews in the gospel, who thought they were sinless and in good standing with God because they had been spared death in a local massacre, we can fool ourselves into feeling that all is well. We also can imagine that we are in good spiritual shape and have no need for repentance precisely because no calamity has come our way. The absence of misfortune does not mean the presence of virtue. One point that comes across clearly in the message of Jesus is that we are expected to be fruitful and perform good works which are pleasing in God's sight.

Often it is not what we do wrong but the things that we leave undone which prevent us from growing in the love of Christ. The real heartache is that we are guilty of sins of omission and neglect of which we are hardly even conscious. Our lack of concern for others reveals too clearly this form of personal selfishness and highlights our failure to live the christian life to the full. Without exception each one of us needs to make a better effort in caring, sharing, loving and being available to our neighbour. It is not possible to do this unless we undergo a rigourous discipline of denying ourselves the comforts and luxuries we crave.

The Lenten invitation to repentance is not merely a call to turn away from evil but a plea to produce the fruits of good living. The biting question is whether our love of God is evident in our treatment of others. We can begin under our own roof at home and make a start at being more aware of our partner and more sensitive to our children and the other members of our family. It is easy to take our family for granted and to forget that they are individuals in their own right, who deserve respect. Outside of the family circle there are so many ways of showing love in the community. We can meet God by caring for the poor, the sick, the old and the lonely. All of us have received a tremendous amount from others. How concerned are we about giving something in exchange? Are we takers and not givers? Reaching out to others in need demands getting out of ourselves and putting aside our selfish ways. The warning about the unfruitful tree is not given to frighten us but to remind us that the time for doing good is limited and is fast running out. We cannot keep putting off good works in-definitely, otherwise there will come a time when there is no tomorrow and we will be found wanting.

Lent is an opportunity for taking a hard look at our lives and asking how do we stand before God right now. If we find that we are so caught up with material concerns that we have given a back seat to spiritual things, then we have forgotten the real purpose of why God gave us life. The challenge confronting us is to hoe the ground around our hearts in the expectation that it will produce good fruit.

Prayer of the Faithful

In this celebration of praise and thanksgiving for the Lord's ever-present goodness we pray to the Father for a clearer understanding of his nearness and for a readiness to accept him in our lives.

1. For our Holy Father, our bishops and priests, that in their ministry they may be strengthened by the power of God working in our lives. Lord, hear us.
2. For peace in the world, in our country, in our homes, in our hearts – peace which springs from acceptance of and respect for others, especially those who are different from us in any way. Lord, hear us.
3. For all who suffer, for those whose lives have been blighted by misfortune or calamity, that in their darkness of spirit they may have strength to reach out to the Lord who is always near at hand. Lord, hear us.
4. For all here present celebrating this eucharist, that we may bring the presence of Jesus home with us to sanctify our week. Lord, hear us.
5. For all humankind, living and dead, that we may see the face of Jesus and remain in his presence for ever. Lord, hear us.

God, our Father, accept these prayers which we offer in faith. Let us know the love and peace of Jesus your Son and our mediator with you. We ask this and all our prayers through Christ our Lord. Amen.

Fourth Sunday of Lent

This gospel about the merciful father and his two self-centred sons is one of the best loved stories in the scriptures. The younger, a wastrel, tells us something about greed and its consequences but also about the virtues of humility and repentance. The elder, a complainer, speaks multitudes about human nature and how easily envy, jealousy and resentment arise when other people are treated well. The younger son, in a hurry to meet life, gets what he can out of his father, gathers together his bits and pieces and off he goes to live it up and do his own thing. When his money runs out his friends leave him and he finds himself reduced to living like an animal. Down in his luck, he comes to his senses and realises he has made a fool of himself. Hoping for forgiveness, he heads back home to face his father and is overcome with the welcome he receives. The older son, a solid citizen who has never put a foot wrong in life and is resentful of his brother's notorious living, cannot come to terms with the easy pardon and refuses to join the celebrations. His type would never have experienced the shame of coming home in disgrace, knowing full well that the tongues of the town were wagging and buzzing with gossip.

The star of the show is the father who welcomes his son home without a word of reproach or recrimination. Irrespective of what has happened, he can not change the one basic fact of the case. His son is still his son and he will always be received with open arms. The father in the story is someone whose love never changes and is present all the time as much when the son goes off as when he returns. That's where the gospel story tells us something about the gracious goodness of God – his warmth with sinners and the length of his merciful arm. God never changes. Somehow in a way beyond our understanding he knows the weakness, the waywardness and the perversity of the human heart and makes allowances. His love for us remains; he is always willing to forgive.

Lent is a time for growing in an appreciation of the beautiful and comforting truth that every person has a place in the heart of God. This story is drawn from real life with existing situations and if we are honest we can see shades of the elder and younger sons in ourselves. We have been wandering, disobedient and selfish children who hold grudges and are unwilling to forgive one another. We have forgotten our ever-loving Father who even after our most stupid mistakes and tragic sins is always ready to welcome us with open arms. The gospel tells us what coming home to God is really like.

Prayer of the Faithful

With confidence we place our needs before God our Father, who in loving kindness overlooks our faults and greets us with a loving embrace.

1. That the church may be a living sign of true concern and dedicated care for those who are rejected by our society. Lord, hear us.
2. That, like the prodigal father, we may be generous in showing forgiveness to those who have hurt or disappointed us. Lord, hear us.
4. That all those who are suffering or sick may realise that they are loved by God from the care and attention shown to them. Lord, hear us.
5. That eternal light may shine upon all our departed brothers and sisters who have left the shadows of this world behind them. Lord, hear us.

Heavenly Father, and lover of all you have created; guide us through life secure in your love. Help us to learn the lesson of forgiveness and put it into practice in our daily lives. We make our prayer through Christ our Lord. Amen.

287

Fifth Sunday of Lent

Adultery always makes for public comment and scandal head-lines. It's one of those sins which raises moral indignation because it threatens acceptable standards of behaviour. When it is known, tongues in the community inevitably start wagging. Here we have the Pharisees, with resentful and bitter hatred in their eyes, dragging before Jesus a woman caught in the act of adultery. With no regard for her feelings nor shred of concern for her as a person, they point accusingly at the adultress while asking Jesus to pass judgement and approve of her death by stoning. Compassion never enters into their hearts. Not wanting to be involved in their hatred or party to their condemnation Christ avoids the issue and indicates his lack of interest by tracing some idle lines with his fin-ger in the dust. After this display of indifference he goes to the heart of the problem saying: 'Let the one who is without sin cast the first stone.' The accusers drift away with embarrassment and the woman is left standing alone with Christ in mute and misera-ble repentance. He utters the immortal words: 'Has no one con-demned you? Neither do I. Go in peace.' Without condoning her sinful action Jesus restores her to peace and friendship with God.

We are reminded forcefully of the readiness of God to for-give sin, bind up broken lives and restore people to his friendship. The church wants us to focus our attention on the plight of the sin-ful woman because before God all of us stand silent in our sinful-ness. The good news is that what Jesus does for her he is willing to do for us. Her story of sin committed and sin forgiven is not an iso-lated event but an example of the inexhaustible mercy and com-passion shown by Jesus to sinners. When we express sorrow for our sins Christ also says: 'Neither will I condemn you. Go and sin no more.' The lesson is not that sin is unimportant but that God in his goodness extends pardon to the sinner. Nothing is equal to the mercy of God as shown to us in Jesus Christ, who took the weight of our sins upon himself when he gave his life for us on Calvary. Lent is an invitation to take a close look at our lives, acknowledge our weaknesses and start anew in the friendship of God.

Christ's offer of forgiveness and compassion to this publicly humiliated woman points out our call to be a forgiving people, dedicated to reconciliation. In many ways we are as self-righteous as the Scribes and Pharisees. There are times when we are only too ready to spread scandal with a bit of spicy gossip. Doesn't the tone of our conversation about the unmarried mother, the alcoholic and the shop-lifter amount to looking down on them and passing judgement? It's so easy to criticise and condemn others, yet when our own faults are revealed we need the welcoming and merciful hands of God. We should all be overjoyed that on the last day God will be our judge and not our neighbour.

Prayer of the Faithful

With heartfelt sorrow for our faults and failings let us pray to God our Father that, like the adulterous woman brought before him to be condemned, we too will hear the words, 'Go in peace and sin no more.'

1. For all who minister in the church, that in their work they will always show true forgiveness and understanding like Jesus. Lord, hear us.
2. We pray for ourselves, that we may refrain from passing judgement or condemning others, but look firstly at our own lives in the sight of God. Lord, hear us.
3. That those weighed down with hardship and worry may realise that God is never far away from them. Lord, hear us.
4. May all who are old, lonely, in pain or sick learn from the example of Jesus to bear their suffering with courage and love. Lord, hear us.
5. Grant eternal rest to all the recently deceased. May they find happiness and peace in your warm embrace, Lord, hear us.

Heavenly Father, help us to be forgiving toward people who treat us badly. May we show them the same compassion that your Son Jesus extended to the woman caught in adultery. We make our prayer through Christ our Lord. Amen.

Passion Sunday

Palm Sunday commemorates the triumphal entry of Jesus into Jerusalem. Acclaimed as king and hailed as a conquering hero by the cheering crowd he seemed to have arrived at the fulfilment of his earthly mission. For Christ, it's the beginning of the last week of his life, a week of violent contrasts, which will end in grief and glory. The palms will soon be formed into crosses and the cheers will turn into jeers calling for his death. Throughout the passion our attention is focused on Jesus who appears as a person completely absorbed in prayer, responding quietly and sensitively to each new moment of sorrow.

Before his triumphant resurrection he has to go through a disgraceful death. In the garden of Gethsemane he is deeply troubled, and he sweats blood as he prays for the Father to remove the chalice of suffering and death from him. Betrayed and taken prisoner he is mocked, blindfolded, beaten and spat upon, while a convicted murderer is set free. He undergoes a final wrench of pain when Peter denies him and the apostles forsake him. His sense of abandonment by God is increased by the desertion of his friends. On Calvary he is crucified between two thieves and dies as a common criminal. Mary alone stands at the foot of the cross faithful to the last.

During this most solemn week of the church year we are invited to take the road with Mary and those few friends who follow Christ to Calvary, and to be silently at his side. He wants the work of his cross to touch our lives, to break our sinful ways so that we may be changed and know God. The decisive test of our faith is one day to reach the point where we are ready to accompany Jesus to Calvary along the same path into destruction and death. The sufferings of Christ which we recall in a special way during Holy Week have been a source of strength to countless people throughout the ages. His passion gives us at least a tiny glimpse into the mystery of suffering that surrounds us on all sides. In times of trials, suffering and mental torture often what keeps people going and gives them strength and inspiration is the knowledge that they are at one with Jesus who suffered in the same way before them.

In Holy Week we are confronted with the primary christian symbol – the cross – without which we cannot become his disciples. It affords us an opportunity to ponder as to what is the cross that we are taking up daily or refusing to face? Where is our sharing in his passion? There is not much point in dwelling on the crucifixion of Christ during this solemn week if it is an isolated event and not linked with the drama of suffering that goes on in our lives for the rest of the year.

Prayer of the Faithful

In the glory of his passion, Christ offered up prayers to his heavenly Father, aloud and in silent tears. With confidence we make our needs known to the Father and so we pray.

1. That the church may be faithful to God's will and in times of trial show the same generosity and forebearance as Jesus did in his passion. Lord, hear us.
2. That we may find through prayer and fasting the courage and vision to do all that is necessary to return to God. Lord, hear us.
3. We pray for all who suffer from poverty in the world because of our excesses. May we find ways to change our lifestyle so that no one need go without the necessities of life in order to provide us with luxuries. Lord, hear us.
4. For the sick and the suffering. May they experience the healing presence of Christ in their loneliness and pain. Lord, hear us.
5. That all those who have died may share in the joy of the risen Christ who fully shared in our human life. Lord, hear us.

God our Father, we ask you to listen to the many needs of your peoples Give us courage to face hardship through the inspiration of your Son, Jesus Christ who suffered and gave his life for us. We make our prayer through Christ our Lord. Amen.

Easter Sunday

There is no day to compare with Easter Day. It stands out from the conflicts and turmoil of our broken world, lifts our minds and enlivens our hearts with a joy and love so complete that it conquers death. Early on the first Easter morning a mighty act of God took place – Christ rose from the dead, altered the past and shaped the future. Nothing can be the same again. That is what makes Easter the greatest occasion of the year and Good News for all time. All our hopes and happiness stem from that event. Easter announces that there is a way forward out of darkness, transformation is possible and change can take place in our lives.

The resurrection of Jesus from the dead affirms that death is not the end of us. We are meant for more than this present life and are not anchored to this world. Human life is no longer limited by the cycle of birth to death. Easter is the answer to all the tears that we shed at the graves of our loved ones because it reminds us that we have a future greater than we dare believe in, provided we open our hearts to the grace that Jesus won for us. Christ has shared the gift of his life with us and his resurrection from the dead points to the resurrection of all people.

Easter is the turning point inviting us to live in an entirely new way that goes beyond the limitations of this world. We are challenged to become part of a new creation, inspired by the life of God, which is poured into our souls at baptism. Life depends on how we look at it. It can be seen as an empty tomb, full of bitterness and confusion or full of joy and hope. The challenge is to appreciate God and to see his plan in the ordinary events surrounding us. We can only do this if we are faithful to our baptismal promises, tuned into Jesus and switched on to his power in our lives. He will help us to find the face of God in the bits and pieces of life and in the hearts of all whom we meet.

The gospel tells us that on the first Easter morning the stone at the entrance of the tomb of Christ was rolled back. The question we must all face is: have we arisen to new life with Christ, or are there boulders weighing us down and keeping us imprisoned in our tombs? The Good News is that by God's power the boulders that hold you and me locked and buried can be rolled back and we can be set free.God is in charge. It is his world and he has breathed eternity into our bones. The best way we can give thanks to God for the gift of his life within us this Easter, is by opening our hearts to the risen Jesus and by allowing ourselves to be sent out into the world to proclaim the Good News of Christ's love.

Prayer of the Faithful

Our hearts are filled with joy on this Easter Day. With renewed confidence we bring our needs before God the Father in prayer.

1. For those who have been reborn in baptism that they may find joy within the christian community. Lord, hear us.
2. That the Risen Lord's gift of peace may dwell in our hearts, our homes and in our country. Lord, hear us.
3. That we may show evidence of the faith which we claim to have in the resurrection by our concern for the poor, the deprived and the handicapped. Lord, hear us.
4. For those who are sick in mind or body. May they feel the healing power of Christ uniting them in his body for the glory of God and the good of his people. Lord, hear us.
5. Let us pray for all those who have died. May they rejoice in the presence of the risen Christ. Lord, hear us.

God our Father, we thank you for the joy of this Easter. May all who celebrate the resurrection of your son experience his power in their lives. We make this prayer through Christ our Lord. Amen.

Second Sunday of Easter

The prayerful atmosphere of this gathering of disciples is rudely interrupted by the stubborn disbelief of Thomas. The only way he will believe that Jesus is risen is to put his fingers into the wounds of Calvary. Good Friday had ended all the hopes he had pinned on Christ. It shattered his faith to the point where he makes no attempt to hide his doubts. Thomas is a precious figure and he does us all a favour in demanding proof of the resurrection. In actual fact he is only echoing the doubts and voicing the uncertainties which darken our minds and cloud our faith from time to time, when dreams are crushed by an unexpected death, a broken relationship or some such heavy cross. The gospel points out that faith does not always come easily. Sometimes believing is not a problem, at other times it can be a struggle against despair and a real challenge. Ultimately it is faith that makes life meaningful because it's an adventure of the spirit searching for an encounter with God.

It is worth remembering that the faith of the apostles was no overnight experience but something gradual which increased as they became more intimate with Christ. The same is true of our faith, it will grow and deepen provided we are more Christ-like in our daily living. The biggest obstacle to the spread of christian faith today is not so much intellectual doubt as the unchristian lifestyles paraded by so many of us who regard ourselves as good christians. We are very much citizens of this world, content to look on religion and worship of God as a Sunday obligation which has little or no relevance to the rest of the week. Half-hearted and lukewarm followers do untold damage to the cause of Christ. The challenge of Thomas, for all who profess to believe, is to be more outgoing and to touch people in such a way as to bring hope and encouragement to their existence. By the witness of our lives we produce unfailing evidence that Christ is risen. We show the fruits of our faith in our care for the under-privileged of the human family. In this way doubters will have the closed doors of their minds opened to see Christ, to touch his wounds and to be touched by him in return.

Like Thomas we are a strange mixture of belief and unbelief. We have faith in our hearts and doubts in our mind. It is no small wonder we pray: 'Lord, I believe. Help my unbelief.'

Prayer of the Faithful

We pray now to God our Father, in the spirit of his risen Son, so that he may touch our lives, heal us of our doubts and restore our faith.

1. That the church will be filled with the spirit of the Risen Lord and be a witness of new life to the whole of the world. Lord, hear us.
2. That as members of the believing community, we may live lives of commitment to Jesus Christ which is the greatest proof of love. Lord, hear us.
3. Lord, help us to see and touch the wounds of the body of Christ in the victims of poverty,unemployment and crime. Lord, hear us.
4. We pray for the sick of our community, that their faith in the risen Lord may give them courage and comfort in their suffering. Lord, hear us.
5. We pray for those who have died. May they rest in peace with God forever. Lord, hear us.

God our Father, help us to lean upon your great strength trustfully and to await the unfolding of your will patiently and confidently. We make our prayer through Christ our Lord. Amen.

Third Sunday of Easter

Eager to put the trauma and disgrace of Good Friday out of their minds, the apostles have slipped back to life as it was before the call of Jesus. They have just come back from a night's fishing, empty-handed. A stranger on the shore urges them to cast their nets once more and the result is a miraculous catch of fish. At that moment they recognise the Lord and accept his invitation to share breakfast with him at the lakeside. In Pilate's courtyard Peter with curses and an oath had denied he knew Jesus and now the memories of how badly he had acted on that occasion were making him uneasy. Jesus knew exactly how he felt and offered him an opportunity to proclaim his love and loyalty to the risen Christ. Peter's authority, lost by his denial, is now restored through his confession of faith. His position as head of the apostles is clarified and he is given the commission to guard the whole flock in Christ's name, a role that will lead to a violent death. The Good Shepherd leaves his church in the charge of a man who has failed, which shows that Christ's call does not exclude falls. Peter came to know God's grace through failure. Often failure can be the finger of God pointing the way, awakening within us an awareness of our own helplessness. Whatever it was about that lakeside gathering it restored Peter's confidence, gave him the strength to renew his faith and throw himself into the spreading of the gospel.

The challenge which Christ presented to Peter, 'Simon, son of John, do you love me more than these others do?' is the same challenge facing us. We are to plunge into the waters of life and risk everything for the sake of the Lord. The miraculous catch of fish symbolises the bringing of all people into the reach of God's mercy. The church will gather, into one unbroken net, men and women of every race, colour and nationality. Like the apostles, everyone has been summoned by Jesus to extend God's kingdom everywhere. We are to bear effective witness, to go out and preach in his name to a world that does not always want to hear the truth. To be faithful to the ideals of the gospel requires courage, because it is never easy to do what is right when it means we have to go against popular values. Our life's work is meant to be one of living service for the glory of God. All of us can find some role where we can be helpful to others, whether it be modest, spectacular, important or insignificant. We are presented with

daily opportunities to help the elderly, to listen to bereaved neighbours and to give human contact to the lonely, provided we are
willing to take time out. It's as good a day as any to reflect on the
way in which we perform or neglect these functions.

Prayer of the Faithful

*Mindful that we are sent on the same mission as Peter, we ask God the
Father to strengthen our faith.*

1. We pray for our Holy Father and for all who are called to exercise responsibility and authority in the church, that they may be
guided by the Holy Spirit. Lord, hear us.
2. We pray for our worshipping community, that others will see us
as a people radiating the peace and love of the Risen Lord. Lord,
hear us.
3. We pray for sinners. May they draw encouragement from the
Lord's forgiveness of Peter, and never lose hope. Lord, hear us.
4. We pray for the sick and for those who are in distress in any
way, that the Lord will be close to them in their suffering. Lord,
hear us.
5. For our beloved dead, whose faith was known to God alone.
May they receive light, happiness and peace. Lord, hear us.

*Heavenly Father, you sent your Son to save the world through the work
of your church. May we be inspired by the example of Peter to labour for
the spread of your kingdom on earth. We make our prayer through
Christ our Lord. Amen.*

Fourth Sunday of Easter

There is such a need for religious vocations in the church that the Holy Father has set this Sunday aside as a world day of prayer that the Lord of the harvest may send labourers into his harvest. We all have a mission in life, because the word of God, which came to birth in our souls at baptism, is waiting to blossom forth in a more total way in each of us. God has created us for some definite service. While we may not be able to gauge with any real accuracy the effectiveness of our lives, there is nowhere we walk in life without leaving the imprint of who we are upon the ground we tread. We can be a little bit of Christ in our own homes and do our best to co-operate with his invitation to 'come, follow me.'

The gospel picks up the idea of Christ the good shepherd calling each of us by name as we journey through life by different ways. Youth is a time of great generosity, idealism and hope. Evidence of this is in the way young people give of their time and talents to deprived groups in society. In these loud and frantic days it may be more difficult for them to hear the voice of the Lord calling, so we should pray that, as they face the decision about their future role in life, they will leave open the possibility of a religious vocation and ask God's help to make the right choice in their calling. There are enormous riches within the hearts of youth – riches that are theirs to spend lavishly during life. Many of them are unaware of their giftedness and never draw on their talents because they are afraid to take the risk of faith which is needed. By opening their hearts in prayerful service, God, and not material things, will be the focus of their attention. The special calling facing them is to be Christ to others in times of need, to be healers in times of sorrow, towers of strength in times of distress and a shoulder to lean upon when support is needed.

It is always easier to wash one's hands of the responsibility of proclaiming the gospel than to become involved. However, the duty of fostering vocations is the concern of the whole believing community and we discharge that responsibility by living full christian lives. Parents, vocations come from families like your own, where there is a climate created within the home based on solid christian values, and where encouragement is given to follow the Lord in a special way. Your support is particularly important, because your child's faith grows through the example of your own faith, by the practice of prayer in the church and in the family. We preach not something exterior but the life we live and lead. God does not knock at every door looking for someone to respond to a religious vocation. If he happens to knock at your door, be generous enough to let him in. How otherwise will the needs of the flock in the next generation be met?

Prayer of the Faithful

Mindful that the kingdom of God has the need of dedicated young people prepared to spend their lives in living service, we make our prayer to God the Father:

1. For the Holy Father, bishops and clergy that they may be strengthened in serving the spiritual needs of their flock with joy and courage. Lord, hear us.
2. When we become anxious and upset because the daily trials of life bother us, make us remember that we are the sheep being looked after by Christ the good shepherd. Lord, hear us.
3. For those whom God is calling in a special way in the preaching of his word and in the spreading of his kingdom, may they have the courage to respond in generosity. Lord, hear us.
4. That the sick of our community may experience the healing hands of Christ. Lord, hear us.
5. For those who have died recently, that Christ the good shepherd may lead them safely home. Lord, hear us.

Almighty Father, we your people place our prayers before you in complete trust and confidence through Christ, our Lord. Amen.

Fifth Sunday of Easter

It may come as a surprise to realise that Jesus gave us the command to love one another at the Last Supper shortly after Judas had left the upper room on his mission of betrayal. This was the new order the Saviour had come to bring, and the sign by which the world would recognise his followers. Christ paid a great price to love us. It meant crucifixion and death on the cross at Calvary. If we are to live by this new commandment we must undergo many trials, for this love makes as many demands upon us as it did upon Christ. We need to learn how to go about loving others for the sake of God because, in the evening of life, we will be judged on how well we have loved.

Christ's rule for living life properly may not present problems as far as loving our friends is concerned. Most of us are fairly good at overlooking their faults, making allowances for their shortcomings and forgiving their failures. It is easy to love those who are kind and loving towards us but christian love calls us to do more than this. Nobody must be excluded from our loving. What about our enemies – those who have done us harm and perhaps still do? We fail miserably when we retaliate and our good intentions are shattered as we gossip maliciously about them. The making of ourselves into real christians is the work of a lifetime. Conversion does not take place overnight and requires much patience.

The one thing we all need to experience is the kind of love that Jesus lived and preached. It's a love which finds its source in God, is a fragment of eternity within our being and without which our lives have no meaning. This is the one Commandment on which we are called to base every action and it is the very core of the gospel. Love has the power to give meaning to impossible situations, to bring light into darkness, to inspire people, fill them with hope and give them the courage to continue on the road ahead. The Lord may not be walking our pathway today in his physical body but in every age he continues the work of making the whole of creation new through his disciples. The good news is that we have been chosen to be instruments of his grace, channels through which others may experience his love. It may simply be a smile which costs nothing but means so much, because it comes from our heart. In one sense the only failure facing any christian in life is the failure to love.

The gospel is an invitation to look into our hearts and see how we are answering this call to love in our lives and within our families. There is always the danger that we may be in love with ourselves instead of with one another. The presence of God so easily fades into the background when we give way to this inner selfishness. The real test of love is how we respect others. No-one can be a friend of Jesus Christ who does not love his neighbour.

Prayer of the Faithful

As a community united in love and filled with concern for one another, we call upon God the Father and ask for his support in our pilgrimage.

1. We pray for our Holy Father, the bishops and all those entrusted with authority and the responsibility of leadership in the church, that God may fill them with his spirit of love and service. Lord, hear us.
2. We pray that as a parish community we may show love, encouragement and support for one another not merely in words but in deeds. Lord, hear us.
3. For those who find it hard to forgive. Banish hatred, bitterness and revenge from their hearts and make them channels of your peace. Lord, hear us.
4. Bless the sick, comfort them in their illness and sustain them with your love. Lord, hear us.
5. For those who have died. Grant them peace and eternal rest in your kingdom. Lord, hear us.

Heavenly Father, listen to our requests and deepen our awareness of your tender love. Help us to remain faithful to your son's new commandment of love. We make our prayer through Christ our Lord. Amen.

Sixth Sunday of Easter

Occasionally we all experience the wrenching pain caused by saying goodbye. Here we have Jesus gently breaking the news of his departure to his disciples. The thought of his going away was so painful that their minds were almost numbed to what he had to say. Without him the future would be bleak and meaningless, as the whole focus and direction of their lives was gone. Yet Christ did not abandon them for, as his parting gift, he left the offer of peace which the world cannot give. This deeper peace, of walking with God, is difficult for the unspiritual mind to grasp. It was not a promise to preserve them from hardships and suffering, but a pledge to bring them safely through all trouble to eternal life. The peace Jesus was offering was the confidence of being loved, the assurance of knowing that God can be relied upon and trusted in hard times. It flows into our lives when we open our hearts and allow God's healing presence to work within us. His strength is a powerful help to ease the tension and restlessness of life's difficulties which afflict our minds and souls. This peace which Christ makes available is not easily won as it comes from striving consciously to live according to the known will of God.

Peace which means the absence of war, a lack of noise, the avoidance of conflicts, an hour without pain and suffering, was not the peace announced by the angels at Christ's birth, nor willed at his death. The peace which is proclaimed is achieved by victory over sin due to the power of God, and Christ could speak of it on the night before he died. To obtain it means shutting out of our lives all that is selfish and greedy, all hatred and bitterness, and putting in their place forgiveness and the desire to help others and share with them the good things of life. The basis of peace is God. The secret of peace is trust, but the soul of peace is love which comes from the love of God and expresses itself in our love for people.

The question we have to ask is whether we are at peace with ourselves, which is the wonderful effect of being accepted by God. If his Spirit dwells within us we can accept others in his name. Excluding others from our company means we are erecting barriers which prevent God's love and peace from reaching us.

Prayer of the Faithful

We pray now to the Father in the name of his son and ask him to pour out upon us the gift of his spirit of peace.

1. We pray for our Holy Father and all who minister in the church. May they receive the grace to live the gospel of peace which they preach. Lord, hear us.
2. May all the homes of our parish be blessed with the joy and peace of Christ – a peace which the world cannot give. Lord, hear us.
3. We pray that peacemakers and lovers of reconciliation may be blessed and that they may influence everyone they meet. Lord, hear us.
4. That those who are suffering in their old age may receive our attention and care which will make them aware of the peace of Christ. Lord, hear us.
5. Give us, Lord, the grace of a peaceful and happy death and may we one day see our faith in you fulfilled. Lord, hear us.

Heavenly Father, take pity on our restless hearts and troubled minds and grant us the peace and love of your kingdom where you live for ever and ever. Amen.

Ascension of the Lord

By virtue of our calling as christians, we are meant to be optimistic people, full of hope and deep rooted confidence about our future. The ascension, which marks the final departure of Christ from his friends on earth, celebrates that hope. It proclaims that Jesus, who spent his life in Jerusalem and the surrounding countryside, achieved the work he was sent to do and is now in heaven in the company of God the Father, beyond the boundaries of death and decay. What the feast does is to give us a glimpse of the destiny that awaits us. It spells out in no uncertain terms that our home-land is heaven. Where Christ has gone we hope to follow, once our earthly journey is over. In his own person Christ has made available a sharing in his complete happiness which death cannot take from us or interrupt. This is the joyful hope we have as a safe and sure anchor for our lives. The Ascension assures us that the longing for happiness and fullness of life which is deeply imprint-ed within every person can ultimately be realised.

The final words of Jesus to the apostles were brief and to the point. 'I am with you always. Go teach all nations.' No longer con-fined to a bodily presence, he will be with his disciples in a new way, through the power of the Spirit, the Lord, the giver of life. Now that his earthly mission is over, he entrusts the continuation of his work to his friends who believe in him. Their task is to spread out from Jerusalem and to proclaim to all nations the sal-vation that he has won. In the same way as the first disciples, we are called to follow Christ and proclaim his message, by living in this passing world with our hearts set on a world that will never end. The best place to make a start is to get our own lives in good spiritual shape. Actions speak louder than words. We carry on his mission more by what we are than by what we say. If the love of God burns in our hearts, people will see from our joy that life is good, has a purpose and is worth living. We preach the values of Christ in our neighbourhood by our good example. The faithful love of a husband for his wife and the concern shown for the wel-fare of their children speaks more effectively about marriage and the family than any sermon. In the absence of Jesus we are placed firmly at the centre of the stage to busy ourselves being his healing hands, his warm smile and his comforting words. The ascension reveals the work we must do in order to be with Christ forever. Our way to glory is none other than to witness to the Lord by taking up our cross and following in his footsteps.

Prayers of the faithful

On this day of hope and promise, we open our hearts to God the Father, whose power is at work in our lives and we ask his help in all our needs.

1. We pray for our Holy Father and all bishops of the church. May the spirit of God strengthen them to lead lives which correspond to the office they hold and the destiny to which they are called. Lord, hear us.

2. We remember missionaries who are working in all parts of the world to spread the gospel. May their labours in building up the church be fruitful. Lord, hear us.

3. For a spirit of peace, harmony and forgiveness in our homes. May we rise above the anxieties that get us down and the jealousies that prevent us from loving each other. Lord, hear us.

4. We pray for the sick. May they not be discouraged but draw hope and comfort from the Lord's Ascension into heaven. Lord, hear us.

5. For the dead, especially our loved ones who recently departed this life. May they share in the fullness of the life of Christ who, on this day, returned to the Father. Lord, hear us.

God our Father, you have given us your son Jesus to be our guide on our earthly pilgrimage. Help us to follow closely the path which he has traced for us and so enter your kingdom. We ask this through Christ our Lord. Amen.

Seventh Sunday of Easter

A striking feature of the early church was the bond of unity which existed between the various local churches which differed in language and culture. This unity was based on a common faithfulness to the teaching of Peter and the apostles, and it was the distinguishing mark in a pagan world of being a disciple of Christ.

In the gospel, we have just heard Jesus praying aloud to his Father the innermost concerns of his heart. With great intimacy and confidence he pours out his deepest feelings about the future mission of the disciples in the church which he was forming. He appeals to the Father to carry out his plan for the world, which will draw all people together in a common bond of love. The unity in love of these apostles is to be the pattern in his community for all ages. Unity amongst christians announces to the world the love that Christ has for all people and his wish to share his life with them. The main point of his prayer for unity emphasises that we will find this unity not in one another but in Christ. The more we grow like Christ, the more we grow like one another and our differences stem from not resembling him sufficiently. Only by a strong unity of one generation of believers with the next, and of one part of the church with the other can christian oneness be really achieved.

It goes without saying that the greatest tragedy which has befallen the church down the centuries has been the divisions which led to the formation of rival christian churches. This breaks the unity so precious to Christ, who prayed to his Father, 'that they may all be one as thou Father in me and I in you.'

We are living stones in the building of which there is only one foundation, Jesus Christ. Each of us has the responsibility of promoting unity in a world largely indifferent to the church. People will not know Christ is present unless we bear witness and they see his face in our face. Our love must extend not only to friends but to strangers as well and it comes through generous and selfless giving. If Christ's prayer is to be realised our oneness in the Lord must be visible. People should be able to see it. It does no good for believers to proclaim that they are God's children, baptised into eternal life when the image they present to the world is one of division instead of unity and peace.

'Come, Lord Jesus, and unite us in your love.'

Prayer of the faithful

Calling to mind the Father's love which extends all our hopes and desires, we pray for that unity of heart and mind which was the parting wish of Jesus.

1. We pray for our Holy Father. May he have the courage and wisdom to lead the church in these difficult times. Lord, hear us.
2. We pray for the healing of divisions and the removal of prejudices among our people. Give us the grace to walk Christ's pathway of love and peace. Lord, hear us.
3. For a broader vision of life which enables us to appreciate the differing values and religious traditions within our society, so that we can live in spiritual harmony and peace. Lord, hear us.
4. For the sick in our community. May they find comfort in the love and compassion of those who care for them. Lord, hear us.
5. We pray for our dead. Lord, grant them eternal rest and perpetual light in your presence. Lord, hear us.

Heavenly Father, send your Holy Spirit into our hearts, fill us with the fire of your love and remove all bitterness from our hearts. We make our prayer through Christ our Lord. Amen.

Pentecost

The picture painted in the gospel about Pentecost is a colourful description of the spectacular beginnings of the infant church as an active missionary community. The Holy Spirit like a roaring wind descends with tongues of fire on the heads of the apostles, and breathes new life into this faint-hearted band. The immediate impact on the apostles is radical and dramatic. Inspired by the Spirit of God they boldly go out to the market place and proclaim the resurrection of Christ and his conquest of sin and death to those who had only recently crucified their master. They are no longer the terrified and cowardly collection of individuals locked away in the upper room for fear of the Jews. Their world which had fallen apart with the crucifixion and death of Jesus was changed and transformed into a new creation. They emerge full of enthusiasm, gifted with eloquence and with a very clear sense of their vocation.

The thought strikes us that the first Pentecost must have been an exciting time to be alive in the church. The atmosphere was joyful, change was in the air and the outpouring of God's love upon all of creation was like a river in flood. However the coming of the Holy Spirit was not something that happened only at the foundation of the church. The living breath of God is at work in every age as a permanent feature renewing and building up the body of the church. The gift of the Holy Spirit, given at Pentecost, is available to the worshipping community gathered here, provided we are open and willing to receive it. He acts through human persons like ourselves but depends on our response to his promptings. If we are prepared to live our lives according to his guidance and inspiration, by always doing what we sincerely believe is right, there will be no limit to the support he will give us.

This feast, which celebrates the birthday of the church, is an excellent opportunity for evaluating the use we are making of our God-given gifts. The church is built up when we use our individual talents, not for our own personal benefit but for the good of all. We are all labourers whom the Lord asks to go into the harvest. How we love each other and care for each other is a message to everyone we meet and is what outsiders judge our christian faith on. The fact that our gifts are not of the spectacular type which fascinated the onlookers on the first Pentecost, does not diminish their importance. Being a patient father, a loving mother, a good listener and having time for the elderly may not attract the headlines but it witnesses to the fact that God is to be found in the humdrum of a daily routine.

It is in the ordinary that we share most fully in the greatest of God's gifts. As we face the difficulties and trials on our earthly journey we should rejoice that the Holy Spirit is ever present, enlightening our mind with hope and gradually forming Christ in us as he did in the womb of Mary. 'Come Holy Spirit, fill the hearts of your faithful and enkindle in them the fire of your love.'

Prayer of the Faithful

As a community baptised in the Spirit, we turn to our heavenly Father and place our needs before him.

1. We pray that the church, the Body of Christ, may, through the power of the Spirit, open the hearts of the faithful and renew the face of the earth. Lord, hear us.
2. We pray that as a community we may grow in a deeper appreciation of our gifts and put them to use so that we can better care for one another. Lord, hear us.
3. For ourselves, that we may radiate the spirit of love, peace, joy, kindness and gentleness to all we meet. Lord, hear us.
4. By the gentle touch of your spirit help us to develop a deeper compassion for the sick and elderly of the community. Lord, hear us.
5. We remember those who died recently. May the Holy Spirit comfort those who grieve and turn their sorrow into joy. Lord, hear us.

Heavenly Father, send your Spirit into our hearts so that we may become your faithful witnesses and your instruments in drawing all people into unity of life and love. We make this prayer through Christ our Lord. Amen.

Trinity Sunday

When we come to worship, we usually make the sign of the cross. The words that accompany this holy action, 'In the name of the Father, Son, and Holy Spirit,' remind us that there are three persons in God. The feast of the Holy Trinity is a celebration of the mystery of God as a family of love. We have not been left in the dark in our struggle to attempt to understand God. From what Jesus said and did while on earth, we can grasp little pieces of the innermost being of the mystery of God. Throughout his life, Jesus was forever talking about God as his Father, and he referred to himself as God's only Son. He explained also that his mission was to do the will of the Father. Jesus introduces us to the Spirit whom he talks about as being a real person, completely different from himself and God the Father. The Spirit's job is to inspire people to continue in the church the work begun by Jesus and draw everyone into the love of God the Father.

This feast reminds us of a simple truth which we often forget – God's plan is that we share in his life of glory. By our baptism we are raised to a level at which we become sharers in the family life of God. We are born of God the Father, God the Son becomes our brother and the love of God is poured into our hearts by the Holy Spirit. This revelation of his inner life of three persons, in which we have a share, is one of God's greatest gifts to us and it is the model towards which all of us should aim and strive.

Jesus reveals the mystery of the Trinity to us, not just to let us know the truth about God, but also to know the truth about ourselves – as to what is our origin, where is our destiny and how we can arrive at that final point. We only exist, and the world only exists, because God gives life. He is the Father who looks upon us as his children and is closer to us than we are to ourselves. Everyday is a day to love the Father, Son and Holy Spirit so we should strive to make the Holy Trinity a more practical part of our lives. Love is the binding force of the three persons of the Trinity; so when we love we share in that community of love which is the living God.

This celebration of the abundance of God's love is an occasion for appreciating what God has done and continues to do for us. It calls on us to respond to the love of God, poured into our hearts by Christ and the Holy Spirit, and invites us to look forward to the day when we shall share in the glory of God, Father, Son and Holy Spirit.

Prayer of the Faithful

As we worship God, Father, Son and Holy Spirit ,we make our prayer to the Father, through the Son, for all his people.

1. For the church on earth, that inspired by the Holy Spirit it may be a beacon of light to the world. Lord, hear us.
2. For all those who believe in Christ. May they grow in unity so as to reflect on earth the perfect unity of the Blessed Trinity. Lord, hear us.
3. For the families of this parish. May they in imitation of the Blessed Trinity be eager to share with one another the love bestowed on them in life. Lord, hear us.
4. For the sick and the handicapped, that they may experience Gods love in the caring concern of neighbours and friends. Lord, hear us.
5. For our young people who are busy with examinations. May the Lord bless them and inspire them in the work which they are undertaking. Lord, hear us.
6. Let us pray for the dead, especially ... May they be welcomed by the communion of saints. Lord, hear us.

Heavenly Father, in your gentle mercy guide our wayward hearts. May we always experience your presence among us. We make this prayer through our Lord, Jesus Christ your Son who lives and reigns with you and the Holy Spirit one God, forever and ever. Amen.

Body and Blood of Christ

The feast of Corpus Christi was instituted to focus special attention on the real presence of Christ in the eucharist. In a sense it is a repeat of Holy Thursday's Mass of the Last Supper. The sad memories associated with Holy Week tend to overshadow the Lord's breaking of bread and his farewell promise that he would be with his church all days until the end of time. It is a celebration of the generosity of the Lord to us, in offering himself as food to satisfy our spiritual and material hunger as we journey through life. On this day, the church makes us sit down, stop and consider the great miracle of God's presence among us. We thank the Father for the gift of his only Son as our redeemer and Saviour, as our Lord and friend. God has given us everything he could in the life of his Son.

The feast is not only about the eucharist – it is also about the community that assembles to celebrate the eucharist. Hospitality is at the heart of the gospel message. If our hearts are not open and ready to share with those in need in our ordinary life we cannot be united in our celebration. There is no way we can offer the eucharist and not reach out to the poor as Jesus did. It is the daily life that we live during the week that gives us something to bring to the community Mass on Sunday. We cannot take a worldly lifestyle to the altar and celebrate it as christians. By living lives of service for others, we begin to appreciate what the eucharist is all about. It sends us out to touch the lives of neighbours as the healing presence of a helping hand or a sympathetic voice, changing despair into hope and suspicion into trust.

One cannot be truly present at the eucharist without a desire to change and set out on the road travelled by Christ, trying to live as he did in a caring and sharing way. Every celebration is an invitation to give ourselves as completely as possible to Jesus, and to surrender ourselves to his power of love, which will change us and bring us to eternal life. When we are deeply scarred by sin the eucharist binds up our wounds, restores our strength and pours peace into our troubled souls. The very fact that we celebrate this feast indicates that we are a people of thanksgiving, a community which knows how to praise God for the basic gifts of life, family, friends, food and clothing. Above all we thank God because of what he has done for us in Christ.

312

Prayer of the Faithful

Filled with a deep sense of gratitude and joy at the great gift given to us in the eucharist we approach our heavenly Father with our requests.

1. We pray for our Holy Father and the leaders of the church. Keep them true to their calling, open to God's will and eager to serve Jesus Christ. Lord, hear us.

2. We pray for those young people who are making their First Holy Communion at this time of year. May they be enriched in love and strengthened in faith. Lord, hear us.

3. We pray that the generosity which Christ has shown to us in the eucharist may be reflected in the care we show to the poor, the lonely and the unwanted. Lord, hear us.

4. We pray for the sick. May they experience Christ's peace and healing power. Lord, hear us.

5. We pray for the dead. May they rest in peace, in the company and friendship of Jesus. Lord, hear us.

Heavenly Father, grant that the unity we share with you in the eucharist may transform our lives so that we may become what we receive. We ask this through Christ our Lord. Amen.

Second Sunday of the Year

After a little coaxing and gentle persuasion from his mother to save a wedding feast from catastrophe, Jesus performs the first of his miracles at Cana in Galilee. However, there is more to his action of changing barrels of water into vats of wine than appears at first sight. He is not merely saving a couple of newly-weds from public embarrassment because their wine is running short. What he is really doing is talking to each one of us personally about the shortages in our own lives. Could it be true that after a few years of marriage, gone are our dreams? Our love has dried up, we've lost our ideals and no longer have the sparkle for living. Bored and weary we have settled for humdrum routine. John is telling us that we need to be refreshed, to let Christ touch the water of our lives, and bring greater understanding.

Christ came on earth to change people and to make all things new. He came to change us just as he changed water into wine. His presence among us is an invitation to change our ways and a call to a new manner of life. Christ is the spirit of new life who is continually bursting into a world that is weary of meaningless living. His words are spirit and life and have a message for every age. A few weeks ago we welcomed in a New Year which speaks of new beginnings and a fresh start. With it comes our old familiar resolutions to be better people and transform our living. If we really want to change our lives we have got to turn to Christ and call on his help. Wherever Jesus is found, life is always changed for the better. He enriches the very ordinary, makes it precious and gives an eternal value to the commonplace. Given the opportunity, Jesus will be at work in the most unexpected of ways, transforming us, making us like himself. The joy and happiness he brought into the lives of the newly-weds at Cana by his presence is ours for the asking provided we follow the simple instruction given by Mary, 'Do whatever he tells you.' As our pleading mother, Mary, is always anxious to show her concern by bringing our human needs into the mission of her Son. Our big mistake in life is that when we run short we forget to turn to Jesus for fresh supplies of what we need. It is only when we go to him with open hearts and empty hands that he can touch us and make certain that the wine of love and joy will always be part of our lives.

Prayer of the Faithful

Confident that we can expect the same compassion shown by Jesus to the newly-weds at Cana in Galilee we make our prayers to our heavenly Father.

1. That the church may always give of its best to a world that is short of ideals, as Christ gave the best wine to the newly-weds. Lord, hear us.
2. For all couples who are planning to marry this year. May they invite Jesus to strengthen their lives. Lord, hear us.
3. For married couples whose dreams have turned sour and whose relationships are dull and threadbare, that in their need they may find the help of Christ. Lord, hear us.
4. Let us pray for those who are sick or housebound. May they experience the healing power of your love in their lives. Lord, hear us.
5. May all who have died in Christ enjoy his eternal banquet in heaven. Lord, hear us.

God our Father, we ask you to hear our prayers spoken and unspoken so that we may experience your Son's gentle and loving presence in our lives. We make our prayers through Christ our Lord. Amen.

Third Sunday of the Year

A great moment in Jewish religious history is recalled in today's gospel. Jesus was the centre of attention when he declared the Lord's year of favour as he preached in the synagogue of his home town of Nazareth, where he had been brought up. He opened the scroll and read that passage from the prophet Isaiah, who many years before declared that the long-awaited Messiah would bring Good News to the poor, proclaim liberty to captives, give sight to the blind and set the down-trodden free. When he had the full attention of the congregation, he calmly and deliberately announced, 'This text is being fulfilled today even as you listen.' It was a declaration that the moment of salvation had arrived and that he was the long-awaited Messiah, the fulfilment of Israel's hopes and dreams. The effect was stunning as the locals tried to come to terms with the fact that the holy one of God had turned out to be one of their own. The hope of ages had been born in their midst. There was an air of expectancy at the realisation that God, far from abandoning them, was near at hand, concerned and interested in their well-being.

The message of the gospel, first preached in Galilee, is to be spread today through us. The word of God which first came to birth in our souls at baptism is anxiously waiting to burst forth and take root in the lives of others. Every year is a year of favour from the Lord. There are so many ways we can make these words of Christ, about bringing glad tidings to the poor, liberty to captives and sight to the blind, our very own and have them fulfilled in our hearing. When we help those whose hearts have grown cold and are heavily weighed down, the love of God shines through us and we make them realise that Jesus Christ is not a memory but is living among us today.

We can touch people's lives and be healers in times of estrangement, sympathetic listeners in moments of sorrow and towers of strength and loving care on the occasion of tragedy. To be successful channels of his message we have first to put our own house in order, by accepting the good news of Jesus, inviting him into our lives, so that he can show us the way. If we are privileged to receive the gospel, then the challenge arises as to what extent do we pass on this portrait of God's favour to others by what we are. A question for all of us to ponder – what is the Good

News proclaimed by my life to others today? There is nowhere we can walk in life without leaving the imprint of who we are, good or bad, upon the ground we tread.

Prayer of the Faithful

We turn now with confidence to the Father whose son Jesus proclaimed the year of favour in the synagogue at Nazareth:

1. That the whole church may be guided by the example and teaching of Jesus Christ in the preaching of the Good News. Lord, hear us.
2. That those in government may be mindful of their obligation to show true concern for the poor and the neglected in our society. Lord, hear us.
3. That we may have the courage to take the necessary steps to make our lives conform with the gospel message. Lord, hear us.
4. For the sick, that the Lord may comfort them through our healing words and actions. Lord, hear us.
5. For the dead, that they may obtain eternal rest. Lord, hear us.

Almighty God, you sent your son Jesus to give his life that we might be free. Save us through his merits and restore our world to harmony and peace with you who are God forever and ever. Amen.

Fourth Sunday of the Year

When Jesus began his public ministry in his home town, the initial reaction of the locals to his preaching was very favourable. He spoke fluently and simply but with authority and they loved his words when they first heard them. However, as time passed they felt threatened because they realised that they were being challenged to change their ways. The message of Jesus was a disturbing one and they could not accept it. In a mad frenzy they ganged up against him and made an attempt upon his life. When Jesus made the comment that no prophet is ever accepted in his own country he was clearly identifying himself with the long line of prophets who suffered a similar fate. He was not in the popularity game. He had come to preach the Good News regardless of how well it would be received. What happened that day in Nazareth was to be repeated over and over again during his ministry, with crucifixion as the inevitable final outcome.

Although today's gospel is about the rejection of Jesus Christ, the greatest prophet of all, the work of prophecy continues in every generation as people are invited to witness to Christ, not simply with words, but with their lives. This mission of Christ points to our mission which we received at baptism, to witness to the values which he represents. Every christian is by nature an apostle to whom God has entrusted other people. We are to take a stand with Christ against friend and foe and often a stand against our own weaknesses. At home it may be the call to love more tenderly, showing patience when irritated by shortcomings among friends and neighbours, a readiness to excuse and overlook sharp words, at work a dedication to the job in hand and a refusal to tolerate shoddy workmanship.

God has called us to this particular work but he has not promised easy success or popularity. There will be moments when we will have to stand up and be counted, and our moral worth severely tested. To go against the trend and shake people out of their complacency may not be well received but there is the call to be a prophet. People are too comfortable in their sin and they resent interference. As it was with Jesus so it is with his church. Christ is in every one of us. Either we honour him or deny his presence, but what we do to him is done to ourselves.

Prayer of the Faithful

As we come together around the table of the Lord, we bring all of our needs and worries and we ask God the Father to listen to our prayers.

1. Let us pray for the leaders of the church, our Holy Father, our bishop, our priests, religious sisters and brothers. May they be blessed by God in their preaching and teaching of the Good News. Lord, hear us.

2. For courage and strength to proclaim generously and fearlessly the gospel message in our homes and neighbourhood. Lord, hear us.

3. For those whose love is unsung: parents of handicapped children, those who care for aged parents, and all those suffering at home or in hospital, who bear a silent witness to the love of God in prolonged illness. Lord, hear us.

4. We pray for all young people: those at school and those leaving school. Help them to get employment suited to their ability, and lead them, through strong faith in you, to know and accept the way of life in which they can best serve you. Lord, hear us.

5. Lord, comfort those who are sad because of the death of someone they love, especially those who have died as a result of violence in our country. Help us all to work together to bring about a true peace, founded on principles of justice and equality. Lord, hear us.

Heavenly Father, we call on you with confidence to hear the prayers of these your people, since we make them in the name of Jesus Christ our Lord. Amen.

Fifth Sunday of the Year

By human standards the command Jesus made to Simon Peter: 'Put out into deep water and lower your nets for a catch,' was as foolish as Simon's acceptance of the instruction. Fish only come to the surface for food at nightime – during daylight they remain on the bottom of the sea. Human experience was weighted against success, so a haul was highly unlikely. Yet something in Jesus must have struck a chord in Simon's heart which prompted him, against his better judgement, to obey. The outcome surpassed his wildest dreams. His faith and perseverence were rewarded when Jesus put him in the way of a bumper catch. Realising what had happened, Peter was ashamed and overcome by a deep sense of his own unworthiness. It dawned on him that he was in the presence of the almighty Lord, who alone could rescue him from his sinfulness. He fell on his knees and said: 'Leave me Lord, I am a sinful man.'

What happened to Peter is what happens to us. When we recognise our own sinfulness the power of Christ becomes available to enrich us, so that we can offer ourselves to God, faults and all. The discovery of our spiritual poverty opens our souls to receive what God is offering and awakens us to an awareness of his call. We should not be looking for God in strange places because he speaks to us in ordinary situations where he finds us, in the humdrum bits and pieces of our every day experiences. We are more likely to hear his call in our pain than in our plenty. When we discover the hand of God at work in our lives, the impossible becomes possible.

The challenge facing all of us is to detect the voice of God in our lives and to have the courage and generosity to answer promptly. God expects us to share in his work of spreading his love and mercy. Peter offers an inspiring example in leaving his nets to become a fisher of men. Up to this time, he was engrossed in his own work. Launching out into the deep meant putting his faith and trust in Jesus who was directing him on a new pathway in life. Jesus wants us to go through life with our hand in his hand. There will be times when we are called to take a new direction and face the unknown. Our response should be no less generous than Peter's if we are to meet the challenge of the vocation to which we are called.

Prayer of the Faithful

Jesus tells us that if we ask for anything in his name the Father will give it to us so we now offer our prayers to the Father in his name.

1. We pray for our Holy Father, for bishops, priests and for all who have been called to be fishers of men, that they may have the courage and perseverance to cast their nets in deep waters. Lord, hear us.

2. We remember all who work at night, fishermen at sea, staff in hospitals, and all who provide a nightly service for their community. Let us pray that they are aware of God strengthening them in their labours. Lord, hear us.

3. We pray for young people who are launching out into the unknown to face a difficult future that they may put their trust in Jesus and leave everything to his will. Lord, hear us.

4. We pray for the sick, the sorrowing and the troubled and those who suffer in mind and body, that the Lord may touch their lives with his tenderness and strength. Lord, hear us.

5. We remember our dead and those who grieve for their loved ones. We pray that God may keep them in his love and peace. Lord, hear us.

Lord God, you have called us to be part of your family, the church. Bind us to one another in faith and fellowship and shower your blessings upon us. We make our prayer through Christ our Lord. Amen.

Sixth Sunday of the Year

The Beatitudes are such a familiar part of the gospel that when we hear them read during the liturgy we can easily miss their meaning. The message they contain may take a lifetime to learn, but unless we take it to heart there will be no entry into the kingdom of heaven. They explain how to spend this life in order to attain everlasting happiness in heaven. Following Christ is not meant to be easy and it is a challenge we must face every day. We are invited to do things that do not come naturally to us like being humble, showing mercy and opening our hearts to those in need. On the surface, the gospel might appear to be a plea for poverty and a condemnation of riches. Jesus does not idealise poverty as a value to be sought for its own sake but as a means to giving us greater freedom to follow Christ without compromise.

If we take Jesus seriously, we will come to realise power and affluence are two of the greatest threats to the christian way of life. We live in a world which praises efficiency, glorifies success and worships power. Society announces that happiness comes from wealth, affluence and freedom from any form of pain. The trouble with reliance on such material resources to bring happiness is that, in the final analysis, it does not work. The truth is we have not got a steady grip on life, for death is a reality which has always plagued the human race. Even if all other problems were suitably resolved we would still have to contend with death. Jesus is not against our striving for true happiness; but he bluntly warns us against putting our trust in material comforts because, in the long run, it will turn out to be a misplaced confidence. There is more to life than superficial passing things. We are created to share God's joy, and anything that calls us away from this goal is not good for us.

The message contained in this gospel is both severe and challenging because it is at odds with our customary way of thinking. Many of us who profess Jesus to be our Saviour, live life without any thought for our religious beliefs. As we face the task of developing a proper relationship with God, we are frightened by the deep demands which the beatitudes make on us. We are called not to worship wealth, food or comfort, but to worship the God who alone can grant us all good things.

Prayer of the Faithful

Aware of the danger arising from putting our trust in the pleasures of this world, we lift up our hearts in fervent prayer to the Father.

1. We pray that the church throughout the world may be an effective sign of the way to everlasting happiness and eternal life. Lord, hear us.

2. That we may learn to place our trust in spiritual values which enrich our being, and not in material possessions which bring discontent to our soul. Lord, hear us.

3. That we may never close our hearts to those in need, but consciously involve ourselves in Christ's work of healing and reconciling. Lord, hear us.

4. For the sick and disabled. May they experience the Lord's care through the love of their neighbours and friends. Lord, hear us.

5. We pray that our deceased relatives and friends may enjoy peace and rest with the Lord in heaven. Lord, hear us.

Heavenly Father, look with compassion on the needy. Enlighten our lives with your truth and give us the grace to live out the high ideals put before us by your Son Jesus Christ, who lives and reigns with you forever and ever. Amen.

Seventh Sunday of the Year

One of the key tasks facing any christian community is to put into action the gospel of forgiveness, by refusing to harbour thoughts of hatred and revenge for our enemies. Anger, bitterness and resentment are the moral cancers of our age and set us on the road that leads to disaster and destruction. We have long memories for injuries inflicted and a frightening capacity for nursing old sores, all of which poison our spirit and destine us to a life of misery. While the world goes its way of retribution and revenge this gospel tells us that the standard of behaviour for a follower of Christ is the way of friendship and love. The real test of love is the regard we have for those we find little reason to like; those people who are bent on insulting us and causing us harm.

Christ calls us to a radical re-ordering of our lives when he warns us to be on our guard against the all too natural temptation to retaliate by paying back one wrong with another. Instead we are to demonstrate generosity of heart by seeing beyond our hurts and injustices. Our enemies are given the benefit of the doubt on these occasions when we are gracious enough to offer pardon on the grounds that a person is bigger than his wrongful actions. Furthermore, so much hatred is often the result of ignorance or misunderstanding. Forgiveness is about removing the barriers which block the flow of love and, as a result, damage friendly personal relationships. It is costly and the gospel is the story of the price God had to pay so that our sins could be forgiven. It meant the crucifixion of Jesus Christ on the hill of Calvary so that we could be reconciled with God.

If we are intent upon pleasing our heavenly Father, a consideration of his limitless mercy should prompt us to put the teaching of Jesus into practice. Each of us here can start forgiving right now by curbing a sharp tongue of criticism, suppressing the revenge instinct and accepting the irritating behaviour of a neighbour. The gospel ends with a plea to show compassion for those who have done wrong. Compassion is the outgoing love of God which gives us the ability to appreciate and share the joys and troubles of a neighbour. We can often live in close proximity with people and be unaware of how they really feel and how much they are in need of our help and understanding. As we gather round the table of the Lord, we pray that our hearts may not be insensitive to the sufferings of others but a source of hope and encouragement to those in distress and in need of our help.

Prayer of the Faithful

With confidence we now approach the all-forgiving Father whose mercy towards us is limitless and without bounds.

1. We pray that the church on earth may be a living example of the forgiveness and compassion shown by Jesus. Lord, hear us.
2. Bless with your kindness all those who have hurt us, injured our family or caused us hardship in any way. Lord, hear us.
3. Through my own troubles, help me to feel the sufferings of others. May I know your joy and peace and share it with them. Lord, hear us.
4. Look with compassion on the sick, the old and the neglected. May our concern keep the flame of hope alive in their hearts. Lord, hear us.
5. Bless and reward with eternal life those who have departed this world. Lord, hear us.

Almighty and compassionate Father, we thank you for the forgiveness you have offered through your Son. Help us to show your forgiveness to others. We make our prayers through Christ our Lord. Amen.

Eighth Sunday of the Year

Our attention is drawn to a number of practical points on christian living, which are broad in scope and rich in truth. Following
Jesus is a serious occupation and leaves no room for comfortable
complacency. Our words and conversation, the fruit of our
tongues are a true indication of our spiritual health and our christian life. When we open our lips we should be intent on praising
God and refrain from hurting our neighbour. We are asked to
search as carefully for our own faults as we do for the faults of
others, because concentrating on ridding ourselves of the big
blotches in our personal lives will leave precious little time for
comment on the failures of others. The person who is aware of his
own weaknesses and is striving to overcome them is slow to
judge and swift to give benefit of the doubt.

When preaching, Jesus drew his examples from the obvious
in everyday life and here we have him commenting on the people
who are preoccupied with spotlighting someone else's faults and
yet are blind to their own. The appealing thing about fault finding
in others is that it takes the focus off our own deficiencies and
helps us to feel ever so self-righteous. How miserable it all becomes when it spills over into spiteful personal gossip. It's no ex-
aggeration to say that gossip is the most vicious and dangerous
type of talk. All this business of tittle-tattle, passing on scandalous
tales about people, does untold damage as it results in tearing rep-
utations to shreds. All who have been the victims of wagging
tongues know the pain inflicted. Socrates once said that nature
has given us two ears, two eyes and only one tongue so that we
should hear more than we speak. If we cannot say something
good about another person then it is better to remain silent. Isn't it
lovely when occasionally we meet someone who isn't interested
in people's failing but only in their good points.

The lesson on how dangerous it is to pass judgement on
others stands at the heart of the gospel message. Jesus was never
in the judgement business. He used words to heal, restore and to
bring back life, joy and hope. Our striving to imitate the Lord and
produce the fruits of good living is seriously hampered when we
allow judgemental attitudes to take root in our lives. The honest
and perceptive christian will pay more attention to personal

short-comings, knowing that it is only with God's help that they can be overcome.

Prayer of the Faithful

Confident that he will grant us what we ask, we make our prayer to God the Father with a sincere heart.

1. We pray for our Holy Father, that the Lord may grant him wisdom and courage, to guide and govern the church. Lord, hear us.
2. May we always use the wonderful gift of speech to praise and thank God and to comfort and encourage our neighbour. Lord, hear us.
3. That we may be able to see our own faults and refrain from passing judgement on the failures of others. Lord, hear us.
4. For the sick, the lonely and the handicapped. Grant to all of them Lord, healing, courage strength and hope. Lord, hear us.
5. For our dear departed relatives and friends. Grant them the joy and peace of your heavenly kingdom. Lord, hear us.

Heavenly Father, you are our strength in time of need. Open our hearts to your grace and lead us into your kingdom. Through Christ our Lord. Amen.

Ninth Sunday of the Year

By any standard the centurion standing in the street at Capernaum is an outstanding personality. First and foremost he is an individual, both in character and in faith, but what makes him extra special is his attitude to his servant. In days when servants were little more than slaves, he cares for the sick man as if he were his own son. He is grieved that his servant is dying and is determined to do everything in his power to save him. In dire distress he waives protocol, swallows his pride and approaches Jesus. It may well have been his unexpected compassion which so moves Jesus and prompts him to say, 'I tell you I have never found so much faith among the Israelites.'

What is being emphasised in this gospel is not so much the cure of the servant, as the faith of the centurion. There is nothing narrow, crippled or bigoted about his outlook on life. Here is a man who is an outsider, a pagan, a detested foreigner with no church to go to, yet the depth and quality of his faith contrasts so much with the lip-service of the Jews. He has the calm assurance of someone who has placed his problems in the hands of God and is willing to take Jesus at his word and trust him. By the way he behaves, we can see that he realises that God's house is open to all – that God has a place for everyone who calls on his name and that there is no such thing as a foreigner as far as Jesus is concerned.

Several times throughout the gospel we find Jesus commenting on the lack of faith among his people. What disappointed him most were the many who believed only with their lips. It prompted him to say, 'These people honour me with their lips but their hearts are far from me.' Nothing repels people from religion more than the hypocrisy of lip-service. The faith of the centurion expresses itself in a very practical way – in the love he has for his servant. His action shows that goodness is not confined to churchgoers. The willingness to take God at his word is not restricted to religious people. The strange thing about faith is that it can blossom in unlikely places and people, and that it can wither and die within the very doors of the church. So, let's not mistake religious practice for faith.

Faith is not some kind of lucky charm which helps to ensure

a comfortable passage through difficulties. It is a person's way of looking into life and making meaning of it. The depth and strength of our faith shows up and is reflected in our dealings with other people. The centurion was open, warm and friendly to those around him and gives us an insight into how to approach God with simplicity, sincerity and full confidence. Even in the brief appearance he makes on the stage of the New Testament story the centurion proves to be one of the most attractive characters in the gospel. His memory lives on in the moving words put on our lips just before we receive Holy Communion: 'Lord, I am not worthy that you should enter under my roof; just say the word and my soul shall be healed.'

Prayer of the Faithful

Inspired by the gift of faith which God has given us, we present our prayers to the Father.

1. Let us pray for all who minister in the church that they may bring the light of the gospel to all mankind. Lord, hear us.
2. May we, in our lives, show the same love and compassion that the Centurion had for his servant, to those who need our help. Lord, hear us.
3. Lord help us to understand and accept those people in our community who differ from us in race or creed. Lord, hear us.
4. May the old, the lonely and the sick of our community receive the comfort of God's love in their distress. Lord, hear us.
5. We remember in our prayers the faithful departed. May they be raised to the fullness of new life by the power of God's will. Lord, hear us.

God our Father, help us to grow in compassion and give hope to all those who touch our lives. We ask this through Christ our Lord. Amen.

Tenth Sunday of the Year

There is really no problem identifying with today's gospel story. Many things cause tears to fall but the greatest offender of all is death. Here a young man dies and with him the hope and dreams of a widowed mother. Her whole world has fallen apart. She is burying her only son and the entire community is mourning with her. They can console her with their presence, but have no power to bring her son back to life. As the story goes, it happened that Jesus is coming into town just as the son's funeral is heading out for burial. The sight of the widowed mother's distress moves his sacred heart with compassion. Everyone present is struck with fear when he intervenes and restores the young man to life. There's no doubt about it, God has visited his people. The power of Jesus raising the dead man to life is recorded simply and without fuss.

Let's not forget that the widow's son has only been granted an extension to his life. He has been merely brought back to life for a while – perhaps a few years. At a later moment, death will have its way, with all the grief and heartbreak that it brings. However, by restoring him to life, Jesus is pointing dramatically to the need we all have for his healing spirit. He is telling us that he has come on earth to raise all people to life, a life that will never end. His raising of the widow's son is a sign of the spiritual resurrection offered to all people. He is showing concern about the need for us to be spiritually alive here and now.

We are all familiar with the saying, 'Every day we die a little.' As christians we begin to die at baptism. Death in small portions enters all our lives a thousand times before the final event. Its shadow falls across life from the cradle to the grave. Some of us are so tortured, mixed up by circumstances and situations that in times of despair we put the question: 'Is life before death worth living?' At moments like that we are the living dead. In a sense we are as unconsolable as the widow at the loss of her son. Only Christ can give us true life by filling our suffering with his presence and by pointing a way out of our entanglement.

We are being challenged by today's gospel to become channels of God's compassionate and healing love. If we are in any way serious about our christianity, we must translate concern for others, who are sorrowing, into action and do a little of what the Lord did in Nain. Our little deeds of love transform the broken-hearted and help them experience God as the Father who has come among his people – in a way it's the only real job any of us has got to do.

Prayer of the Faithful

We place our needs with confidence before the Father, through his Son Jesus, who came on earth to raise all men to new life.

1. For our Pope, the bishops, and the clergy that through their voices the care and hope of Jesus will be shown to all people. Lord, hear us.
2. For those who care for the sick daily that they may be channels of Jesus' compassionate and healing love. Lord, hear us.
3. For those who have recently suffered the loss of a parent or relative, that they, with God's help, may recover their faith in life. Lord, hear us.
4. We remember the sick of our community, that like the widow's son they may experience the healing hand of Jesus in their sufferings. Lord, hear us.
5. For the dead, that they may be raised to the fullness of life in God's presence. Lord, hear us.

God our Father, guide us by our gestures to touch the broken-hearted and help them experience your Son who has come among us. We make this prayer through Christ our Lord. Amen.

Eleventh Sunday of the Year

While many of us have not got a keen awareness of our own sins, we find no difficulty in pointing out the faults of others. Personal shortcomings are difficult to admit but a neighbour's failings are always a topic of conversation. The temptation to join Simon in the chorus of wagging tongues about such a woman faces everybody. We may well pride ourselves on our own goodness and yet be quick to condemn and pass judgement on those who are not up to the mark. Because Simon dismissed her as a sinner, he hadn't a kind word or shred of sympathy for how she felt. Jesus, in his approach to her, was gentle and loving because he saw her as the person that she could become – a far cry from our way of thinking. Contrary to expectations, he did not show his disapproval of her lifestyle because he had not come to judge sinners but to show them mercy and forgiveness. The greatness of the woman's shame and disgrace was as apparent to him as her dishonour. He understood human weakness and how people can be bent and broken into so many shapes on life's journey.

Forgiveness is one of those words we bandy around without really thinking what it means. It slips easily off our lips but rarely penetrates our hearts. Deeds are far more eloquent than words. The prostitute anointing the feet of Jesus is a great example of the sorrow for sin that leads to healing. She shows that nobody is debarred from receiving God's forgiveness, which is there for the asking. We must never forget that we are God's sinful people, before whom we all stand empty-handed, in need of the courage to face our faults and repent.

What Christ is asking of us is a totally forgiving attitude towards our neighbour and a deep awareness of our own personal need for God's forgiveness. Christ does not say that it is easy to forgive, but that we must learn to forgive. We come to know ourselves and others better when we patch up quarrels, misunderstandings and disagreements. Too many family feuds which begin over children playing, animals straying or rights of way never heal. Often the rift becomes so great that generations on both sides of the quarrel grow up without ever meeting or knowing each other – and yet all of them consider themselves to be quite good christians.

The intense sorrow of the woman kneeling at Christ's feet was the passport that brought her a new life. She was heavily burdened but she found peace and rest in Christ. We too can experience the same when we realise that forgiveness flows from lowering our defences and admitting our wrong-doings. God can not help those who deny their sin.

Prayer of the Faithful

Placing our confidence in God the Father, who shows loving mercy in his treatment of sinners, we make our prayer.

1. We pray for all church leaders. May they carry on the work of Jesus in forgiving sins and binding up hearts that are broken. Lord, hear us.
2. For the openness and honesty to be aware of our sins and to know ourselves as God knows us. Lord, hear us.
3. We pray for those who are searching for God in their lives. May they find Christ who is the light of the world. Lord, hear us.
4. We pray for those who are sick and for those who care for them. May they experience the healing presence of the Lord through a caring christian community. Lord, hear us.
5. We pray for the dead especially ... that they may be cleansed of their sins and enter forever into the light, happiness and peace of your kingdom. Lord, hear us.

God our Father, we offer you our thanks for your goodness to us. When we grow careless and wander off the right path, guide our footsteps once more in the direction of your Son who is the way, the truth and the life. We make our prayers through Christ our Lord. Amen.

Twelfth Sunday of the Year

At a critical moment in his public ministry Christ puts a question to the apostles concerning his true identity. He was anxious to know what people thought of him: 'Who do people say that I am?' It comes as no surprise that the vast majority were confused and mistook him for one of the prophets of old. Very few were interested in discovering accurate details about the private person behind the public face, who didn't bribe people with empty promises but stated that there was a price to pay for discipleship. The only one that gave the correct answer was Peter, but while he spoke the right words his appreciation lacked depth. When the crunch came at Calvary he turned his back and denied all association with Christ. 'I do not know the Man.' Recognising who exactly Christ is, and what he means in our lives, is undoubtedly a priority for all of us who call ourselves christians. We cannot hope to form a meaningful relationship with Christ, and dedicate our lives to him, unless we know who he really is.

It is easy to say, 'You are the Christ,' but the real answer depends on our readiness to follow him in our daily lives which involves taking up our cross, embracing suffering and often going against the tide of public opinion. Each day brings its own share of trials and difficulties and the gospel states that we only give proper recognition to Christ when we are prepared to follow the path of pain, sorrow and distress that he trod. This means accepting that suffering and hardship have a place in our lives, leading as they do to salvation and final glory. Suffering and the cross present us with a problem, because they go against the grain of life. We all want ease, comfort and luxury. Most of us are quite willing to follow Christ, but when trouble comes our way we are forced to realise that we cannot have christianity without tears. The cross and suffering stand fair and square in the centre of life and are a great mystery. Jesus is showing us that suffering is the measure of a person, the test of love for friends, and a necessary requirement of his followers.

We find the cross everywhere in life, and do not have to go searching for it. It's already on our shoulders in parenthood, unemployment, in the loss of life's partner, in the death of a child and in the pain of a family feud. All we need to do is to carry it willingly by offering up our daily sufferings with those of Christ.

One of the paradoxes of the gospel is that life comes from death. In the midst of this season of growth when the countryside is teeming with life, Jesus reminds us that only when we die will we truly live.

Prayer of the Faithful

Confident that nothing in life or death can separate us from the love of our heavenly Father, we make our prayer of petition to him for all those who are suffering.

1. We pray for our church leaders. May they have the courage and willingness to suffer for the sake of the gospel so that the message of Christ may be heard in all its fullness. Lord, hear us.
2. We pray for all who are suffering physical hardship; the poor, the sick, the handicapped and prisoners. May they never fall into despair but experience the comfort of your personal love. Lord, hear us.
3. Help us realise that we cannot be truly christian unless there is self-denial in our daily lives. Lord, hear us.
4. Lord, give your comfort to the sick, especially ... Bless all who care for them and show them your loving kindness. Lord, hear us.
5. That our dead, especially ... may be one with God and their loved ones in heaven for all eternity. Lord, hear us.

God our Father, the suffering and death of your Son, Jesus, brought life to the world. Help us to recognise the cross and suffering, not just in the great trials of life, but in our day-to-day choices. We make this prayer through Christ our Lord. Amen.

Thirteenth Sunday of the Year

The call and the cost of christian commitment are heavily emphasised in this gospel where the life of discipleship and its qualities
are laid out before us. There is nothing about being a follower of
Jesus that does not demand effort. As all existing responsibilities
have to take second place, discipleship is not something to be
entered into casually. On his journey to Jerusalem, Jesus meets
three men who are anxious to follow him but who are unfit and
unprepared for the challenge involved. The young man bursting
with enthusiasm who, with whole-hearted response, vowed to be
a follower wherever he would go, must have been surprised to
hear Jesus dampen his spirits and warn him off with the caution,
that the Son of Man did not have a home to call his own. Jesus is
only being fair when he makes it clear in very direct speech what
is expected of those who wish to join his group. If we want to
accompany him we must know what we are doing and be aware
of the harsh realities of life. To follow Jesus to Calvary can be no
casual accompaniment of a wandering preacher. The message is
harsh but clear – if anything at all stands in our way or takes priority over Jesus in our lives, then we are not free to follow him.

Every day we are faced with a situation similar to these
three young volunteers.In the midst of our work, as we are hurry-
ing about our business, we encounter Jesus who beckons us to
come and serve. He longs for us to acknowledge his loving presence in silently carrying out his will. It's an on-going challenge
requiring practical daily choices which are not always easy to
make. Sometimes it may involve a serious conflict of loyalty or it
may be a simple call to be friendly or neighbourly. Our journeying with Christ began at baptism with the promise to make his
way of life our own. Growing in closeness to him is the result of
making daily sacrifices, but the grind of monotonous living gets
to us all and is evident in our half-hearted responses.

We love the call but we quibble about the cost to our personal
freedom. Sunday Mass affords us a wonderful opportunity to
deepen and renew the relationship which we have established
with Christ as a believing community. It's a time to pray for the
grace to follow him whole-heartedly without wavering or reser-
vation. The Lord's call requires an immediate response and is not
just something to be fitted in after we have attended to all the

important business; like maintaining our status, our popularity and all the other goals we set ourselves. Whatever invitation comes our way, our reply should always be: 'You are my God. It is you who are my portion'.

Prayer of the Faithful

We place our needs before God our Father whose Son has gone before us and has called us to follow him. With confidence we pray for the grace to accept that calling.

1. We pray for the leaders of the church, and all those engaged in preaching the word of God, that they may persevere in their commitment to follow Christ. Lord, hear us.
2. We pray for the community who worship in this parish, that they may be renewed from day to day through faith in the word of God calling them to a better life. Lord, hear us.
3. That those of us who have lost hope because of our sins may realise that Christ our leader walks with us and shoulders our burden. Lord, hear us.
4. We pray for those who are weakened by sickness or infirmity. Assure them that in your love they do not stand alone. Lord, hear us.
5. We pray for the dead who have followed Jesus through the gateway of death. May they enjoy God's presence forever in heaven. Lord, hear us.

Father in heaven, in our desire to follow in the footsteps of your Son, make us one in mind and heart through Christ our Lord. Amen.

Fourteenth Sunday of the Year

Christ sent his disciples ahead of him to announce, with a message of peace, that the reign of God was at hand. We can feel a sense of their joy and wonder that their mission was a success as people flocked to listen and welcome the word of God. The church's task of sending out missionaries is an urgent one and goes on in every age. 'God wishes all men to be saved and to come to a knowledge of the truth.' (1 Tim 2: 4) Since Christ's own life and mission were confined to a small area of Palestine around Jerusalem, he was looking out on the world and thinking of people of all times and places when he spoke the words: 'The harvest is great but the labourers are few.' He realised that the harvest of souls was countless, the opportunities for saving them plentiful, but that too few people would volunteer for the work of spreading his gospel message. The world would be far more ready to receive the gospel than his followers would be to announce it.

The invitation to take part in the work of the Lord, to be the salt of the earth and the light of the world is extended to our generation. Our mission is to bring the peace of Christ wherever we go and to all we meet. No special training or education is needed for the work, as the word of God is waiting to come to birth in a more total way in each of us. All that is required is an effort on our part to allow the goodness of God to shine in our lives. Since the Lord relies on us as his helpers, Christ will be judged on our showing of him. In an age when many are confused and disillusioned, and are searching for meaning in drugs and shallow relationships, we can open their hearts to faith and arouse in them a thirst for God by treating them with courtesy, charity and respect. In the midst of plenty, people are hungering to be wanted, loved and recognised. God alone can satisfy the desires of the human heart and overcome the darkness from within.

Everyday is a harvest day and in every place there are things we can do for Christ which will otherwise remain undone. We are all responsible for some small part of the Lord's work and it is up to us to reap the harvest. We cannot sit back and expect the peace of Christ to appear unexpectedly from heaven without our involvement. To give to others the peace of Christ is the vocation we all share as disciples and the task committed to us. We are called not merely to be good people but to spread the gospel.

Prayer of the Faithful

We turn now in prayer to the Lord of the harvest and we pray for the needs of the church and of the world.

1. For the church, that all the faithful may be aware that they are called by God to spread his kingdom of peace in the world. Lord, hear us.
2. For our parish community that we may be more conscious of our vocation to announce the Good News of the gospel to the people in our neighbourhood. Lord, hear us.
3. We now pray for farmers who till the soil and work the land that they may have good weather and reap an abundant harvest. Lord, hear us.
4. We pray for all who are sick or who find life difficult. May they know that God cares for them through the concern of their families. Lord, hear us.
5. We pray for all who have died. May the love and friendship of their lives blossom forth into the flower of eternal life. Lord, hear us.

Heavenly Father, help us to take part with joy in the work of spreading your gospel by the example we show in our lives. We make this prayer through Christ our Lord. Amen.

Fifteenth Sunday of the Year

The parable of the Good Samaritan is one of our Lord's best known short stories. When a lawyer approaches Jesus inquiring as to who his neighbour is, Jesus directs his attention to what being a good neighbour entails. He paints a portrait of a man who was robbed on the road from Jerusalem to Jericho and beaten within an ace of his life. The Priest and the Levite passed by on the other side of the road, because to touch the dead body would have meant their exclusion from religious service in the Temple. Their brand of worship was not inspired by the love of neighbour but by religious duty. The unlikely hero of the story turns out to be a Samaritan who acting out of sheer love and generosity instead of a sense of duty, opened his heart and recognised a neighbour even in a despised Jew.

Neighbourliness is not a general attitude of helping those who are good to us, but a matter of being ready to come to the assistance of those in need, even the perfect stranger. There is to be no picking and choosing or limit to the scope of our giving. Nobody is excluded from a claim on our help because we are all God's children. The story is easily understood and painfully true but difficult to put into practice. It forces us to think about ourselves and to reflect on the quality and quantity of our acts of charity – to ask the question: 'Are we doing what Jesus would want us to do in his name?' When it is a matter of putting ourselves out for people we can all find suitable excuses to avoid unpleasant duties and let the opportunity to do good pass by. Our spark of compassion is easily snuffed out as we look the other way. The road from Jericho to Jerusalem runs through our neighbourhood and is strewn with wounded people. There is a world crying out for mercy at our very door. If we are alert and sensitive we can come in contact with people who are lonely, hungry for love and attention, crushed by disappointment and failure, guilt-ridden and wounded by sin.

The Good Samaritan represents Jesus Christ who, reaching out in love, came to the rescue of the human race in its pitiful condition and healed our wounds by dying on the cross of Calvary. That act of love cost him his life. He expects us to stop and help those in need even though it will cost us time, trouble and expense. The gospel is at pains to emphasise that there is no love of God without love of our neighbour who is in distress.

Prayer of the Faithful

We are reminded today that God the Father has given each of us the ministry of being a good neighbour. With confidence in his love, we come now to ask his help in serving our neighbour.

1. We pray for the church throughout the world. May all its members realise that in service to others they bear witness to Christ in word and action. Lord, hear us.
2. Teach us to stretch out a helping hand to bring consolation, strength and encouragement to those who are in distress and who feel neglected. Lord, hear us.
3. We remember all in our local community who work in organisations dedicated to the needy and neglected. May the knowledge that they are furthering the work of the good Samaritan, help them persevere. Lord, hear us.
4. For those in our midst who are sick or suffer from depression or worry, that God may heal and comfort them. Lord, hear us.
5. For all those who have died that they may be happy forever in paradise. Lord, hear us.

Heavenly Father, open our hearts to receive your mercy and compassion. Give us the grace to recognise Christ in all who suffer and are downtrodden. We make this prayer through Christ our Lord. Amen.

Sixteenth Sunday of the Year

Most of us at one time or another have experienced the fret and fuss of a Martha and Mary clash of temperament in the home. The hardworking Martha gets irritated with the idling Mary and on the spur of the moment says out straight what is in her mind. She thinks that her sister should be engaged in something more important than listening to Jesus. The problem with this gospel story is that we are not all at ease with Christ's comment; Mary's behaviour seems so unfair. The kitchen dosser gets the praise and is commended by the Lord for having chosen the better part. It comes across as a picture of blatant injustice and our sympathy is with the long suffering Martha. St Teresa said: 'If Martha had imitated Mary, Christ would have gone without his dinner.' We are left wondering just how does the Martha-Mary story fit into our lives and what exactly the Lord is saying to us through it?

Perhaps we might get a better insight into the incident if we remember that at this time Jesus was on his way to Jerusalem and, with the cross before him, all he wanted was a break from the crowds. He calls in to his friends Martha and Mary, not to avail of lavish hospitality, but for a brief rest, to leave behind his cares and concerns. Mary chose the better part because she took time to listen and to give her undivided attention to Jesus. She understood his needs at that moment, realising that time spent in the Lord's company was more important than fussing around making him comfortable. The problem with us is that we are often so busy doing the work of the Lord in the good deeds which we perform for our neighbour that we forget the Lord of the work – who is the motivation for acts of christian charity.

The gospel is telling us that no matter how busy we are we should take time to sit quietly and find the Lord in our world of work and to be guided by him. It is easy to get our priorities wrong because all our working moments are busy ones with little time for sitting at the feet of Jesus, reflecting on our lives. The danger is that if we do not take time to listen to the word of God and to pray, we become slaves of our duties. We rush about and yet the important things can be forgotten and remain undone. One of the great difficulties in life is that we neglect people because we do not have the time to sit down and listen to them. Our approach is often based on what we can do for others; how we can smother them in kindness, whereas, what they are really looking for is our company. Time spent visiting a lonely soul in a home for the aged can also be time spent in the company of God. For what we do to others we do to Christ. All the everyday happenings of life are part of our religious lives and provide an opportunity for working out our salvation.

Prayer of the Faithful

There are many things which occupy us, but what really counts is listening to the voice of God, who speaks to those who are willing to listen. In a spirit of hope we bring our prayers before him.

1. We pray for the church throughout the world. May all who are homeless and wandering find a welcome within her walls. Lord, hear us.
2. We pray for ourselves, that like Mary we may choose the better part and welcome Jesus into our hearts and lives. Lord, hear us.
3 For all who are preoccupied with the passing distractions of life. May they come to appreciate the value of listening more attentively to God's word. Lord, hear us.
4. We pray for the sick. May they experience the healing power of Christ through the love and support of their friends. Lord, hear us.
5. Grant eternal rest to the faithful departed. May they dwell in the Lord's own house forever. Lord, hear us.

God our Father, you have sent your Son Jesus to show us the way to eternal life. May we always welcome him into our lives and have a place for him in our hearts. We make our prayer through Christ our Lord. Amen.

Seventeenth Sunday of the Year

What better introduction could we have to prayer than the direction given to us by Jesus, who is the master of the art of prayer. One of the reasons why people were attracted to him and sought his company was the long periods he spent in private prayer and the importance he attached to it. The success of his daily activity flowed from prayer. Our inbuilt thirst for God expresses itself in the fact that almost everyone would like to pray better. However, the problem is that we often give up on prayer because we are not sure how to pray, what to say and whether our prayers are heard. At one time or another we have all made comments like: 'What's the point of praying? My prayers are never answered!' 'I don't pray anymore – God does not seem to be listening'. The truth is that we give up before we start. Like the disciples, we need encouragement and must turn to Christ and say, 'Lord, teach us to pray.' When they put this request to him he spoke spontaneously from his heart to his Father in heaven.

The traditional and familiar words of the Our Father make it a community prayer for all times and every occasion. The tone of the prayer is both intimate and also mysterious. It is simple, short and yet a profession of faith because it reveals God as our Father whose kingdom we seek, and who can be trusted to provide for our genuine needs. Prayer is talking to God – it's an intimate and loving conversation which we carry on as family members with our heavenly Father. It's walking in his company, paying loving attention to his presence and deepening our relationship with him. God wants us to be real, so we can drop our inhibitions, come as we are and speak to him with all honesty in a human way. We all have our own style of communication – lengthy speaking and many words are not necessary. The joys and disappointments that make our days, give us much to converse about. We can place our petitions before him and they will be answered as he sees fit. Whatever his response, we can be sure it is for our good.

It has been said that he who prays rises from his knees a better person. It always happens as we come to know God more, we come to know ourselves better. Prayer makes us realise how much we need God and deepens our sense of dependence on his saving help. We become aware that we stand before God in weakness, powerlessness and yet in the hope that his grace can make something of us. In the rush and noise of life, which drowns out the voice of God, we must find a time and a place of silence to pray. It is only in silence we can speak to God and God can speak to us.

Prayer of the Faithful

Christ has told us we can call God, our Father, so with firm hope we place our petition before him.

1. We pray for the church throughout the world, that she may always express a deep trust in the coming of the Father's kingdom of love, justice and peace. Lord, hear us.
2. Amidst the difficulties of life help us to go on praying and never give in to temptations. Lord, hear us.
3. That we may have sufficient bread to meet our daily requirements and the greatness of heart to forgive our enemies. Lord, hear us.
4. For those members of our community who are sick, that the Lord will help carry the cross of their illness. Lord, hear us.
5. We pray for our dead. May they see the Lord face to face, in his eternal home in paradise. Lord, hear us.

Heavenly Father, we thank you for listening to our petitions. Help us to trust always in your loving ways and to accept your will in our lives. We ask this through Christ our Lord. Amen.

Eighteenth Sunday of the Year

A sobering comment on the worthlessness of working unnecessarily for material possessions is the old saying that there are no pockets in a shroud. Every generation learns, often through bitter experience, that life is brief and entrance into heaven cannot be bought with riches. We leave the world the same way we came into it so what is the point of hoarding, when someone else, who may care nothing about us, will inherit and perhaps waste all we have worked to achieve. The rich fool found this out to his cost because death exposed his real poverty. During his life he behaved as if he was going to live forever. He failed to realise that what counts when we die is not wealth but the person we become in the process of living. Greed cut him off from God and other people. It showed up the foolishness of thinking that happiness can be attained without taking God and death into the reckoning.

In case we are in the process of switching off, because we think that this gospel applies only to the rich, it's well to remember that Christ preached this parable to people who were very poor by our standards. This is the story of the person who spends life without any reference to God. Christ is really warning us against going it alone, and trying to hold our future in our hands – of wasting our time, gloating over possessions and setting ourselves down securely in this life's comforts. This is a caution about greed and the hold which possessions exercise over the human heart. Greed and meanness are not confined to the wealthy but the most common of human failings and all of us can become victims of them in our struggle to earn our daily bread. They spell disaster for us and blind us as to where true values lie. The frustrations, disappointments and incomplete joy that the pursuit of material possessions bring are a reminder that happiness does not come from having what we want, but being content with what we have.

We can overcome the temptation to greed by helping those who are less fortunate than ourselves. What is given to others is not lost but is transformed into a treasure for eternity. In the evening of life we will be measured by the good we have done. Rather than wrap money around our hearts, we are urged to give our money to the poor. In the light of what Jesus says, each of us has some hard thinking to do about our attitude towards possessions. God is at the end of the line waiting for us when life is over.

Prayer of the Faithful

With unlimited confidence in God's care for us we open our hearts to our heavenly Father for the gift of wisdom, in order that we may realise what is truly important in life.

1. For our Holy Father, our bishops, priests and religious, that they may continue to make the presence of Christ known in the world through the simplicity of their life-styles. Lord, hear us.

2. Lord, help us to be sensitive towards the disadvantaged who are in trouble and distress and who are in need of our help. Lord, hear us.

3. That we may not value people by what they possess, the job they hold or the place they live. Lord, hear us.

4. For those who are sick or suffering. May they experience the richness of your presence in their lives, and realise that through their illness they can proclaim your gospel. Lord, hear us.

5. Lord, in your mercy grant light, peace and eternal rest to those who have died recently. Lord, hear us.

God our Father, we thank you for the abundance of your blessings. Help us to handle the possessions we have carefully, and never regard them as unqualified good. We make our prayer through Christ our Lord. Amen.

Nineteenth Sunday of the Year

For those who believe in God, life is a journey of searching in the valley of shadows and darkness, full of fear and doubts. Every man remains to himself a mystery and an unsolved problem. We are dissatisfied with our present life – in terms of this world it does not add up or reach fulfilment. We see ourselves as strangers and exiles on this earth, pilgrims in search of a homeland and a better country beyond our present situation.

The only beacon of light we have on our passageway is faith. It is our attempt at solving the dark mystery of where we came from, why we are here, and where we are going. We believe that there is a purpose to life and a divine providence at work within us. Somehow the hand of God is in action weaving a pattern in and out of our lives, shaping our destiny. It is God's world and he knows what he is doing with it. This is our belief – it is our faith. It is not something we can really describe. Faith is a type of window we look through which helps us to see life from a viewpoint beyond this world, enabling us to take God at his word when he makes promises about the future and calls us to be his people, in a special way.

The Jews could never think about trust in God and not recall the story of Abraham their father in faith. He left family, friends and country and went as a pilgrim on life's journey. The only thing he had was a promise from God. His faith was so unshakeable that on one occasion he drew a knife and was willing to sacrifice his only son Isaac if God wanted it that way. Abraham never knew where the road of life would take him but he believed at the end of it he would meet God.

The call from God to go forward into the unknown, moving step by step as light or darkness allows, is made to all of us. We, no less than Abraham, are called to leave behind the old ways of sin and selfishness and to put our trust in God, who calls us to walk the way he has planned for us. We cannot settle down in this world. Each day we have countless opportunities of showing our faithfulness as christians. To have faith in Christ, we must live his life and do the works appointed by him, willing to expose ourselves to the wear and tear of caring for others.

Every day we are presented with opportunities of demonstrating our faithfulness as followers of Christ. If we avail of them we will be prepared and ready for the arrival of the master of the house at whatever hour he chooses to come.

Prayer of the Faithful

As descendants of Abraham we place our faith in God the Father as we bring before him the needs and concerns of our lives.

1. We pray for the church throughout the world, that she may always show a deep faith in God our Father who guides world events. Lord, hear us.
2. We pray for an increase of faith in order to be confident of what we hope for and assured of the things we cannot see. Lord, hear us.
3. For those who have lost their way in life, that the Lord will open up new paths and lead them safely home. Lord, hear us.
4. Let us ask the Lord to give strength and support to those who are sick and to all who are denied good health in mind and body. Lord, hear us.
5. For those who have died that they may enjoy forever the fulness of God's saving power for which they have always longed. Lord, hear us.

Heavenly Father, we know that anything we ask for in your name will be granted. May your word always have a place in our hearts. We ask this through Christ our Lord. Amen.

Twentieth Sunday of the Year

A gospel story where Jesus tells us that he came to bring division even within family circles, cannot fail to make us sit up and take notice as it puts us on edge. After all there is nothing so agonisingly painful as a family feud, and yet there is no escaping from this fact of life. We find these words puzzling and strange, accustomed as we are of turning to the Lord for comfort and peace in the midst of strife and division. What we have here are a few pithy and profound remarks which Jesus made on the way to Jerusalem about the outcome of his mission. They give us a rare glimpse of the inner conflict within the heart and soul of Christ, as he foresaw the suffering of his passion. His mind is a mixture of anxiety about what is going to happen and impatience to have it over and done with. At this time opposition to his mission was mounting and he was being honest in facing the fact that his work could not be carried out without suffering and death. His message was not welcome because, as far as the Jewish establishment was concerned, he had rocked the boat and they did not like it. They felt threatened and were going to silence him by getting rid of him. Division and conflict would inevitably result from his mission as many would reject his offer of salvation.

Few of us like to be unpopular or stand up and be counted, even when principles are at stake and our voice needs to be heard. We are part of the silent majority lacking the moral courage to speak out. The gospel is forcing us to face the fact that if we are to be followers of Christ, conflict and tension are unavoidable. Jesus never promised that the journey would be without its crosses. They are the inevitable part of being a christian.

The teaching of Jesus demands acceptance or rejection. There is no escape route in trying to play the role of an anonymous christian. If we accept Christ's teaching, we will be opposed and ridiculed by those who reject it. What is at stake is the uncompromising nature of the gospel message, which is the light exposing the darkness of a crooked world. Somewhere along the line we must make the choice of whether we are going to be followers of Christ or not. It's a serious decision and not to be taken lightly. The call to be prophets by modelling our lives on Christ will automatically mean saying goodbye to a cosy and comfortable existence. If the teaching of Christ does not cause us to question the way we are living, we are falling short of being whole-hearted. The fire of Christ is not burning within our hearts.

Prayer of the Faithful

Trials and troubles may come our way but we are confident that God the Father will not fall short of his promises to those who are faithful and who perservere.

1. We pray for the leaders of the church in countries where they are openly persecuted and suffer for their beliefs. May they be given the courage and strength to remain constant in their faith. Lord, hear us.
2. May parents have the strength and courage to guide their children in the ways of faith and the christian life. Lord, hear us.
3. May our young people have the strength to resist the alien influences of the bewildering world in which they live. Lord, hear us.
4. We pray for all those who are caring for the sick, that they may show them care patience and compassion. Lord, hear us.
5. We pray for all those who have died. May they be happy forever in the kingdom of the Father. Lord, hear us.

God our Father, you sent your Son to help us in our struggles. Comfort us in our pain and give us the strength to act always with trust in your word. We ask this through Christ our Lord. Amen.

Twenty-first Sunday of the Year

Life is a pilgrim journey full of doubts, difficulties and tensions. Heaven is at the end of the road; salvation is offered to all, but it is not given freely. The question about how many will be saved has occurred to all of us at some time or another because there is no sure way of knowing who's in and who's out. It reflects our anxiety about getting to heaven and our own chance of making the grade. The mystery of salvation remains, to this day, an open question and Jesus leaves it in the hands of his eternal Father. We see from the gospel that it is the wrong question to ask, and Jesus will not answer it. The question that should be asked is: how does one attain salvation? In urging us to enter through the narrow door, Jesus seems to be warning us against having an over-confident approach. We cannot sit back and take our salvation for granted, expecting God to do everything for us. Entrance to heaven is not easy. It is a case of struggling rather than strolling in. If we want to make the journey, we cannot afford to be complacent. We have to exert ourselves. A serious effort is needed as we must measure up. The words 'depart from me' are a stark reminder that the danger of missing eternal life is a terrible reality facing everyone. It would be foolish to turn a deaf ear to the warning. The stakes are high – eternal salvation and nothing less.

We do not want to run the risk of ending up like the Jews, God's chosen people who counted themselves first and ended up last. God has no established favourites and nobody is on the inner track as there is no such thing as automatic membership. We cannot pin our hopes on the mere fact that we are paid up, church-going people. Sunday Mass-goers who confine religion to the church and sabbath and whose worship has no bearing on their week-day lives are guaranteed absolutely nothing. Such worship is an empty ritual of lip-service, a mere pretence, and a going through the motions of being christian. The test of Sunday worship is how we live at home, behave at work and treat our neighbour during the week. The gospel is a call to deepen our christianity and to respond whole-heartedly to the invitation of Jesus, who wants us to live seriously in this light. The terms of entry are about loving God and our neighbour. There is no substitute for making the following of Christ our life's work.

One fact is urgent and clear: the door will not remain open

indefinitely. The idle, the indifferent, and those who put salvation on the long finger may well be too late. Salvation depends somehow on our co-operation, our personal decision and the intensity of our efforts. If we make a response, God will not fail us, because his generosity is not measured sparingly. He wants everyone to be saved, his love is unlimited and we shall surely be pleasantly surprised at the company he keeps.

Prayer of the Faithful

We turn now to God our Father who has called us from every nation to become his sons and daughters and pray humbly for our needs.

1. For the leaders of the church, that they will have the courage to speak the word of God without compromise. Lord, hear us.
2. That we may take our christian obligations seriously and strive earnestly to enter by the narrow door that leads to eternal life. Lord, hear us.
3. Grant that parents will give their children the proof of a true love which will give them security in the years when the words of Christ are most strongly challenged. Lord, hear us.
4. For all those who are suffering in mind and body. That they may accept their cross patiently, realising that it is a training ground for life with God. Lord, hear us.
5. For the recently deceased that they may be welcomed into the kingdom of heaven. Lord, hear us.

Merciful Father, help us to bear our sufferings and to transform them into a source of growth and grace. We make our prayer through Christ our Lord. Amen.

Twenty-second Sunday of the Year

We are all familiar with this gospel passage which encourages the practice of humility. At a banquet to which he is invited, Jesus is not at all impressed by the sight of the guests, pushing themselves forward, scrambling for the good seats and skilfully manoeuvring themselves into the places of honour. He makes a comment about good manners at table and from it draws conclusions concerning an invitation to an even greater banquet to which we are all called – the eternal banquet in the kingdom of heaven.

Humility does not get good publicity these times. In a world of power and privilege where the fittest survive, and where those who push themselves forward succeed, it does not rate highly. In fact it is often associated with spinelessness, weakness and a poor self-image – but it is none of these things. Humility is an attempt to try and see ourselves as God sees us. It's taking an honest measure of ourselves without being boastful, pompous or proud, realising that we are what we are before God and nothing more. It is an admission that our talents come from God who has seen fit to work through us. We are conditioned to view our gifts as if they are our own, without realising that they are to be used for the good of the community. The truth is that we are all vessels of clay and have much to be modest about. In one sense we are worthless, merely dust and ashes but God took hold of our worthless dust and gave it eternal value by turning it into his own image and likeness. Our lives only have meaning when we are sincere in relation to God. We need to practise humility if we are to be true to ourselves and God. It is a key which opens the gate of heaven for us.

This gospel warns us against all forms of pride and self-glorification. The message is so obvious that we may fail to give it serious thought. We should take a hard look at ourselves for what we are. Pride is a road going nowhere. Like a frost which nips our spiritual growth in the bud, it makes us so self-centred and full of our own importance that there is precious little place for God in our lives. Pride cuts us off from reality and makes us prisoners of ourselves. In God's eyes the proud man takes a very lowly place because God rejects the proud and raises up the humble – for everyone who exalts himself will be humbled and the man who humbles himself will be exalted.

Prayer of the Faithful

The better we know God, the more we realise our total dependence on him. Aware of our limitations, we pray in our helplessness to God the Father.

1. We pray for the leaders of the church that they may give their lives unsparingly in the service of Christ. Lord, hear us.

2. For true generosity of heart, so that we may break through our pre-occupation with self and grow in our need to meet Christ who is meek and humble of heart. Lord, hear us.

3. We pray for a true spirit of humility in our dealings with the poor and oppressed so that we may recognise in them the features of Christ. Lord, hear us.

4. As we begin another school year, we remember our teachers, pupils, parents and ancillary staff. Help them to make their school into a community of love. Lord, hear us.

5. We pray for the sick of our parish. May we support them in their illness by our caring. Lord, hear us.

6. We remember our dead who have gone before us. May we be united with them once more in the kingdom of your love. Lord, hear us.

Lord God, father of the poor, conscious of our weakness and our pride, hear the requests of your needy people. We make this prayer through Christ our Lord. Amen.

Twenty-third Sunday of the Year

The world is full of wishful thinkers who dream and talk but never succeed because they are unprepared to make an effort. While addressing a large crowd who are eager to join up and be his disciples, Jesus bluntly dampens their enthusiasm by challenging them in a way that is off-putting. He is not interested in gaining a large following by softening his words and watering down the requirements needed, so he leaves his listeners under no illusion about the cost of discipleship. Nothing short of total commitment, even life itself, is required. In fact he is saying something like this: 'If you want to be disciples of mine, you have got to think seriously. Do not act on the spur of the moment or on impulse because it's not for the starry-eyed. Give careful consideration to what it's going to cost because I have no time for half-hearted recruits. I'm not inviting you to walk in my foot-steps for a day, a month or even a year but for a lifetime. What's more I am looking for followers who will measure up to my expectations.'

The gospel presents us with a series of sayings on what the demands of a life of discipleship involves in terms of suffering and self-sacrifice. The life to be lead and the conditions laid down are anything but easy: you give God everything and hold nothing back. Whole-hearted service is demanded and there is no room for compromise. The price to be paid is the heavy burden of cross-carrying and it may mean the parting of company with close friends. The journey to God is so valuable that it is worth stripping our lifestyles down to the bare essentials. By doing this we realise that discipleship is more important than acquiring possessions.

This gospel makes us feel uncomfortable because our lives should demonstrate that we are carrying the cross. When the cross is absent from our lives then Christ is not present either. Putting God first in our lives is a choice we must make every day. We can hardly consider ourselves as feeling the pinch and standing up for what we believe if all we have got to show is Sunday Mass with communion and a few prayers hastily said. At moments when the struggle becomes too great, it is good to remember we are not alone; Christ is walking along every step of the road with us. We are called to be disciples at home, in the family, in our place of work, in our dealings with our neighbour, treating them all as our friends and appreciating their true worth. To follow Christ through time into eternity costs nothing less than everything.

Prayer of the Faithful

We pray to God the Father, who welcomes us as his own children for the strength to meet the demands which genuine christianity places upon us.

1. We pray for those who lead the church of God that they may be guided by the Holy Spirit in the decisions they make to build a better world. Lord, hear us.
2. We pray for ourselves, that we may not turn our back on suffering but may accept the crosses that come our way. Lord, hear us.
3. That we may realise that a life dedicated to God entails a life of suffering service. Lord, hear us.
4. We pray for the sick and the neglected, that they may have the courage to persevere in their sufferings. Lord, hear us.
5. We pray for our deceased relatives and friends who have shouldered Christ's cross in this world. May they now enjoy eternal happiness in heaven. Lord, hear us.

God our Father, you know the many different needs we have in this life. Give us the courage to take up our cross and follow in the footsteps of your Son Jesus. We make our prayer through Christ our Lord. Amen.

357

Twenty-fourth Sunday of the Year

Running through the bible is the consoling message of the forgiveness and mercy of God towards sinners. Christ preached the story of the Prodigal Son to answer the bitter criticism of the Pharisees, who accused him of lowering moral standards by associating with public sinners, and spending too much time with the dregs of society. These high-minded people were scandalised by his indifference to bad company and they grumbled at him for eating with outcasts. In this classic passage on forgiveness the focus is on the Father, in order to tell us something about God. We are in a family relationship with God whose kindness is beyond words. He welcomes his wayward children home and treats them as if they had never strayed.

In this story we feel the overpowering might of the mercy of God, who withholds no sign of affection for those who have walked a crooked path. This spirit of forgiveness must surely touch, console and give hope to sinners. Jesus wants us to know that, even after our most stupid mistakes and tragic sins, he will be looking to take us back with open arms and restore us to his love, because God is tireless in seeking out sinners. It is comforting to know that should we stray away a loving father joyfully awaits our return.

In our world today there are a lot of lost souls, people who are adrift morally, spiritually and in need of healing. Like the prodigal son, they have sown their wild oats, have led a life of debauchery and are on the hard shoulder of life, feeling the pinch. They are bewildered and confused because, in their plight, they have not experienced God as a loving Father. The closer we feel to the elder son, who neither appreciated the Father's pain of loss or joy of re-union, the more we are an obstacle to their return. The older son needed a change of heart every bit as much as his younger brother. If we have taken God's unfailing pardon in our own lives for granted, then we have muffled his message of mercy. God the Father expects his love and forgiveness to be imitated by us. How else can he seek and save the lost except through our co-operation? His pardon is brought into the world by the love and mercy we show sinners. Our ability to welcome home the lost shows how much we treasure our own friendship with God. What we receive from him we must pass on to others.

358

Prayer of the Faithful

We offer our prayers with one heart and mind to the Father, who not only forgives sin but heals the wounds caused by sin.

1. We pray for the church, that it may be a sign of God's mercy, pardon and forgiveness to the world. Lord, hear us.
2. Let us pray for all those who have drifted away from the church into sin, that they may discover the forgiveness that Christ has to offer. Lord, hear us.
3. Let us pray for families who are divided and estranged, that they may be brought together by God's healing love. Lord, hear us.
4. For the sick of our community. May our prayers and good works bring them comfort. Lord, hear us.
5. For those who have died, that they may now enjoy the light of eternity. Lord, hear us.

God our Father, help us bring your pardon, forgiveness and peace to all those we meet. We make our prayer through Christ our Lord. Amen.

Twenty-fifth Sunday of the Year

In the light of what Jesus has to say concerning wealth, every-one of us has to do some hard thinking and sincere praying about our attitude towards material possessions. The gospel is especially warning us against making money the goal of our existence. Money plays such an important role in our daily lives that it influences us deeply, whether we have it or not. In a world where values are out of focus, money talks, opens doors and is a voice that is always heard and listened to. Given the emphasis society places on having lots of riches, it's hard to remain indifferent to its power. Money is something we have to use but, at the same time, watch, in case it gets a grip on us and destroys us by becoming our god. At the end of our life, what will count is the person we are and the good we have done, and not what we have accumulated in material possessions.

The saying, 'Money is the root of all evil,' contains a certain element of truth. When money dominates our lives, we easily forget the distant goal of life's destiny. Our values become muddled and our christian commitment to God is drained of all its strength. Greed creeps into our hearts, deadens our conscience and dulls our sense of responsibility to the poor of the community. This gospel seeks to discover whether God is taking first place in our lives or whether the pursuit of riches is a more important consideration. If we are using our earthly wealth to attain our heavenly goal, then we are on the right road. This is the only real possession worth striving for, as death cannot take it away.

Experience teaches that the longing for happiness and security is not satisfied by any created thing. Our life is not made secure by material wealth because we have a heavenly destiny. We are here today and gone tomorrow, but we are here for a purpose. The closer we come to eternity the more material possessions lose their value. When life draws to an end, riches prove worthless and have got to be left behind. We can take nothing with us from this life except the good we have done. The gospel message is summed up in the quote, 'Money is an instrument that can buy everything but happiness, and purchases a ticket to every place but heaven.'

Prayer of the Faithful

We make our prayers to the Father who has called us to be faithful stewards in using the goods of this earth for the benefit of all.

1. We pray for our Holy Father and bishops that they may be conscious of their responsibility to spread social justice in the church. Lord, hear us.
2. We pray that as a christian community we may be generous in giving to the poor in our midst. Lord, hear us.
3. We pray that employers and workers may have a sense of honesty and respect for each other. Lord, hear us.
4. For the sick, that they may be given the gift of patience in their illness. Lord, hear us.
5. For those who have departed this life, that they may be received into eternal glory. Lord, hear us.

Heavenly Father, make us realise that it is only through our concern that your love and care can reach the poor and the neglected. Help us to be generous in the time we spend with them. We make our prayers through Christ our Lord. Amen.

Twenty-sixth Sunday of the Year

There's a very damning picture painted of the rich in today's readings. They are enjoying lives of luxury, eating and drinking of the best, totally out of touch with real life, while people on the fringes of society are rife with poverty. Time runs out for them, roles are reversed, poverty is changed to wealth, and riches to misery. But do not go off with the idea that only the rich are being reprimanded. The people to whom Christ addressed this story were poor by our standards. It had a message for them and it has one for us. This is a gospel call to brotherly care. If we love, we share our possessions and our time with the marginalised. Greed gets to us, because we are basically selfish. The gospel costs us our comforts because it makes inroads on our pockets. When our own interest is involved, self-deception is all too easy.

Take Dives for instance: he did not beat Lazarus nor was he deliberately cruel to him, neither did he deny him food. However, he did not take Lazarus under his notice or recognise him as his brother. That was his sin: he did nothing. How often is it ours? We do nothing wrong; we just do nothing. Dives is cut off from God, sent into torment in Hades not for being rich, well fed, or distinctively dressed, but because he cut himself off from helping his brother. He ignored the poor man standing at his doorstep and closed his heart in the face of human misery that confronted him daily. Lazarus provided him with an opportunity to exercise charity, overcome selfishness and attain eternal salvation. Heaven is prepared for while we are on earth.

The dialogue between Dives and Abraham at the end of the gospel, where Dives asks to be allowed to convey a special message of warning to his five brothers, misses the point because his brothers are insensitive and uncaring. They have the words of scripture and that is shock treatment enough.

We are the five brothers who are still alive. God's message is there for all of us to hear. The words of scripture, 'I tell you solemnly, in so far as you did it to one of the least of these brothers of mine you did it to me,' (Mt 25: 4) are addressed to us. Now is the acceptable time, now is the day of salvation. Nobody is exempt from responsibility for the less fortunate members of society. We have obligations to the poor at home and in the third world. The little we have we must share. If we ignore the pleas of the orphan and the widow, the sick and the lonely we will pay the price.

This is an occasion to ask the question: what am I doing personally for the poor? Am I generous to the point of hurting myself? Do I take notice of the poor and oppressed in my neighbourhood? Wherever we look there is sorrow to be comforted, need to be supplied, pain to be relieved. We cannot say we do not know. Do we realise that to have a job in the present economic climate is to be privileged? Are we conscious that the unemployed are the new oppressed in our society, part of the new belt of misery on the fringes of every town? The poor are a challenge. By our attitude we can show that people matter more than possessions. People are more precious for what they are than the job they do or the money they earn. We are to make ourselves shining examples of faith in these difficult times of growing injustice and self-seeking.

Prayer of the Faithful

We come before our God who shared his riches with everyone, by sending his Son into the world, as we remember the special needs of the poor:

1. We pray for the leaders of the church. May they show forth the compassion of Christ for the poor in their striving for a more just society. Lord, hear us.
2. May all who are tempted to become slaves of wealth and security realise that spiritual poverty arises from refusing to share with others. Lord, hear us.
3. That we may all have the grace to show mercy and compassion, generosity and understanding to those in need. Lord, hear us.
4. Let us ask God to strengthen the sick of the community with the warmth of his loving presence. Lord, hear us.
5. For those who have died. May they share in the happiness and peace of God's kingdom. Lord, hear us.

Heavenly Father, in your love and mercy, fill us with the abundance of your generosity and help us to reach out to the less fortunate. We make our prayer through Christ our Lord. Amen.

Twenty-seventh Sunday of the Year

As they approached Jerusalem, the apostles sense the mounting opposition to the master's mission and feel isolated. They are tempted to despair. In a conversation with Jesus, they ask for an increase in faith in order to accept his words more easily and obey them more readily. Jesus emphasises, in his reply to their request, the explosive power of the smallest possible amount of faith and uses the image of the tiny mustard seed uprooting a mulberry tree to express it. A faith that is deep-rooted can achieve the impossible, because life takes on a new significance when the power of God is at our disposal.

The tragic happenings that are part of our daily lives call us to share in suffering, but prompt us to question the ways of God. At times, as we seek instant solutions to our problems, we bitterly complain of his absence. God so often seems to be silent and we are left dumbfounded. The challenge is to remain faithful to God and religious values especially at moments when they do not make sense. Whatever the evils of the world the person of faith will always emerge victorious because he is in communion with God. For that reason we can join the apostles in their request to Jesus for an increase in faith.

This is a gospel call to give our lives to Jesus and make a special effort to push ourselves to our christian limits. How many of us, who profess to be christian, have a casual approach towards prayer, the observance of the commandments and the exercise of charity? Faith and good works are not alternatives for the christian – they are inseparable. God's gifts to us require that we are open-handed to others. No matter how we look at it, the kind of faith we have is best shown by the type of life we lead. This is a proper indication of our christianity. If we believe in the person of Jesus, we will give him unswerving allegiance in our everyday lives, by living as he would have us live and by loving God and our neighbour. Even if we have done what he asks from each of us we have done nothing remarkable in his service. God owes no gratitude to us for our service to him.

Prayer of the Faithful

As God's priestly people who have been blessed with the gift of faith ,we present our requests to him with confidence and trust.

1. We pray for the church, that all who profess the name of christians may grow in faith and love for one another. Lord, hear us.
2. We pray that our own faith may increase and make us acknowledge our complete dependence on God. Lord, hear us.
3. For those whose faith has grown cold and who are overcome by despair. May they be fired with a new enthusiasm to renew their christian commitment. Lord, hear us.
4. Let us pray for the sick and the handicapped, the aged and the house-bound. May their faith never desert them in their suffering. Lord, hear us.
5. May Christ our Saviour welcome those who have died and forgive them their sins. Lord, hear us.

God our Father, realising that by ourselves we can do nothing, help us to cling steadfastly to you in faith. We ask this through Christ our Lord. Amen.

Twenty-eighth Sunday of the Year

Ingratitude is perhaps the most common of all human failings. Nothing is so hurtful as to be taken for granted without a word spoken in thanks or praise. What causes most pain is the neglect and coldness of those for whom we have done our best. One of the most satisfying experiences in life is to receive a word of praise as a mark of appreciation for a service rendered. While we are ready to deplore the ingratitude of others, we are often unaware of our own ungratefulness.

As Christ headed towards Jerusalem and the cross, he met deep and amazing ingratitude along the border between Samaria and Galilee. Ten lepers huddled in their misery, cried out to him for help, 'Jesus, master, have pity on us.' Leprosy then was akin to aids today. The victims were treated as outcasts and isolated from the community. Their prayer was answered and they went off rejoicing because they were cleansed. When only one leper thought it worthwhile to return and say thanks, Jesus expressed genuine disappointment at the attitude of the nine who stayed away and failed to praise God. He made the very human and moving comment, 'Were not ten made clean? Where are the other nine?'

The leper with the grateful heart is an example to us all, because he got full benefit from his encounter with Jesus. By acknowledging the source of his new-found health, his spirit as well as his body was healed. The other nine lacked something in failing to show any appreciation to Jesus by keeping everything for themselves and giving nothing back. They missed the great richness and inner joy that comes from giving thanks. The story reminds us of how often we fail to express thanks to God as the source of all goodness, for favours granted.

The best things in life are appreciated more when they are in danger of being lost. After an encounter with serious illness, we are filled with a sense of gratitude for our health and feel a new joy in living. The real worth of our love for God flows from our ability to recognise the countless blessings, great and small, which come our way daily. Coming together for the celebration of the eucharist makes it clear that the giving of thanks to God is an essential part of our worship and prayer life. The more we thank God for his generosity, the more we will be open to receive the joy of his blessings. Since the whole of our existence depends entirely on his will we should not let a day pass without thanking God for the good things of life and the crosses and trials that put us to the test.

Prayer of the Faithful

We entrust to the Father all our cares and needs, especially our desire for a better spirit of thankfulness.

1. We pray that the church throughout the world may always be aware of the importance of being a truly thankful people in word and deed. Lord, hear us.
2. Let us thank the Lord for the gifts of life, health and happiness and for the warmth of family and friends. Lord, hear us.
3. May we always give thanks, in every aspect of our lives, for the love that God has lavished on us by adopting us as his children. Lord, hear us.
4. For the sick, that they may learn to link their suffering and pain to the victorious death of Christ. Lord, hear us.
5. For the faithful departed. May all who have gone before us in faith enjoy the victory of the risen Christ. Lord, hear us.

God our Father, we thank you for our lives and the new life given to us in the risen Lord. We make this prayer through Christ our Lord. Amen.

Twenty-ninth Sunday of the Year

Jesus urges us to pray continually and never to grow discouraged. He encourages us with the assurance that our prayer will be answered and that we will not be disappointed. The widow, with her dogged determination to gain justice from the careless judge, is put before us as an example of perseverance in prayer. Persistence is her strong point and she exercises it relentlessly without losing heart. Despite the odds, she keeps up her petition and wears the judge down until he eventually grants her justice for the sake of his own health.

In an age where we have become accustomed to instant results and are impatient with endless delays, Christ's message is to keep on praying, to keep on knocking and not to give up easily because the values we cherish are not instantly available and take time to establish. Making prayer a daily habit means that we appreciate its importance and are prepared to make room for it in a busy routine. When something becomes precious to us we don't leave it to chance. Continual prayer somehow, like breathing, is a necessity if we are to avail of God's help and strength in getting safely through this life to heaven.

Prayer is talking to God, and when we pray we are to speak our hearts in a real human way, making use of the style which suits us best: We need be under no pressure to be other than what we are and what we feel at that moment. It doesn't matter whether we are joyful, depressed, angry or frustrated. There is no reason to be ashamed because we are in the presence of a friend who understands. We pray because there is confusion in our lives and because we need guidance to make the proper decisions. There are our wrong-doings for which we need forgiveness, and our successes for which we ought to give thanks. One pressing problem is that, while we expect immediate results, God seems to remain silent and inattentive to our requests. It is good to remember that we are not telling God anything that he doesn't know, so we can be assured that he hears our every prayer. He will not refuse what is for our benefit and will grant us what we ask in his own good time and as he sees fit. If we get our praying right, the rest of life will fall into place. Prayer is the oil that keeps the lamp of faith burning brightly, drawing us closer to God and enabling us to produce good works.

Prayer of the Faithful

We approach God the Father with confidence and place before him all our needs.

1. We pray for the leaders of the church. May they persevere amidst all their trials and tribulations and never lose confidence in proclaiming the gospel. Lord, hear us.

2. May all those, who are discouraged and are tempted to give up the struggle in leading a good life, find new inspiration in the faithfulness of God. Lord, hear us.

3. For those who find prayer difficult. May they grow in fervour and make room for God in their daily lives. Lord, hear us.

4. We pray for the sick, that they may persevere in their sufferings and never lose heart. Lord, hear us.

5. We pray for the dead. May they receive the heavenly reward for their perseverence on earth. Lord, hear us.

Heavenly Father, we entrust our needs to you. Show us the way to pray continually so that we may always be united to you. We ask this through Christ our Lord. Amen.

Thirtieth Sunday of the Year

The Lord presents us with a picture of two people at prayer in the temple, one a pharisee, the other a tax collector. The pharisee is a good-living, generous man and the essence of Jewish respectability. As he stands in praye,r his mind is focused on how, as a loyal church member, he has kept the rules of fasting, alms-giving and worship. His piety is outstanding and his religion without fault. He has staked all his life on God and has a great feeling of security in his own uprightness. Oozing with pride, he looks over his shoulder and, without a glimmer of guilt, he falls prey to the temptation to compare himself to the tax collector, who is a social outcast. Conscious of his wrong-doing, the tax collector sorrowfully confesses his sinfulness and asks God for mercy. His humble prayer touches the tender heart of God and wins acceptance.

Although this parable needs no explanation, it does merit some personal reflection if we are to apply the message that it contains to our lives. This gospel puts into words shameful attitudes that many of us possess but are reluctant to admit. The strange thing is that, as we listen to the story, our sympathy goes out to the tax collector, whose broken heart has nothing to offer God except sorrow for his failings. However, in real life we are more inclined to imitate the pharisee. Our style of behaviour may be less obvious but it's there all the same. It expresses itself in our thirst for recognition, in our desire to be centre stage and in our seeking out preferential treatment. In everyday life when we boast, brag, put ourselves on pedestals and appear better than we are in reality, tinges of the pharisee emerge in our character. We pride ourselves on our achievements and we forget that pride eats away at the core of the human heart. It is only when we empty ourselves of pride that we come to realise how totally dependant we are upon God, and can develop a reliance on him.

Prayer must come from a sincere and humble heart if it is to be heard. We have all got to be honest about our sinfulness and worthlessness in God's eyes, and our need for his mercy and forgiveness. This gospel contains a warning for all church-goers about the danger of becoming spiritually smug and of presenting ourselves as a deserving subject of God's mercy because of the good works we have performed. We have not earned our salvation, for grace is the gift of Jesus from the cross. When we compare ourselves to the life of Jesus and the holiness of God, all that is left to say is: 'O Lord, be merciful to me, a sinner.'

Prayer of the Faithful

Standing firm in hope we approach God the Father who assures us that the prayer of the humble person never goes unanswered.

1. We pray that the leaders of the church, through the witness of humble lives, may point us to God the Father's heavenly kingdom. Lord, hear us.
2. May we realise that only when we are conscious of our weakness, sinfulness and wretchedness, is the mercy of God made available in our lives. Lord, hear us.
3. May we rid ourselves of pride and be rooted in the recognition that we are nothing before God except weak human beings. Lord, hear us.
4. We pray for the sick at home or in hospital and those burdened with loneliness, worry and anxiety. May they find consolation in your loving care. Lord, hear us.
5. We pray for those who have died and especially for all those near and dear to ourselves. May they be received into your kingdom of love and peace. Lord, hear us.

Heavenly Father, trusting in your power to save we walk humbly in life so that we may be brought safely into your heavenly kingdom, where you live and reign with your Son and the Holy Spirit, God, for ever and ever. Amen.

Thirty-first Sunday of the Year

This is a delightfully touching gospel story about the boundless love that God has for sinners. It shows the forgiveness that he offers, with open arms, to the worst of us. Zacchaeus was the most hated man in the community. People boycotted him and wouldn't bid him the time of day because he was a cheat, a quisling and a tax-collector for the Roman forces of occupation. Popular estimation had written him off as lost. Yet Jesus made him feel special. He saw beyond the idle curiosity of the little man up the tree, into the pain and turmoil of his heart. He made the first move and called: 'Hurry, come down, I must stay at your house today.' His whole being called out to Zacchaeus and the little man's selfishness crumbled before the gaze of Christ. Zacchaeus desperately wanted to get outside of himself and make a break with the past. He was wealthy but not happy and he saw Jesus as the answer to his troubled conscience. The encounter made him mend his ways and think about his behaviour in a new light. He now saw something more worthwhile in life than lining his pockets with money. Close contact with Jesus had awakened in him religious impulses and opened his eyes to his real faults.

The message that Jesus is trying to get across to us is that nobody is beyond redemption. There are no limits to the possibility of salvation offered by Jesus. God's grace is able to turn a life upside down and change a sinful person. The greater the sinner the more forgiving he is. There is no past, however shameful, that cannot be given a fresh start. Lurking within each one of us there is a sinful Zacchaeus, seeking out the Lord to save us and give us new hope.

The call of Jesus, 'Hurry, because I must stay in your house today,' goes out to everyone in the congregation. We must take full advantage of his passing, by acknowledging our sins and opening our hearts to his goodness. The real focus of the story is on the last line of the gospel: 'The Son of Man came to seek out and to save the lost.' Before Jesus, all men are sinners like Zacchaeus. The Lord has come to save you and me and he meets us at the point of our need, with no strings attached. He is waiting to change our lives as soon as we show a willingness to open the door of our hearts and let his salvation get to work in the very centre of our being.

Prayer of the Faithful

We open our hearts to God the Father who wills the salvation of everyone by sending his Son to seek out and save what was lost.

1. We pray for the leaders of the church. May they continue the Lord's work by being channels of reconciliation and healing to sinners. Lord, hear us.

2. We pray for those who exploit the poor and make profit at their expense. May they see the errors of their way and like Zacchaeus make a break with the past. Lord, hear us.

3. We pray that we may be prepared to welcome the Lord whenever he comes into our lives and allow him to make his home in us. Lord, hear us.

4. We pray for the sick whose daily calling to holiness is accepting the cross of ill-health. Lord, hear us.

5. We pray for the dead. May they be rewarded with everlasting happiness in the life of the world to come. Lord, hear us.

God our Father, fill our hearts with your love, give us your saving help when we fall, and keep us always in your care. We make our prayer through Christ our Lord. Amen.

Thirty-second Sunday of the Year

Out of sheer malice the Sadducees asked what they considered a tricky question. They presented Jesus with the problem of the one bride for seven brothers to try and force him into a denial of the resurrection. Jesus readily evaded their mockery by stating that life in the resurrection would be of a completely different quality and an altogether new experience. It would not be a return to, or a continuation of the normal pattern of life as we know it. Life after death remains clouded in a great mystery and we would all like to know more about it. We wonder what it will be like, when will it begin, where will we be going? Our dreams are about being reunited with our loved ones who have gone before us and who are with God our Father. Christians have as many questions to ask about life after death as anyone else.

The Mass today forces us to reflect on the meaning of life and the purpose of death. Going through life, we meet death in its many forms – slow, sudden, young and old, after an accident or prolonged illness. The path of life leads to the grave. It's the one appointment we cannot cancel. There is no sorrow comparable to the heartbreak experienced at the graveside. Death crushes and destroys earthly ties and it's a time for grieving and bitter tears. No departure leaves us so isolated as the death of a loved one. The church gives us hope and brings meaning to this otherwise unacceptable and painful occurrence in our lives. The coming of Christ into the world has given new meaning to every departure and has taken the sting out of death. As christians, we believe that our human existence cannot adequately be explained in terms of this earth only; life does not finish with the grave; it's open-ended, beginning here on earth but finding its completion somewhere hereafter, beyond what we call death. Death is the doorway leading to eternal life. It is our leap into eternity with God calling us to the fullness of life.

At Mass, in our profession of faith we say, 'We look for the resurrection of the dead and the life of the world to come.' Perhaps these words slip meaninglessly from our lips. Is our notion of death bound up only with thoughts of despair and remorse or is it a feeling of sorrow mingled with joy because we share in the glorious resurrection and the life of Christ? The month of November is here with its short days and long dark nights. The year is dying. It's a suitable time to remember our dead, not with fear and despair, but in the hope of joining them in eternal life. The spirit of the dead lives on in the memory of the living.

Prayer of the Faithful

Standing in need of the comforting love of God the Father we place ourselves in his presence and make our prayer.

1. We pray for the church throughout the world, that it may continue to preach the Good News of the resurrection and the life of the world to come. Lord, hear us.
2. We pray that in our daily lives we may bring the light of hope to those who live in darkness and despair. Lord, hear us.
3. We pray for the poor, the homeless and the needy. May they experience the Lord of life in the love and generosity of those who are kind to them. Lord, hear us.
4. We pray for all who are sick or suffering, that they may discover the healing presence of Christ in their lives. Lord, hear us.
5. We pray for those who have died. May they find new life in the company of Jesus. Lord, hear us.

God of the living, may this eucharist give us a longing for the eternal banquet which you have prepared for us, where we will enjoy the happiness of your presence forever more. We make our prayers through Christ our Lord. Amen.

Thirty-third Sunday of the Year

As the church's year draws to a close and another year of life slips quietly by, our thoughts are directed towards the end of time. Jesus paints a picture foretelling the end of the world in terms of the destruction of the Temple in Jerusalem, and warns his followers in the meantime to be prepared for tension, conflict and a difficult struggle ahead. The world which Christ describes, has a familiar ring about it and sounds similar to the one we live in. People of every age share the curiosity of the disciples in wondering when will the end come. It's exact timing is unknown and as a result there has been no shortage of self-appointed prophets to quote scripture out of context and exploit people's fears by announcing that the end is near.

One message that becomes clear is that our state of readiness to meet the Lord depends on the type of life we lead. Where we will stand on Christ's arrival is decided by what we are trying to be at this moment. Our future happiness is shaped out of our present efforts to turn to God and live life properly. It's comforting to know that, whatever the future holds by way of disappointment or failure, the Lord is in control and will not abandon his people. We must not lose hope because the trials, troubles and tribulations of the present time will one day make way for a happy ending.

At this moment, the challenge facing us is to put our lives in order and turn our backs on such things as the practice of dishonesty, and the taking of short cuts to solve our problems no matter how serious they may be. Selfishness can cut us off from God and close us in on ourselves. How we appear before God when Christ comes will not be a matter of luck, but will depend on whether we are messengers of hope and bearers of light in troubled times. The gospel gives us encouragement by announcing that God is on our side and longs for us to be saved. Having called us to salvation he will not abandon us against our wishes.

Prayer of the Faithful

God our Father, we humbly place before you all our needs in the hope that we may be ready to answer your call when the curtain of life falls.

1. For the Pope, bishops and church leaders, that they may follow the example of Jesus by serving all who seek their help and encouragement. Lord, hear us.

2. We pray for ourselves. May we remain faithful to the word of God and constant in our hope of heavenly life. Lord, hear us.

3. We pray for all who are unemployed and have lost hope in the future. May they realise that the Lord will not abandon them. Lord, hear us.

4. We pray for those who are burdened with sickness at this time. May they find comfort in the love and trust of those who take care of them. Lord, hear us.

5. We pray for those who died recently. May they experience a merciful judgement and everlasting peace in the company of the Lord in heaven. Lord, hear us.

Father in heaven, help us to always remain faithful to your word so that in our difficulties we may have the strength to persevere. We ask this through Christ our Lord. Amen.

Our Lord Jesus Christ, Universal King

Today's gospel reminds us of the end of time by drawing our attention to the last moments of Christ's earthly life. He was crucified on the cross between two thieves, for claiming to be a king, yet the only crown he wore was braided with thorns. Over his head was written, 'Jesus of Nazareth, King of the Jews.' Only his mother Mary and a few friends were faithful to the last. At the moment of his greatest human agony he welcomed the repentance of the good thief and gave him the personal assurance and guarantee of eternal life. 'Today you will be with me in paradise.'

While earthly kings rule from palaces, Christ the King reigns from the cross. His kingdom is not a place, but a people who give their hearts lovingly to him by shaping their lives according to his will. All that is good and elevated in our human nature flows from Calvary where he became the Saviour of the world and won for us a life of eternal joy with God. His death on the cross is our signpost to heaven and the road to be followed if we are to make sense of our lives and open up the vision of a new world.

For those of us who have lost sight of the truth that heaven is our final destination, the feast of Christ the King invites us to start living our lives as Jesus taught us to live them. In all we do we seek to grow more like Christ, for he becomes our king only when we give him our allegiance. In practice we often withhold that loyalty. How many of us can truthfully say of family life that Christ is the head of our house, the unseen guest at every meal and the silent listener to every conversation. To recognise Christ as the king of our lives may mean a change of heart, like the good thief, and a more honest approach in our way of living. Decisions may have to be made on our part about abandoning the short cuts we have been taking in our daily dealings with others. Selfishness, hatred and injustice must give way to Christlike attitudes if we are to follow his message.

The kingship of Christ is made real by allowing God to do his work in us and through us. It is a life-long process involving a daily invitation to conversion. He calls us, who are his subjects, to take his side in the struggle of furthering the growth of his kingdom.

Prayer of the Faithful

God's kingdom is one of justice, love and peace. We now pray to our heavenly Father for the grace to play our part in building it into our lives.

1. We pray for the church throughout the world. May it more and more become a sign of Christ's love and compassion for all people. Lord, hear us.

2. We pray for ourselves, that we may prepare for the coming of the christian kingdom with kindness, truth and justice in our homes and neighbourhood community. Lord, hear us.

3. We pray for those who do not believe. May their minds and hearts be open to the wonder and majesty of God's plan to save souls. Lord, hear us.

4. We remember the sick, the aged, the handicapped. May they be shown a spirit of care and kindness by those who minister to their needs. Lord, hear us.

5. We pray for those who have died. May they have a place in God's everlasting kingdom. Lord, hear us.

Almighty Father may your Son Jesus Christ give you glory by gathering your church into the kingdom you have prepared for it. We make our prayer through Christ our Lord. Amen.

Immaculate Conception

Mary is the world's most remarkable model of an Advent figure. At a given moment in salvation history, God asked her to mother his Son. It was a demanding invitation and one which troubled her greatly. When she gave her reply to the angel Gabriel, 'Let it be done to me according to your word,' the salvation process began and from her humanity came his flesh and blood. To be worthy of such an honour, God graced her with freedom from original sin from the first moment of her conception. Mary had to be immaculate, untouched by sin from the first moment of her birth. The mother who was carrying God's son, not for herself but for a world in need, could have no hand, act or part in sin. Mary became Christ's first disciple and the very model of what discipleship means.

This feast celebrates the humility and faith of a woman who accepted the challenge which God put before her. She is an example of what human life is capable of achieving when touched by the grace of God. Like many a mother she gave a child to the world while remaining unaware of the details of God's plan. We should not think that because Mary was free from sin her life was without struggles. She was subject to the same doubts and anguishes that we all face. Like her son, she shared all our problems and difficulties showing us the value of patience amidst our own trials, by turning sorrow and trouble into hope and joy.

Mary reminds us of the goodness of God which is the source and root of our life. What he wills for Mary he wills for all of us. In sending his Son into our world, God wanted to share the very best of himself with us, by making us his adopted sons and daughters. God calls each of us like Mary to welcome Jesus and to make room for him in our lives. If we give him co-operation in living his word and sharing his cross, he will shape us into a worthy dwelling place for his Son. Mary teaches us what it means to abandon ourselves completely to God's will and to be fully at his disposal. We are fortunate to call Mary our mother and to claim her as the model to imitate to the best of our ability. Of all creatures, she is the closest in love to God, nearest to his heart and everything a human being should be. Her Immaculate Conception calls us to be more freely and totally ourselves according to God's eternal plan.

Prayer of the Faithful

With confidence we approach the Father who is gracious to all who call upon him and make our prayer.

1. We pray that the church on earth may be a beacon of light and hope, reflecting closely the holiness of Mary. Lord, hear us.
2. That those who are deeply troubled and steeped in worry may find in Mary compassion and comfort in their suffering. Lord, hear us.
3. We pray that, by giving Mary a place of honour in our lives and in our homes, we may deepen our appreciation of her son. Lord, hear us.
4. Support and comfort the sick with your love and keep them in your grace. Lord, hear us.
5. We pray for the faithful departed. May they enjoy the vision of God in everlasting life. Lord, hear us.

Heavenly Father, we thank you for the message of peace that Mary brings to our troubled world. Help us to overcome our sins and raise us from the depth of our weaknesses. We make our prayer through Christ our Lord. Amen.

Solemnity of Mary, Mother of God
(Years A,B,C)

As a fresh and unstained New Year opens before us we go through a gateway to walk a path we have not known before. The old year may have had its days of sorrows, misfortune, loss and pain but all that was good about it we still carry with us as memories that can always warm and gladden our hearts. We feel a twinge of sadness about its passing and a reluctance as we look towards the future, for each New Year is a time of great expectation. Before this year comes to an end some of us may have completed our earthly journey and entered the house of our eternity.

A week ago, we celebrated the birth of our Saviour, born of a pure and humble virgin; the angels sang, the shepherds came and went, the Magi following a star emerged from the mist, offered their gifts and faded into the shadows. The gospel tells us that Mary treasured all these happenings in her heart. What her thoughts were then we do not know, because her child was wrapped in mystery. She had to live her life as a mother, relying heavily on her trust in almighty God. She must have often recalled the events of Bethlehem and pondered deeply about their meaning. All the visitors who arrived there had eyes of faith for her son.

The New Year begins with the Solemnity of Mary, the Mother of God, a feast which celebrates a mysterious union between God and a woman. 'When the appointed time came God sent his Son, born of a woman, to redeem the subjects of the Law and enable us to be adopted as sons.' (Gal: 4. 4-4) The church puts forward Mary to guide us on our journey of faith through this valley of tears. Although she was singled out to be the mother of our Saviour, she was a woman who had to walk in faith and for whom belief was a constant struggle. She did not enjoy an easy life. At the birth of her Son she had nowhere to call a home. At his death she stood silently at the cross, hardly understanding all that was happening. As a mother, she was the great giver who formed Christ and made him fully human. She will form us and bring us close to her Son if, in the coming year, we put ourselves under her protection. Even our sorrows and sacrifices will be turned into joys and gladness beyond our imagining. There is surely no better way of starting the year than celebrating the day that Mary became the mother of God.

Prayer of the Faithful

Mindful of Mary's faith and courage we bring our needs before God the Father at the beginning of the New Year.

1. We pray for the leaders of the church, that under the patronage of Mary, by word and example they may bring God's people closer to Christ. Lord, hear us.

2. Let us ask the Lord to make it a year of constant growth and development in living faith, in radiant hope and in a love that reaches to all those whose lives we touch. Lord, hear us.

3. For those who, in recent times, have been heavily burdened by sorrow and the cross, that they may find peace and inner contentment as they reflect on the sorrows of Mary. Lord, hear us.

4. For our parish community, that we may welcome the word of God into our hearts and respond to it with the generosity of Mary. Lord, hear us.

5. We ask Mary, the mother of God, to look down with compassion on those who are sick in our midst. Lord, hear us.

6. We ask God the Father to welcome into his presence our departed brothers and sisters. Lord, hear us.

Heavenly Father, you chose Mary to be the mother of your Son. Help us through her intercession to treasure the mystery of his life, death and resurrection. We ask this through Christ our Lord. Amen.

Saint Patrick

On the feast of St Patrick, people the world over rejoice and give thanks for the rich christian heritage which finds its roots in the life and work of St Patrick. Christianity began in Ireland because he was able to forgive his enemies and bring about reconciliation and peace between himself and them. Irish raiders, plundering the coastline of Wales, snatched him away from his family, deprived him of his freedom and took him as a prisoner to Ireland. He spent six years, cold, hungry and exhausted as a slave herding swine on a bleak Antrim hillside. In captivity, the pain and loneliness of exile ate into his young heart but in his plight he turned to Christ and discovered the real meaning of life and the importance of prayer. God took complete possession of him and he became a man of faith.

According to his 'Confessions', which he wrote in his old age and is the story of his soul, he prayed one hundred times a day and as many more by night. When the opportunity arose he escaped to his homeland and began his studies for the priesthood. We could hardly blame him for not wanting to have anything to do with the Irish. However, one night in a dream he heard the voice of the Irish asking him to come back and walk once more among them. To respond to God's call to return and convert the people who had taken him prisoner, was surely a grim and difficult decision. He returned to Ireland as a bishop and the people received his preaching with enthusiasm and took to the faith. The conversion of Ireland from paganism in his lifetime borders on the miraculous. Our tradition pictures him as a man of great faith, a spiritual giant and a humble priest of heroic sanctity. His wish was that he would never be separated from the people he had won for God at so great a price.

Every nation has its flower and for Ireland it is the shamrock but there is more to being Irish than wearing a sprig of shamrock, and walking in a parade. All of us can sow seeds of peace and reconciliation among those whom we come in contact with in our community. Patrick speaks a message to every generation of our countrymen. He enkindled in our land that vital spark of faith which has never gone out. However, the spreading and rooting of the faith is not a one man effort. Our rich spiritual heritage is due in no small part to the successive generations who saw that it took a firm hold. If we are to remain a people ruled by gospel values, we have to take his message seriously and to heart. As we celebrate Patrick's memory we pray that the faith of the Irish may be renewed and strengthened and that the peace of Christ will come and take possession of our land.

Prayer of the Faithful

Today as we celebrate the feast of St Patrick who brought the faith to Ireland, with joy in our hearts we make our prayer to God the Father.

1. We pray for the leaders of the church in our country, that a spirit of justice, forgiveness and peace may be evident in all their work. Lord, hear us.
2. We pray that the christian faith, which was first sown by St Patrick, may always burn brightly within us and be the guiding light of our daily lives. Lord, hear us.
3. May the blessing of St Patrick be upon all those who are away from their homeland, especially those faced with loneliness, heartbreak and fear. Lord, hear us.
4. We pray for the poor, the elderly, the handicapped and the infirm. May they always find friends who will share their lives with love, care and respect. Lord, hear us.
5. We commend to God's loving mercy all who have died and for whom we have been asked to pray ... Lord, hear us.

God our Father, we place all our prayers before you knowing that you will always grant what is best for us. We make our prayer through Christ our Lord. Amen.

Assumption

The Feast of the Assumption places before us the final act of Mary's earthly pilgrimage. The young girl from Nazareth, who gave Jesus to the world, was spared death and was brought up body and soul into heavenly glory, where she remains with her son to welcome her children. Mary was so totally possessed by her son that, when her life drew to a close, she had to be with him immediately. Conceived and born without taint of sin, there was nothing in her life to keep her from heaven. Mary has done what we all hope to do, to rise triumphant from the dead and spend an eternity of happiness in heaven. As a young woma,n she lovingly accepted God's plan to bear his Son and bring him into the world.

We are inclined to forget that Mary had little idea of what faced her when she responded to the angel Gabriel. It was with faith and trust, but with little knowledge, that she kept going through fair days and foul, making the same effort as we do to discover the hand of God in what was happening. As a woman with a human heart and human personality she experienced the sunshine and shadow that is part of everyday life. In the gospel we see Mary making her way on a road winding through valleys and over hills to visit her cousin Elizabeth who was expecting a baby. From the cradle to the cross, Mary is the silent background figure in the Saviour's life. Christ, who needed her at Bethlehem, must surely have been consoled by her presence at Calvary where she shared in his crucifixion.

In Mary we see the fullness of the response we must make to God in our own lives. The whole of her life was a proclamation of the greatness of God. She realised that she was no self-made woman, but that God was working through her. ('The Almighty has done great things for me ...') Her assumption into heaven should inspire us to see the worth of making every effort to live life properly, for she is a living symbol of what God calls us to be. As we journey on our pilgrim way, Mary has so much to teach us, because she points forward to where we hope to be. She shows us that loyalty to Christ and a willingness to suffer with him is rewarded by complete happiness in heaven. If we follow the pattern of her life we will share in the glory of her son.

It is right and wise to heed Mary who, like the morning star preceding the dawn, beckons us forward to the fullness of life. In the midst of the sin and suffering of this valley of tears, our greatest hope is that one day we will stand with Mary before God the Father and give praise to her son, Jesus Christ.

Prayer of the Faithful

We pray now to God the Father who accomplished great things in Mary and brought her into the glory of the resurrection. We ask him to make known to us our many needs but above all our need for him

1. We pray for the whole church that, following the example of Mary, it may be strong in faith and a sign of hope and comfort. Lord, hear us.
2. Give us the grace, Lord, to accept the sorrows and sufferings of life with the same faith as Mary. Lord, hear us.
3. May devotion to Mary, which inspired former generations, be our constant guide and encouragement. Lord, hear us.
4. May the motherly care of the Blessed Virgin Mary heal the sick and comfort those who are in sorrow. Lord, hear us.
5. May the prayers of Mary intercede for the souls of the faithful departed and bring them into eternal glory. Lord, hear us.

Lord God you have taken Mary into heavenly glory. We ask you to keep us in your love and, like Mary, lead us to share in the joy and triumph of your resurrection. We make our prayer through Christ our Lord. Amen.

All Saints

On the Feast of All Saints we remember all the unsung heroes of the christian past who are enjoying eternal happiness in heaven, reaping the rewards of their good lives on earth. These are the countless souls in heaven who are not canonised and do not appear on the church's official list. Their names are only known in the hearts of a small circle of people, whose lives they shaped and touched. Many lived in obscurity, died unknown and all memory of them has been forgotten. Their lives were not marked by any great occurence, their accomplishments too insignificant to be recorded, but they lived through all the stresses and trials of everyday humdrum existence. Like ourselves they were weak as we are weak, tempted as we are tempted and when they fell into sin they got on their feet again and made their peace with God. The way they lived their lives was more important than the recognition they attained.

Popular opinion places holiness beyond our reach. Many people have the mistaken notion that being a saint is beyond their grasp. For them saints are unusual types, people who never commit a sin in their lives and know nothing of wrong-doings. They forget that becoming a saint is the long and painful struggle of a lifetime. Jesus tells us that the good person is prepared to put up with hardship, overcome selfishness and to change his ways.

Holiness is achieved by doing ordinary things well. What fills us with great joy is that among this vast multitude of saints are people from our own neighbourhood and from our own family circle, with whom we share intimately and who, until recently, lived among us. Their lives influenced us greatly because they had the strength to live the gospel message in simplicity and with undivided hearts. The great example of their goodness is not wasted on us. Contemplating their victory gives us courage to fight the good fight with prayer, penance, perseverence and works of mercy. Our prayer is that God may enter our lives and make his home in us so that one day we may be numbered with them also.

Prayer of the Faithful

In union with the saints in heaven, who remained true to their calling in life, with confidence we place our needs before God the Father.

1. We pray that the members of the church may always respond in faith and hope to the gospel message of the Beatitudes. Lord, hear us.

2. Inspired by the example of the saints, may we always remain faithful to our baptismal promises. Lord, hear us.

3. That we may always accept the hardships of life in order to receive peace with Christ. Lord, hear us.

4. For the old, the lonely and the sick, that they may place their trust in God alone. Lord, hear us.

5. We pray for all those who have completed their earthly journey, that they may be brought into the heavenly presence of Christ. Lord, hear us.

Almighty God, may we always imitate the saints in our lives and so work towards a share in your life in heaven. We ask this through our Lord Jesus Christ. Amen.

Thematic Index